In Defence of Fantasy

A Study of the Genre in English and American Literature since 1945

Ann Swinfen

Routledge & Kegan Paul

LONDON, BOSTON,
MELBOURNE AND HENLEY

First published in 1984
by Routledge & Kegan Paul plc

39 Store Street, London WC1E 7DD, England,

9 Park Street, Boston, Mass. 02108, USA,

464 St Kilda Road, Melbourne,
Victoria 3004, Australia, and

Broadway House, Newtown Road,
Henley-on-Thames, Oxon RG9 1EN, England

Set in 10/12 Sabon by
Inforum Ltd, Portsmouth
and printed in Great Britain by
Redwood Burn Ltd
Trowbridge, Wiltshire

Library of Congress Cataloging in Publication Data

Swinfen, Ann.
In defence of fantasy.
Bibliography: p.
Includes index.
1. Fantastic fiction, English—History and criticism.
2. English fiction—20th century—History and criticism.
3. Fantastic fiction, American—History and criticism.
4. American fiction—20th century—History and criticism.
I. Title.
PR888.F3S94   1983   823'.0876'09   83–11164
ISBN 0–7100–9525–2

For David

O imaginativa che ne rube
    talvolta sì di fuor, ch'om non s'accorge
    perché dintorno suonin mille tube,
chi move te, se 'l senso non ti porge?
    Moveti lume che nel ciel s'informa,
    per sé o per voler che giù lo scorge.

                Dante, *Purgatorio* XVII, 13–18

Contents

Acknowledgments

Extracts from *Tree and Leaf* by J. R. R. Tolkien (Copyright © 1964 by George Allen & Unwin Ltd) are reprinted by permission of George Allen & Unwin Ltd and of Houghton Mifflin Company.

Extracts from *The Earthsea Trilogy* by Ursula Le Guin are reprinted as follows: from *A Wizard of Earthsea* (Copyright 1968 by Ursula K. Le Guin) reprinted by permission of Houghton Mifflin Company and of Victor Gollancz Ltd; from *The Tombs of Atuan* (Copyright © 1971 by Ursula Le Guin) reprinted by permission of Atheneum Publishers and of Victor Gollancz Ltd; from *The Farthest Shore* (Copyright © 1972 by Ursula Le Guin) reprinted by permission of Atheneum Publishers and of Victor Gollancz Ltd.

Abbreviations

· 1 ·
Fantasy and the Marvellous

The modern fantasy novel might hardly seem to need a defence, were it not for the curiously ambivalent position it occupies in the contemporary literary scene. On the one hand, many post-war writers have employed the genre with considerable skill and variety, some phenomenal publishing successes have occurred in this field, and an increasing number of universities throughout the English-speaking world now include the literary criticism of fantasy as part of their English Literature courses. On the other hand, some critics and academics condemn the whole genre with a passion which seems to have its roots in emotion rather than objective critical standards.[1] Relatively little has been written on post-war fantasy, except for studies of individual authors. This is an attempt to redress the balance, by taking what it is hoped is a wide-ranging and comprehensive view of fantasy – what it is, what it tries to achieve, what fundamental differences distinguish it from the realist novel. This study covers modern fantasy published over the three decades after 1945.

To some extent the precise period has been arbitrarily chosen, for there is no special significance in the terminal dates. However, the period as a whole has been selected deliberately, for it witnessed a considerable expansion in the publishing of works in this genre and the emergence of a number of notable novels by a new generation of writers in both Britain and America. This may be partly due to the influence of J. R. R. Tolkien, but this is not to say that many of these novels are simply derivatives of Tolkien's pioneering work. A great many, indeed, appear to owe little or nothing directly to Tolkien, and some writers may be said to surpass him in imaginative power or philosophical conception. The point is, rather, that Tolkien made fantasy 'respectable'. Since the publication of *The Lord of the Rings* it has been possible for British and American writers with a serious purpose to employ once again the genre of marvellous writing, as they had not been able to do since the growth and dominance of the realist novel. Even so, they have too often been obliged in the first instance to publish as children's writers, only later (as of course

1

was the case with Tolkien himself) becoming accepted by an adult readership. It is quite clear from any prolonged study of what might be termed 'high fantasies' that to label them as children's books is grossly misleading. They operate on an adult level of meaning, and the issue of deciding the dividing line, if such could ever exist, between worthwhile literature for children and for adults seems to be a futile exercise. In any case it is tangential to the current discussion, and no such division will be made here.

While disclaiming the existence of any identifiable school of modern fantasy, this study is founded on the demonstrable fact that many of these writers have some characteristics in common and share similar concerns. Indeed, it is for this reason that the subject is approached broadly on a thematic basis instead of author by author, as has been the case in other works.[2] It becomes clear that fantasies published during the period are frequently imbued with a profound moral purpose and, even when set in a different historical period or, more interestingly, in a complete otherworld, display a concern for contemporary problems and offer a critique of contemporary society.

Yet it would not be wholly satisfactory to deal with this period as if it were totally divorced from what had gone before. Indeed, it might be argued that modern fantasy writers are simply the heirs of a long-standing literary tradition, even perhaps that they could scarcely have existed but for the foundations laid earlier in the development of European literature. Where appropriate, attention to such historical origins will be given in the succeeding chapters. For the moment it is sufficient to point out that modern fantasy employs structures, motifs and marvellous elements derived from its predecessors in myth, legend, fable, folk-tale and romance. Yet it cannot employ such elements in the same way as these predecessors did. In a world governed by materialism and scientific rationalism, fantasy sets out to explore the immaterial and irrational. Moreover, unlike, for example, the writer of a medieval romance in what was virtually a universal Christian culture of Europe, the modern writer of fantasy cannot start from a widely accepted basis of belief. The moral premises must be established within the work itself. In addition, the literal-mindedness of the modern reader militates against the writer of fantasy. With their wider interpretation of what could, or might, constitute human experience, earlier audiences were readier to accept a Grendel or a Green Man. The modern writer must expend much effort in order to induce 'secondary belief'. Hence, although there are similarities with earlier marvellous literature (and indeed without this rich tradition, fantasy could not achieve many of its most deeply moving moments), modern literary fantasy is, of its nature, a different genre.

Some omissions must necessarily be made in a study which ranges over so wide a field of literature in an attempt to clarify and assess its particular characteristics. For example, there is no extended consideration to be found here of the works of Tolkien, for the obvious reason that such a consideration, if properly carried out, would leave no room for anything else, and that in any case his work has already received considerable critical attention. The writings of Mervyn Peake, like those of Tolkien, have been studied elsewhere, and his novels also appear to be rather different in character from the works being discussed here. Some other writers have been regretfully omitted simply for reasons of space. Nevertheless, even with these omissions there remains a large corpus of works, all of which repay close study, and some of which are of notable literary merit. Throughout, the intention is to examine the nature of fantasy as a whole, rather than individual writers in isolation.

Before embarking on a study of modern fantasy novels it will be useful to arrive at some idea of what exactly is implied by the term 'fantasy'. The epigraph which appears at the beginning of this work is one of many passages in which Dante refers to both *imaginativa* and *fantasia*.[3] To Dante *imaginativa* or *fantasia*, the imaginative faculty, which comprehends the art of prose fantasy, was divinely inspired, offering a dimension of creativity going beyond man's empirical experience. *La Divina Commedia* itself is perhaps the greatest poetic fantasy in European literature. Tolkien, who first applied the phrase 'the sub-creative art' to the writing of fantasy, saw such literary creation as the natural outcome of man's own creation in the divine image.[4] As the Creator creates, so man in His image is also a creator. At the same time, the writing of fantasy appears to be closely linked with man's rational being and perception of the natural world. What may at first sight seem to be a paradox lies in fact at the heart of fantasy: that is, that to create an imaginative and imaginary world it is necessary to observe faithfully the rules of logic and inner consistency which, although they may differ from those operating in our own world, must nevertheless be as true to themselves as their parallel operations are in the normal world. The writing of successful fantasy, then, is amongst the most demanding forms of literary creation.

The interchangeability of 'fantasy', 'fancy' and 'imagination' in the terminology employed by various writers at various periods could support a very wide interpretation of the term. Coleridge, in his *Biographia Literaria,* attempted a distinction between imagination and fancy, which allocated to imagination the creative power and to fancy a more mechanical role. However, Coleridge's definitions do not fully account for the nature of fantasy as sub-creation. It is obviously necessary to arrive at a definition of fantasy which is both adequate and relevant to the works to be discussed.

As a starting-point we may take Tolkien's discussion of the concept in his lecture 'On Fairy-stories', delivered at the University of St Andrews in 1938 when he had already published *The Hobbit* and was writing the first volume of *The Lord of the Rings.* As the author of several of the most notable works of fantasy written this century, Tolkien is able to offer particularly significant views on the genre itself. His ideas on fantasy do not simply constitute an *apologia pro operibus suis*. Fantasy, even modern fantasy, does not begin with Tolkien. Going back to the beginning of this century, we find Walter de la Mare's *The Three Mulla-Mulgars* (1910) embodying many of the characteristics to which Tolkien alludes. The nineteenth century had also produced some distinguished contributions to the genre. Tolkien, therefore, was writing at a point when fantasy was already deeply embedded in the English literary tradition. Moreover, such was the influence of his own work, both in offering an outlet to serious writers unwilling, for whatever reason, to restrict themselves to the requirements of the modern realist novel, and also in shaping the subsequent development of the fantasy novel, that an understanding of Tolkien's conception of fantasy becomes indispensable for an understanding of the genre.

Tolkien's lecture is concerned with the nature, origins and purpose of 'fairy-stories', a term which proves not easy to define. A study of the genre reveals that such stories are rarely concerned with fairies. 'Most good "fairy-stories" are about the *aventures* of men in the Perilous Realm or upon its shadowy marches' (*TL*, p. 16). The nature of fairy-story thus depends upon 'the nature of *Faërie*: the Perilous Realm itself, and the air that blows in that country' (*TL*, p. 16). The term 'fairy-story' is thus misleading, and although Tolkien continues to use it in his lecture, it will not be used in this study.

Instead, the term 'fantasy' has been preferred, as having perhaps a wider currency now than in the 1930s. Current usage varies widely, however, even when it is applied in a literary sense, and contemporary writers on the subject of fantasy usually find it necessary to define the term, often at some length.[5] Tolkien defines the term 'fantasy' as embodying both 'the Sub-creative Art in itself and a quality of strangeness and wonder in the Expression. . . . Fantasy (in this sense) is . . . not a lower but a higher form of Art, indeed, the most nearly pure form, and so (when achieved) the most potent' (*TL*, p. 44).

In this study the term 'fantasy' will be taken to mean both the sub-creative art, with its quality of strangeness and wonder, and the kind of novels which such art produces. The essential ingredient of all fantasy is 'the marvellous', which will be regarded as anything outside the normal space–time continuum of the everyday world. Pure science fiction is excluded, since it treats essentially of what does not exist now, but might perhaps exist in the future. The marvellous element which lies at the heart of all fantasy is composed of what can never exist in the world of empirical experience. Elements of the marvellous may irrupt into the normal world, but more often the reader is carried, at least part of the time, into another world, where, Tolkien asserts, he does not undergo what Coleridge described as a 'willing suspension of disbelief' (*BL*, XIV, p. 169). The writer as sub-creator creates a complete and self-consistent 'secondary world', and if he is successful, the result is 'secondary belief' on the part of the reader: 'He makes a Secondary World which your mind can enter. Inside it, what he relates is "true": it accords with the laws of that world. You therefore believe it, while you are, as it were, inside' (*TL*, p. 36).

Our normal experience of the primary world thus leads us to give primary belief to primary realism, while successful sub-creation induces secondary belief in the secondary realism of a secondary world.

Contrary to a widespread misconception, the sub-creative art of fantasy, the expression of man's natural creative capacity, in no way conflicts with the exercise of his other principal faculty, his reason. As Tolkien asserts:

> It [fantasy] certainly does not destroy or even insult Reason; and it does not either blunt the appetite for, nor obscure the perception of, scientific verity. On the contrary. The keener and the

clearer is the reason, the better fantasy will it make. If men were ever in a state in which they did not want to know or could not perceive truth (facts or evidence), then Fantasy would languish until they were cured. . . . For creative Fantasy is founded upon the hard recognition that things are so in the world as it appears under the sun; on a recognition of fact, but not a slavery to it. (*TL*, p. 50)

Indeed, the detailed examination of modern fantasy bears out precisely what Tolkien alleges here, as will be seen later in the discussion of the realism of secondary worlds and of the vital 'inner consistency' of all successful fantasy writing.

In the sub-creative art of fantasy, Tolkien detects three faces: 'the Mystical towards the Supernatural; the Magical towards Nature; and the Mirror of scorn and pity towards Man' (*TL*, p. 28). Unfortunately, by deliberately choosing to exclude two types of tale – the beast fable and the Lilliputian story – Tolkien largely excludes the mirror of scorn and pity. Yet this seems to be one of the predominant characteristics of fantasy, and this study includes a discussion of both these types of tale, and of the mirror of scorn and pity – that is, the use of fantasy to mock or exhort foolish mankind, often through the use of utopias and dystopias.

The magical face of fantasy seemed to Tolkien to be the essential one, and it is indeed the most characteristic of his own work. It is by the magical renewing and refreshment of our perceptions that we come to view the primary world, dulled through familiarity, with newly wondering eyes. 'We should meet the centaur and the dragon, and then perhaps suddenly behold, like the ancient shepherds, sheep, and dogs, and horses – and wolves' (*TL*, pp. 51–2). Fantasy is thus an enrichment of life, for even if dragons exist only in otherworld, our lives in the primary world are richer and more beautiful simply through the imagining of them. Indeed, 'magic' is perhaps not the best term to use for this aspect of fantasy, for magic 'produces, or pretends to produce, an alteration in the Primary World. . . . it is not an art but a technique; its desire is *power* in this world, domination of things and wills' (*TL*, p. 48). Fantasy may be said to aspire rather to the 'elvish craft' of enchantment. At its heart lies creative desire, like Dante's: 'In this world it is for men unsatisfiable, and so imperishable. Uncorrupted it does not seek delusion, nor bewitchment and domination; it seeks shared enrichment, partners in making and delight, not slaves' (*TL*, p. 49). Fantasy draws much of its strength from certain 'primordial desires' for the enrichment of life: the desire to survey vast depths of space and time, the desire to behold marvellous creatures, the desire to share the speech of the animals, the desire to escape from the ancient limitations of man's primary world condition.

The third aspect of fantasy, as the vehicle of mystery, Tolkien feels is the most difficult to achieve, although when successful it produces stories of 'power and beauty'. Tolkien's friend and colleague C. S. Lewis wrote the cycle of Narnian fantasies as the vehicle of Christian mysteries, and these will be studied in subsequent chapters. Other, younger writers like Ursula Le Guin and Leon Garfield have also produced mystical fantasies of great power and beauty. And indeed the mystical nature of fantasy is the source of what Tolkien shrewdly detects as one of the most outstanding qualities of serious fantasy or traditional fairy-tale, the *eucatastrophe*:

> The sudden joyous 'turn' . . . . a sudden and miraculous grace: never to be counted on to recur. It does not deny the existence of *dyscatastrophe*, of sorrow and failure: the possibility of these is necessary to the joy of deliverance; it denies (in the face of much evidence, if you will) universal final defeat and in so far is *evangelium*, giving a fleeting glimpse of Joy, Joy beyond the walls of the world, poignant as grief. (*TL*, p. 60)

This 'glimpse of joy, and heart's desire, that for a moment passes outside the frame, rends indeed the very web of story, and lets a gleam come through' (*TL*, p. 61) – this is the essential quality which distinguishes fantasy from the realist novel, although many distinctions of detail may of course also be made.

It is clear from the foregoing discussion that Tolkien's views of imaginative creation differ quite markedly from those of Coleridge, against whose theories of the imagination Tolkien was largely reacting. Both regard reason as of importance – for Coleridge the imagination is the agent of the reason,[6] while Tolkien asserts that fantasy 'does not destroy or even insult Reason' (*TL*, p. 50) – but it is clear that Tolkien ranks the creative ability as reason's peer, not as its agent. Moreover, Coleridge distinguishes between imagination and fancy, regarding fancy as a mechanical process:

> Fancy. . . . has no other counters to play with but fixities and

definites. The fancy is indeed no other than a mode of memory emancipated from the order of time and space; and blended with, and modified by that empirical phaenomenon of the will which we express by the word *choice*. (*BL*, XIII, p. 167)

Imagination, on the other hand, was for Coleridge a vital and organic faculty which

> dissolves, diffuses, dissipates, in order to re-create; or where this process is rendered impossible, yet still, at all events, it struggles to idealize and to unify. It is essentially *vital*, even as all objects (as objects) are essentially fixed and dead. (*BL*, XIII, p. 167)

To all intents and purposes, Tolkien reverses the terminology:

> The mental power of image-making is one thing, or aspect; and it should appropriately be called Imagination. . . . The achievement of the expression, which gives . . . 'the inner consistency of reality',* is indeed another thing, or aspect, needing another name: Art, the operative link between Imagination and the final result, Sub-creation. . . . I require a word which shall embrace both the Sub-creative Art in itself and a quality of strangeness and wonder in the Expression, derived from the Image. . . . I propose, therefore, . . . to use Fantasy for this purpose: in a sense, that is, which combines with its older and higher use as an equivalent of Imagination the derived notions of 'unreality' (that is, of unlikeness to the Primary World), of freedom from the domination of observed 'fact', in short of the fantastic. I am thus not only aware but glad of the etymological and semantic connexions of *fantasy* with *fantastic*: with images of things that are not only 'not actually present', but which are indeed not to be found in our primary world at all, or are generally believed not to be found there. But while admitting that, I do not assent to the depreciative tone. That the images are of things not in the primary world (if that indeed is possible) is a virtue not a vice.
>
> * That is: which commands or induces Secondary Belief. (*TL*, p. 44)

It is here that Tolkien and Coleridge really part company, rather than in mere use of terminology. Coleridge evolved his theory of imagination in reaction to the associationist theories of Locke and Hartley, but despite his reading of neo-Platonists like Cudworth or such earlier writers as Plotinus and Proclus, he never fully subscribed to the Platonic view that the primary world is a world of shadows cast by ideal realities.[7] Tolkien can be seen as essentially a Christian Neo-Platonist. Coleridge distinguishes between primary and secondary imagination, the former being involuntary and common to all men, acting as an intermediary between sensation and perception, the latter being the agent of conscious will and particularly pronounced in poets.[8] The secondary imagination is the artistically creative one but, while Tolkien probably took the term 'secondary' from Coleridge, Tolkien's sub-creative art which creates secondary worlds is also capable of affording glimpses of joy and eternal truth. Coleridge did not feel that imagination could grasp truths which were beyond the scope of reason, although he believed that religious faith might do so.[9]

Tolkien's belief in the transcendent power of fantasy is closer to Shelley's views on the poetic imagination, set forth in *A Defence of Poetry*.[10] Two of Shelley's arguments in particular are related to Tolkien's: the emphasis on moral quality – 'the great instrument of moral good is the imagination' (p. 118) – and the recognition of the power to penetrate beyond the outward surface of 'reality' – 'Poetry . . . strips the veil of familiarity from the world, and lays bare the naked and sleeping beauty, which is the spirit of its forms' (p. 137). These two aspects of fantasy provide two of the major centres of interest in the present study.

Aristotle asserts in the *Poetics* that art has its origin in *mimesis*, which is an instinctive faculty in mankind. It is, he claims, the desire for imitation which prompts the creative process and also fosters the pleasure which an audience takes in a work of art. While this mimetic tendency has some part in the sub-creative art of fantasy, it does not account for the full range of its literary achievement. The primary natures of such fundamental things as bread and wine, trees and grass, are not simply imitated, they are enhanced by their setting in fantasy. Thus mimesis of the primary world is sharpened by the creation of a secondary world of numinous experience, while both Tolkien's definitions, considered above, of the nature of the sub-creative art, and the subsequent detailed examination of modern literary fantasy, indicate that fantasy like poetry (in Shelley's words):

> defeats the curse which binds us to be subjected to the accident of surrounding impressions. And whether it spreads its own figured curtain, or withdraws life's dark veil from before the

scene of things, it equally creates for us a being within our being. It makes us the inhabitants of a world to which the familiar world is chaos. It reproduces the common Universe of which we are portions and percipients, and it purges from our inward sight the film of familiarity which obscures from us the wonder of our being. (p. 137)

Broadly speaking, this study attempts to analyse two principal aspects of modern fantasy: its nature and its purpose. Initially structures and modes are discussed, beginning with a popular type of fantasy set in the primary world – animal fantasy, in which animals are given anthropomorphic characters or occasionally humans are metamorphosed into animals. From such fantasy located entirely in the primary world, the move is, logically, to the next stage in abstraction beyond the normal space–time continuum, where the primary world and otherworlds are juxtaposed. The secondary world of such pairs of 'worlds in parallel' still maintains close contact with normal experience in the real world and as such may be distinguished from the secondary world which is in no way directly linked with primary experience. The pure secondary world fantasy, some would argue, provides the highest expression of imaginative creation in this genre. The technical side of secondary world creation is considered first, but the philosophical bases of the most powerful secondary world fantasies are provided by deeply felt moral and religious convictions, and frequently result in the presentation of metaphysical concepts as physical realities. A discussion of the use of symbolism and allegory in fantasy leads on to an analysis of the purposes which fantasy seems to serve: the exploration of enhanced imaginative experience of the primary world itself, the deeper religious and philosophical foundations of some of the novels, and the social concern which employs utopias or dystopias as the most effective means of presenting the writers' views. We conclude with an assessment of the whole body of works studied, in the light of our original definition of fantasy and particularly of Tolkien's dictum that fantasy deals not with marvellous beings but in fact with 'man in the Perilous Realm'.

Perhaps one of the most difficult aspects of undertaking a serious critical study of the fantasy novel results from the attitude of the majority of contemporary critics – an attitude which suggests that the so-called 'realist' mode of writing is somehow more profound, more morally committed, more involved with 'real' human concerns than a mode of writing which employs the marvellous. The contention of this defence of fantasy is that this is far from being the case. It may perhaps clarify the issue if we recall that what is now regarded as the 'real' world – that is, the world of empirical experience – was for many centuries regarded as the world of 'appearances'. To our ancestors, more inclined than we by belief and by learning to look beyond the material world for reality, the ultimately real lay in spiritual otherworlds. It is with the reality of such otherworlds that fantasy very largely deals.

· 2 ·
Talking Beasts

In beginning our study of fantasy with animal tales we are dealing with a subject which is not so much a sub-genre of fantasy as a microcosm of the whole. Animal fantasy is not only a popular form amongst modern writers, but it also has one of the longest and strongest traditions of all types of fantasy. At the same time, it provides us with examples of a wide range of the techniques and purposes of fantasy, with which this study as a whole largely deals.

The emergence of beast tales in the earliest days of European literature and their almost continuous popularity ever since emphasize the fact that man's relationship with the rest of the animal kingdom strikes a deep chord of imaginative recognition in the human consciousness. Since the Fall, some might say, man has been trying to heal the rift between himself and his fellow animals, and to re-establish that mutual understanding and rapport which he senses must once have existed and which through the exercise of the literary imagination, if in no other way, might be re-created. This profound sense of man's identity with the rest of the animal kingdom helps to account for the continued fascination with beast tales, but the attempted re-establishment of the old relationship does not exhaust the resources of such tales. In its simplest form, the animal fable has been used for didactic and moralistic purposes, and the tales of Aesop and La Fontaine are only the best-known examples of this genre. The limitations of fables result from their portrayal of animals as human types or as the embodiment of simple human characteristics: the cunning fox, the greedy crow, the conceited rooster. At a more sophisticated level, animal tales can be used to explore the whole range of human character and relationships, by examining human society from the point of view of the animal; or animal metamorphosis may provide an enhanced vision of primary world reality; or the search may be widened to explore not only the individual but the community – how it is created, how it operates, what are its philosophical, religious and political assumptions – through the medium of the animal community. Amongst the works of animal fantasy to be examined in this study examples of all these techniques and purposes will be found, and thus will establish many of the concepts to be developed in the exploration of other aspects of fantasy in subsequent chapters.

Two characteristics, however, distinguish modern animal fantasy, in some degree, from other types of fantasy to be discussed. First of all, modern animal fantasy in most instances is set in the primary world and therefore rarely involves the often numinous experience of otherworlds. Secondly, it would appear that modern animal fantasy is more closely linked to and borrows more heavily from its antecedent literature than most other types of fantasy. It is therefore particularly illuminating in the discussion of recent works of this kind to set them in the context of the long tradition of which they are the latest manifestation.

In one of the oldest and most enduring myths of the world, Genesis, God created the animals, and created man to live amongst them and rule over them. Briefly, in Eden, man dwelt at peace with the beasts. Since the publication of Darwin's *Origin of Species* in 1859, that man is descended from the humanoid apes has been the generally accepted view of human origins, yet in one sense both the traditions of the Old Testament and the researches of modern anthropologists are in agreement: man was once close to the animals and has since parted company with them. However strangely we may have evolved from our primeval ancestors, however much we may seem to differ on the surface from the animals now found on earth, we are still physically animals, and at a very fundamental level of our being we feel a deep affinity with them. It is not only in our physical attributes that we resemble them, as Edward Lee Thorndike has pointed out:

> Nowhere more truly than in his mental capacities is man a part of nature. His instincts, that is, his inborn tendencies to feel and act in certain ways, show throughout marks of kinship with the lower animals, especially with our nearest relatives physically, the monkeys. His sense-powers show no new creation. His intellect we have seen to be a simple though extended variation from the general animal sort. This again is presaged by similar variation in the case of the monkeys. Amongst the minds of animals that of man leads, not as a demi-god from another planet, but as a king from the same race.[1]

The subject of animal intelligence continues to inspire the

researches of scientists, and yet there remains the unsurmounted barrier: our baffling inability to understand the consciousness of animals, to speak their language from within. This urge to leap the gulf which divides men from the animals is shared by the writers of all animal tales, from the most naturalistic to the most symbolic, whatever may be the other motives behind their work. It is, moreover, one of the most ancient desires in the shaping of tales, and was connected in earliest times with totemistic practices – the desire to enter the skin of the animal and assume his very nature and individuality. Even in these modern times, in the midst of a mechanistic age, when the majority of people hardly ever encounter any uncaged animals apart from dogs and cats, the urge still remains. In discussing the 'old ambitions and desires (touching the very roots of fantasy)' which still move us, Tolkien singles this out as one of the most important: 'There are profounder wishes: such as the desire to converse with other living things. . . . Other creatures are like other realms with which Man has broken off relations, and sees now only from outside at a distance' (*TL*, p. 58).

Talking beasts enter man's literature at some time early in the remote past and survive in many of the most ancient and widespread folk-tale motifs. To the earliest composers of folk-tales, the animals were interesting both for their proper nature, and for the magical qualities with which they had been endowed in tribal religion and ritual. On the whole, men and animals treat each other with justice and on terms of equality in these early tales – a man who mistreats the animals is visited with punishment, while one who accords them courtesy and friendship is helped to success by their skill and magic. So numerous are these tales that it would be impossible to attempt to list them, but they will be found, classified and discussed, in Stith Thompson's *Index*.[2] The episode of the Oldest Animals in the tale of *Culhwch and Olwen* in *The Mabinogion* embodies the view of animals as guardians of secret wisdom. These are animals invested with power and majesty, a survival of the beast-deities of early religion, much earlier than *The Mabinogion* itself.

With man's increasing separation from the animals, and his increasing sophistication in literature, a new type of animal tale appeared. Aesop's name is the first to be associated with the animal fable, although it seems certain that some at least of his tales were already old when he retold them, probably in the middle of the sixth century BC. In fables animals become powerful symbols for human characteristics. Their animal nature is only important in so far as it serves this symbolic purpose. Each small tale contains a lesson in human behaviour, and their morality is not religious or spiritual – it is the morality of practical peasant life. Dogged persistence wins the day where self-conceit and bragging fail. When the mighty fall, even their humblest subjects scorn them. Keep your eyes open and trust no one, especially one who speaks with a flattering tongue. Cunning often succeeds where brute strength fails. The cunning fox appealed particularly strongly to the popular imagination, and when the traditional fables were extended and reshaped in the Middle Ages, whole story cycles formed around the central figure of Reynard the Fox.

The use of a cunning animal as the archetypal folk hero, in the same tradition as wily Odysseus, is also to be found in the African stories of Anansi the spider. Retold by the slaves on the plantations of the southern states of America, these tales took on a new form: Anansi evolved into crafty Brer Rabbit, who stays alive and discomfits his pursuers by the use of his wits. Richard Adams employs this tradition as a framework for his tales of El-ahrairah, the legendary father of the tribe and folk hero in *Watership Down*.

The animal fable often took the form of a miniature satiric comment on human foibles and human behaviour, while the collections of tales which gathered about figures like Reynard the Fox or Brer Rabbit composed mosaics of such satires. The Brer Rabbit stories are more directly concerned with the individual's struggle to stay alive in a hostile world – a struggle which any starving peasant anywhere would recognize at once. The Reynard stories, however, gradually developed into a connected satirical beast epic, and began to appeal to a more cultured, although still discontented, level of society. They became immensely popular in late medieval Britain, France and Germany, and contained satirical attacks on the social structure of Europe – the nobility, the clergy and the wealthy merchants. Like the stories of Robin Hood, they appealed to the poorer man's sense of injustice, and to the rebel's eagerness for change. The attraction of the Robin Hood stories lies both in their adventurous nature and in the character of Robin himself – another of the traditional cunning folk heroes. The tales of Reynard the Fox, however, by using animal characters with their traditionally symbolic qualities, are at once more satirical and more radically critical of the whole framework of society, while at the same time continuing to attack widespread human foibles and weaknesses.

Within this context of animal satire as a recognized tool of social criticism, Swift's use of the Yahoos and the Houyhnhnms in *Gulliver's Travels* can be seen as a natural development of earlier forms. Swift's attack was perhaps more searing than those of earlier fabulists and satirists. They had criticized certain of man's characteristics or social structures; Swift's profound disgust with the whole of human nature caused him to wonder whether man could live worthily in any social structure, or whether his nature was so flawed that he must always be a bestial Yahoo or a rational but heartless Houyhnhnm.

Best-known of the modern animal satires is Orwell's *Animal Farm* (1945), which is primarily a political rather than a social satire. Here, as in the most primitive of the fables, animals are used to symbolize human types. The characters of Napoleon, Boxer, Squealer and the rest are more highly developed than those of Aesop's foxes, donkeys and lions, but this is mainly a function of the length of the book. It is never the nature of the animals as animals which is important, only their value as symbols, a value which has been built up through centuries of familiarity with such animal symbolism. The use of animal fantasy as satire will be considered both in the present chapter and in Chapter 8, and it will be seen that in some significant ways its nature has changed and developed.

Towards the close of the eighteenth century and the beginning of the nineteenth, a new type of animal tale began to appear, which used the natural behaviour of animals to point a moral for human behaviour. The animals were not used as symbolic personifications of human characteristics; they were intended to be seen as their natural, animal selves. Unfortunately, the zeal of such writers as Mrs Trimmer and Mrs Barbauld sometimes distorted the picture of animal behaviour in order to make it fit the moral. By trying too hard, they often destroyed the potential impact of their stories, although they never attained to the wild extravaganzas in the interpretation of nature to be found in the medieval Bestiaries. One nineteenth-century writer whose sympathetic and delicate touch combined the natural behaviour of animals with just enough of human consciousness to make them moving, was Hans Christian Andersen. *The Ugly Duckling* (first English translation, 1846) is the classic example of this kind, in which the normal behaviour of farmyard animals and the lonely suffering of the duckling illuminate the theme of illusion and reality, of misleading outward appearances and inner worth. There is no magic in this story, beyond the magic of nature itself. The duckling always was a swan. Nor do the animals personify human characteristics; they are simply themselves. The duckling suffers and endures with a human consciousness, but – as Andersen himself would have argued – how are we to know that animals, birds, even toys, do not suffer as we do?

With *Black Beauty* (1877) the full-length 'naturalistic' animal tale comes into its own. Beauty is a true horse, and behaves like a horse, but thinks like a human. The book itself is, of course, another attack on society – a society which could callously maltreat the animal on which, at that time, it so heavily depended. There have been many fine naturalists' animal tales since, containing a great deal of detailed and unusual observation of wild life, the most notable being perhaps those of Henry Williamson. Such books will not, however, concern us here, for they are not in any real sense fantasies. Human consciousness and speech is accorded to the animals simply in order to present a vivid picture of animal life as animals experience it. Such animals are not surrogate humans, except in so far as it is impossible to give them human consciousness without also giving them something of human emotions.

The writing of what might be termed 'modern' animal fantasies of a complex type began at the end of the nineteenth century, and early attracted writers of talent. Rudyard Kipling's *Just So Stories* (1902) combined the animal fable tradition with the creation myth, and also contained aetiological tales. In *The Three Mulla-Mulgars* (1910), Walter de la Mare set his strange and beautiful story in the medieval quest tradition, but his three royal brothers were monkeys, and all except one of those whom they encounter, mortal or divine, are animals or fabulous creatures. Kenneth Grahame's *The Wind in the Willows* (1908) is a comic piece of social criticism set in the carefully observed landscape of the Thames valley, yet it is also an adventurous epic, with a narrative structure closely modelled on that of *The Odyssey*.[3] In the 1920s and 1930s, Hugh Lofting's *Dr Dolittle* books explored the ever-tantalizing idea of a man able to speak the true languages of the animals.[4]

In the post-war period, writers of animal fantasies have thus had a five-fold tradition on which to draw: folklore, in which animals are the equals or even the superiors of men; animal fable, which employs animals as expressive symbols for human character and behaviour;

animal satire, in which animal groups or communities provide a framework for social or political satire; naturalists' tales, which attempt to present an accurate and faithful picture of animal life itself; and finally earlier modern fantasies, which might combine elements from any of the animal tale traditions with other literary forms. The exceptionally long-established and varied tradition of the animal tale, which has been briefly outlined above, must affect the writer of animal fantasy, whether he draws upon it or attempts to react against it. The animal fable in particular is an intrinsic part of our culture – so much so that it is difficult for us to make unbiased judgments about the nature of animals. Did Aesop choose the fox as his symbol for cunning because the fox really is exceptionally cunning? Or do we believe that the fox is exceptionally cunning because of the fables of Aesop and his successors – fables which we have heard in our earliest childhood and which have thus helped to mould our attitudes? Most of us, influenced by nursery tales of gentle, helpless rabbits and by their soft, fluffy appearance, think of them as fearful, timid creatures. Here it seems that the Brer Rabbit stories (less well known in England than in America) are nearer to the truth, as R. M. Lockley has shown in *The Private Life of the Rabbit*, the book used by Richard Adams in his researches for *Watership Down*. Rabbits are in fact cunning, resourceful, courageous, and fierce both in establishing the hierarchy within the warren and in defending it.

A writer has thus to contend both with his own preconceived ideas about animals, and with those of his readers. His choice of animals as characters in his fantasy will be influenced principally by three criteria: the main actors in the story will tend to be animals which are familiar or attractive, or both; the traditional characteristics associated with animals, in their role as symbols for humans, may influence the type of characters they assume; finally, if the writer is concerned to present the concept of a community, this normally (although not inevitably) limits his choice to those animals which live in communities in their natural state.

Most writers select their animals from a remarkably limited range. The animals most familiar in everyday life are most easily observed and described, and perhaps are also most easily accepted by the reader: dogs, cats, mice, rabbits, rats, frogs, the commoner garden and field birds, farm animals. Domestic animals and most birds are naturally attractive and sympathetic, while mice, with their diminutive size and soft fur, can be forgiven a good deal. The same is not true of rats. Centuries of contending with this predatory, disease-carrying rodent has made him a natural villain in man's eyes. Manny Rat in Russell Hoban's *The Mouse and His Child*, king of the refuse dump, is type-cast as the villain as a result of the habits of his species and literary tradition as well as his own evil character. On the other hand, in *Mrs Frisby and the Rats of NIMH*, O'Brien makes it the ambition of Nicodemus, leader of the rats, to establish an independent, self-supporting community, and so be free for ever of the contumely associated with the rats' traditional way of life. Other familiar but not readily attractive creatures may become attractive if their charm of personality outshines their less than appealing physical form. This was perhaps not too difficult to achieve with Chester in George Selden's *The Cricket in Times Square*, for the happy chirping of crickets makes them potentially charming, but E. B. White scored a real triumph with Charlotte in *Charlotte's Web*. Spiders, unreasonably perhaps, are fairly generally loathed, but Charlotte is a gentle and gallant heroine. Unfamiliar creatures occasionally appear in animal tales. In T. H. White's *The Sword in the Stone*, there is a whole range of now unfamiliar birds of prey in the Mews, but here the author's expert knowledge overcomes the reader's sense of strangeness. In the same book there is a fabulous beast, but one of very respectable pedigree (straight from Malory) – the Questing Beast, or the Beast Glatisant.[5] This dreadful monster is later found pining away in a snow-covered gorse-bush, having lost all interest in life when King Pellinore stopped questing for it. Nursed back to health and happiness, it bounds off once more to be pursued by the dutiful king.

The traditional characteristics associated with animals through their symbolic use in fables are not as widely current now as might be expected, at least not in any simple and straightforward form. One writer who does draw on this tradition is C. S. Lewis, in his depiction of the Talking Beasts of Narnia. This is fully in accord with the whole spirit of *The Chronicles of Narnia*, with their strongly allegorical quality. The kingly lion Aslan, the gentle but foolish donkey Puzzle, the devious ape Shift, the crafty cat Ginger, the earnest and industrious Beavers, the powerful but rather stupid Bear, the thoughtful Owls – all these animals are in the fable tradition. The notable exception is the heroic but absurd mouse Reepicheep, the very paragon of blind chivalry and courtly manners. There are brave mice in the fables, but theirs is a quiet bravery akin to that of the mice who nibble away Aslan's bonds in *The Lion, the Witch and the Wardrobe*. Reepicheep the heroic mouse belongs rather to the tradition of literary parody which also produced L. Frank Baum's Cowardly Lion in *The Wizard of Oz* (1900). Amongst the animal fantasies in the post-war period, the most overtly symbolic is *The Mouse and His Child*, yet this is only partially influenced by the fable tradition. On the whole Russell Hoban fashions his symbols afresh, and his use of symbolism will be discussed later.

One of the most influential concepts lying behind the writing of much modern animal fantasy is the concept of the animal community. A natural development of the animal satires of Swift, Grahame and Orwell, the fantasy based on an animal community is a powerful tool for social or political criticism. Orwell used an artificial, man-made community, the farmyard (as did Chaucer in his animal satire, *The Nun's Priest's Tale*). The modern animal fantasist in general prefers the natural animal community, which therefore limits his choice of animals: the mice of Margery Sharp's books, the rats in *Mrs Frisby and the Rats of NIMH*, the rabbits of *Watership Down*. In Andre Norton's *Breed to Come*, the highly developed cats live in communities for security, but it is an uneasy mode of life; they keep to separate dens or rooms as much as possible, and hunt alone. One problem is presented by the use of animal communities: if a writer chooses only to depict a single type of animal, he cannot rely on variations in physical form and the traditionally accepted characteristics of different species to differentiate his protagonists – each must be as meticulously drawn as human characters in a human drama.

Every writer of animal fantasy makes one assumption about the marvellous: he gives his animals articulate thought and speech. This may be presented simply as human speech, or there may be further elaborations like the stamping signals of the rabbits in *Watership Down* or the whisker speech of the cats in Paul Gallico's *Jennie*. Beyond this basic premise of speech, the degrees of naturalism in animal fantasy cover a wide spectrum. At one end lie *Jennie* and *Watership Down*, the former with its minute and accurate observations of cat behaviour, the latter in which the rabbits' physical actions are limited to what they could do in real life. At the other lies E. B. White's *Stuart Little*, in which the younger son of an American human family is a mouse, but behaves as though he were an adult human – 'wearing a gray hat and carrying a small cane' (p. 2), sailing a boat, driving a car and teaching at a school.

Most fantasies lie between these two extremes. Rosemary Harris's animals are fully natural, but they have also developed a means of communicating with Reuben the animal tamer and his wife Thamar, later Prince and Princess of Canaan. Most of the animals who help to educate Arthur in *The Sword in the Stone* lead physically natural lives, but they possess a store of legends and traditional wisdom (as do the rabbits of *Watership Down*); some, such as the hawks, observe elaborate codes of conduct, and the badger is writing a D. Litt. thesis. The Talking Beasts of Narnia also have traditions and ceremonies, but we see little of their private lives except that of the Beavers, which is totally humanized. Chester has an exceptional talent for music in *The Cricket in Times Square*, and Charlotte an exceptional talent for weaving words into her web in *Charlotte's Web*, but both of these are, as it were, a variation and extension of their natural creative talents. In *Breed to Come* and *Mrs Frisby and the Rats of NIMH* the cats and the rats respectively have mutated from their normal ancestors as a result of man's biological experiments.

The most curious blend of naturalism and the marvellous in animal behaviour is to be found in *The Mouse and His Child*. In the first place, the two characters of the title are mechanical toys, not living animals, but they think, speak and feel, and become more like living animals as they walk onwards in their quest. Rats have naturally dexterous paws, but it is unlikely that before Manny Rat they employed them for repairing wind-ups and turning them into slaves. Most snapping turtles live long years at the bottom of gloomy ponds – one begins to wonder whether this turns others besides Serpentina into philosophers of nihilism. Crows are showy, noisy, extrovert birds, but they do not usually form theatrical companies and perform drama of the Beckett school. One of the main sources of strength in this book is the way the satire grows from the unnatural behaviour of the animals, which in turn grows by slight exaggeration from their natural behaviour. This easy development from one level to another of *The Mouse and His Child* makes it far more convincing as a quest for personal growth and as an attack on contemporary American society than *Stuart Little*, which attempts to achieve much the same ends. The total unnaturalness of Stuart even robs him of significance as a symbol of the social misfit.

Clearly the greatest determining factor for an author in selecting his types of animals and in deciding upon the degree of naturalism which he wishes to employ, is his overall purpose in writing his animal tale. The author of a story like Henry Williamson's *Tarka the Otter* will be working within quite different parameters from those used by T. H. White in *The Sword in the Stone*, in telling the story of the training of Arthur, or by Andre Norton in *Breed to Come*, where men have perished or departed from earth, and cats have become the dominant race. Setting aside the naturalistic tales like *Tarka,* we can see that animal fantasy is used to illuminate the human condition on three different levels, which will be examined in turn. In the first place, an animal tale may be used to analyse human character and human foibles, and also to place man in his proper frame of reference as a member of the animal kingdom. Secondly, the animal fantasy may explore individual morality, the quest for the good life and the right relationship with others. Finally, the animal tale may be more concerned with the community than with the individual, with the morality and organization of society, and in this way animal communities are used to comment obliquely on human society. These three categories are, of course, not mutually exclusive.

The best-known modern example of humans and animals living on more or less equal terms is to be found in *The Chronicles of Narnia*. The relationship between the two owes more to Genesis than to the folk-tale tradition, for in the latter the animals usually possess secret wisdom and magical powers not shared by men, a survival of their origins in the animal-deities of primitive religion. The clue to the role of the Narnian animals lies in the story of the creation of Narnia, in *The Magician's Nephew*. Aslan creates the animals, selects some of them to receive the gift of speech, and appoints a man to rule over them. The Tree of Protection is planted, and for many years the inhabitants of Narnia dwell in pre-lapsarian innocence and peace. Apart from the gift of speech and the length of the period of paradisal innocence, the episode is taken directly from Genesis. Even in Genesis, Eve and the serpent speak together, but it is not clear in the biblical account whether other animals apart from the serpent have this ability. In C. S. Lewis's version, most of the animals retain their innocence and purity throughout the history of Narnia, although a few, such as the wolves (fable types again), turn to evil ways during the rule of the White Witch, whilst others lapse into atheism and sacrilege in *The Last Battle*. Usually, however, despite this purity and innocence, there is an implication that the animals are somehow inferior to man. No animal ever becomes king of the animal kingdom of Narnia. Tradition holds that only a Son of Adam may sit on the throne at Cair Paravel. Women are also clearly inferior to men. They are allowed to be consorts, as sisters or wives of kings, but only evil enchantresses like the Green Lady and Jadis, the White Witch, scheme to rule in their own right. These are amongst the many indications of a covert anti-feminist attitude which is found throughout the Narnian tales.

In *The Horse and His Boy*, in some ways perhaps the most successful of the Narnia books, the horses and the children do for once appear on an equal footing, and indeed the horse Bree, as the oldest and most experienced, often assumes the leadership. His leadership is not absolute, however, for the abilities of each help the companions to escape from Calormen: Aravis's knowledge of city and court life, Hwin's patience and gentle common sense, and Shasta's innate courage and resourcefulness. The note of equality is struck when the four first meet, and as Bree points out, there is no question of ownership between free individuals: 'Hwin isn't *your* horse any longer. One might just as well say you're *her* human' (p. 34).

This sense of equality is the essence of the relationship between Reuben, Thamar and the animals in Rosemary Harris's trilogy about ancient Egypt and the biblical flood: *The Moon in the Cloud*, *The Shadow on the Sun* and *The Bright and Morning Star*. Anak the camel, Benoni the dog, and Cefalu the cat are actors in the human dramas, but they are also sardonic commentators on human weaknesses and on the corrupt bureaucracy of the Egyptian Old Kingdom in the Sixth Dynasty. These animals of Rosemary Harris's have some resemblances to the wise oldest animals and the loyal animal helpers of folk-tale, but apart from speech they have no magic, other than the wisdom of practical experience, the loyalty of friendship, and the true instincts of their animal natures.

Man as but one animal amongst the rest, naked and defenceless in his natural state, is the subject of the badger's D. Litt. treatise in *The Sword in the Stone* – a treatise with a strong flavour of Kipling. When the young King Arthur has learned much wisdom and many skills from the animals, who draw upon their own experience, he goes for his last lesson to the badger – 'Study birds and fish and animals', advises the badger. 'Then finish off with Man' (p. 311). In the beginning, God created all the embryos, which looked very much the same, and allowed each to choose what specialized tools or weapons it wished to make of parts of its body. At the very end of the sixth day, all had been granted their wishes except Man.

> 'Please God,' said the embryo. 'I think that You made me in the shape which I now have for reasons best known to Yourselves, and that it would be rude to change. . . .'
>
> 'Well done,' exclaimed the Creator in delighted tones. 'Here, all you embryos, come here with your beaks and whatnots to look upon Our first Man. He is the only one who has guessed Our riddle, out of all of you, and We have great pleasure in conferring upon him the Order of Dominion over the Fowls of the Air, and the Beasts of the Earth, and the Fishes of the Sea. Now let the rest of you get along, and love and multiply, for it is time to knock off for the week-end. As for you, Man, you will be a naked tool all your life, though a user of tools: you will look like an embryo till they bury you, but all others will be embryos before your might; eternally undeveloped, you will always remain *potential* in Our image, able to see some of Our sorrows and to feel some of Our joys. We are partly sorry for you, Man, and partly happy, but always proud. Run along then, Man, and do your best. And listen, Man, before you go . . .'
>
> 'Well?' asked Adam, turning back from his dismissal.
>
> 'We were only going to say,' said God shyly, twisting Their hands together. 'Well, We were just going to say, God bless you.' (pp. 314–15)

Here White has used the original Genesis myth in a fresh and illuminating way, enclosing in this story-within-a-story his essential theme of man's divine creation and largely underdeveloped potential.

Another way of viewing man as an animal is to locate a fully human consciousness in an animal body and to explore the reactions of such a consciousness to animal life. This is done by E. B. White in *Stuart Little* and by Paul Gallico in *Jennie*. There is a basic similarity of framework in these books: the human consciousness is found in a small solitary animal in a mainly hostile or indifferent world. In itself this produces a number of resemblances between the two novels, but there are marked differences in the authors' treatment of their subjects and above all in their intentions.

The city life of New York and London is the main setting for the two works, although the comfortable gentility of Stuart's New York neighbourhood contrasts strongly with the cruel, bomb-scarred surroundings of London's docks and slums in which Jennie and Peter have to survive. Stuart's story moves northwards to the peaceful New England countryside, where he nearly decides to settle down in 'the loveliest town of all'. There is a brief period of idyllic happiness for Peter and Jennie also, aboard the dirty and chaotic tramp steamer from Glasgow. Significantly, in relation to the authors' differing attitudes, the cats are happy not because they are idle, but because they are working, as accepted members of the crew. They are neither persecuted nor possessed in this small community where there is complete tolerance for each individual's eccentricities.

Stuart never comes to terms with his mouse body, but remains painfully divided between his physical limitations and his human mind and soul. He struggles desperately to live a fully human life, philosophically accepting his small size as a physical handicap like any other, but he seems unable to form any lasting relationships: he callously leaves his family with no thought for their feelings, and even his longing for the bird Margalo is a curiously empty relationship, for she has left him as indifferently as he leaves his family. Stuart's mouse shape is never used to examine mouse behaviour or mouse character – he is simply a small and disabled human. By contrast, under Jennie's careful teaching Peter, the boy turned into cat, learns to think and act like a cat, until his emotions and attitudes become almost entirely feline.

The writers' intentions are very different, although both are critical of a society which maltreats the poor, the defenceless, the misfit. Stuart is an outcast, born to be socially isolated, despite his loving family. We are led to believe, because of his quest for Margalo, that he is an idealist, yet in spite of this, and in spite of his pluck, resourcefulness and good nature, he has an oddly negative character. What he really hungers for are all the material trappings of American urban life, and although the poetic Margalo awakens some response in him, the reader is left wondering what it can be. *Stuart Little* remains an essentially superficial book, although it directs some amusing thrusts at American society, its materialism and its lack of room for the unconventional. It has a melancholy, anxious quality which is never counteracted by any redeeming quality of inner stature in its mouse hero.

Stuart never grows emotionally any more than he does physically.

On the other hand, *Jennie* is mainly concerned with the emotional growth of Peter, which parallels his training as a cat. The child Peter learns to understand and accept adult emotions and responsibilities until in the end he is a fully adult male. This book has much which merits praise: the depiction of cat life and behaviour, the deeper emotional and moral level, the quality of growth. It is unfortunately flawed by Paul Gallico's tendency towards painful sentimentality when talking about little boys and their mothers, which is a sad contrast to his tough and realistic appreciation of the life of stray cats.

The transformation of human into animal is also one of the central elements of *The Sword in the Stone*, and again it forms part of the training of the hero, in this case the training of the young King Arthur (known as the Wart). Here the hero must learn not only the lessons of manhood, but the even harsher ones of kingship, although he does not realize that this is the purpose of his education until near the end of the tale. The story of Arthur, and his character, hold a unique place in the culture of Europe, and especially of Britain. Whether or not there was a historical Arthur, the legendary Arthur has drawn to him elements of folklore and magic, primitive ritual and Christian allegory, strange adventures and courtly chivalry. The character of the king himself – idealistic, tragic and betrayed – has caught the imagination more than any other single character in Western literature. The boyhood of Arthur has rarely been explored, however.

In T. H. White's story of the youth of Arthur, Merlyn does not train his young charge by explanation and exposition of the qualities of kingship, but rather presents him with examples and counter-examples, leaving him to draw his own conclusions. Generally the animals are used to illustrate the positive qualities of kingship, while foolish or wicked humans are used to illustrate its negative qualities. The glorious comedy of the book lies principally in the follies which are the result of excesses of the chivalric code: King Pellinore and the Questin' Beast; the joust in the forest; the games-mad squirarchy, who talk of nothing but joustin' and questin'. The code of chivalry is not simply a target for satire, however, for a man, and a king, needed to be able to fight, to defend himself and his people, as the Wart and Kay learn from Robin Hood. Moreover, the boar-hunt contains one of the most moving moments in the book, when the King's Huntsman Master Twyti, who, ironically, hates hunting, blows the mort for the slain hound Beaumont.

The Giant Galapagas, whose jacket in the illustration on page 273 of the second edition bears the marks both of the swastika and of the hammer and sickle, illustrates the abuse of superior physical strength, and the witch Madame Mim the abuse of learning: both use their power to enslave others. The oppression of the weak and unfortunate is the theme of the story of Wat, the man without a nose, at whom the village children threw stones until he lost his wits. In much the same spirit, H. Sapiens Armatus Georgius Sanctus slew the last dinosaur, the innocent and humble Atlantosaurus, who 'had never killed in her life'. Georgius Sanctus, better known as St George, made the mistake of judging by outward appearances, and the Wart must learn not to make the same mistake. On one occasion only is an animal rather than a human used to illustrate the abuse of power and kingship, when the Wart becomes a fish and meets the tyrant Pike – 'You will see what it is to be a king,' says Merlyn.

'There is nothing,' said the monarch, 'except the power that you profess to seek: power to grind and power to digest, power to seek and power to find, power to await and power to claim, all power and pitilessness springing from the nape of the neck.' . . .

'Love is a trick played on us by the forces of evolution. . . . Pleasure is the bait laid down by the same. There is only power. Power is of the individual mind, but the mind's power alone is not enough. The power of strength decides everything in the end, and only Might is right.' (p. 72)

The Pike teaches the Wart a positive lesson as well as a negative one: learn to rely on your own strength. In his lonely future as a king it will be an important one. In spite of this, love and loyalty are also vital for a king, and the Wart has a loving nature. Moreover, he is instinctively compassionate, not only towards the afflicted Wat, but also towards his difficult, proud, passionate, sensitive and unkind foster brother, Kay. He has a deep love for his home and his foster family, and does not need to be taught 'love your home' by the badger. Courage is, of course, one of the most essential attributes of a king, and when the Wart is transformed into a merlin, to spend a night in the Mews amongst the hawks, he must undergo an ordeal of courage. He survives his ordeal, standing within striking distance of 'the poor, mad, brooding' tiercel goshawk until the peregrine falcon, the senior officer, has rung her bell three times, and the hawks sing him the triumph song. He endures a different kind of ordeal when he .

is captured by Madame Mim. Offered the chance of saving himself, he sends the goat instead for help, and himself remains behind, sure that, if he escapes, Madame Mim will kill Kay. The willing choice of self-sacrifice for others marks Arthur's nature throughout life.

Beyond his personal training in character and courage, the Wart learns many lessons about the creation of the world, the span of history and man's small place in it, and the strangeness of time. Merlyn, who lives backwards in time, disturbs the Wart's (and the reader's) simple notions and makes him aware of the interplay of past and future, and of the subjective nature of our sense of time. His animal metamorphoses are used by T. H. White to explore entirely new perspectives on the nature of time. When the Wart is transformed into a snake, he learns to understand the reptile's long view of history, reaching back to the dinosaurs, while Archimedes the owl takes him in bird form to visit Athene, where he is shown the dream of the talking trees, which moves at the rate of thirty years a minute, and the dream of the stones, most ancient of all, which moves at two million years a second:

> In the last three minutes of the dream some fishes, dragons and such-like ran hurriedly about. A dragon swallowed one of the pebbles, but spat it out.
> In the ultimate twinkling of an eye, far tinier in time than the last millimetre on a six-foot rule, there came a man. He split up the one pebble which remained of all that mountain with blows; then made an arrow-head of it, and slew his brother. (p. 272)

As his training progresses and he grows older, the Wart learns to 'fit things together'. Apart from his veiled hint at the time of the first transformation, Merlyn never indicates that the Wart is being prepared for kingship, but the animals and the simple-minded Wat sense the young Arthur's lineage long before he himself becomes aware of it. The badger stresses the importance of the lesson of why man has become master of all the animals – in the context of the whole novel it can be seen as a parallel to what makes one man a king over others. The Wart himself, who dreams of becoming a knight, although he seems, as a mere foster-brother of Kay, to be fated never to be more than a squire, longs for a heroic destiny:

> 'If I were to be made a knight,' said the Wart, staring dreamily into the fire, 'I should insist upon my doing my vigil all by

myself, as Hob does with his hawks, and I should pray to God to let me encounter all the evil in the world in my own person, so that if I conquered there should be none left, while if I were defeated, it would be I who would suffer for it.'

'That would be extremely presumptuous of you,' said Merlyn, 'and you would be conquered, and you would suffer for it.' (p. 298)

When at last the Wart tries to draw the sword from the stone (significantly on Kay's behalf, not his own),[6] the memory of all his friends – birds, beasts, fish, reptiles, even the trees and stones – is used by T. H. White to give him the strength to perform the task which proclaims to the world that he is indeed the son of Uther Pendragon, Arthur, King of Britain.

All round the churchyard there were hundreds of old friends. They rose over the church wall all together, like the Punch and Judy ghosts of remembered days, and there were otters and nightingales and vulgar crows and hares and serpents and falcons and fishes and goats and dogs and dainty unicorns and newts and solitary wasps and goat-moth catterpillars and cork-indrills and volcanoes and mighty trees and patient stones. They loomed round the church wall, the lovers and helpers of the Wart, and they all spoke solemnly in turn. Some of them had come from the banners in the church, where they were painted in heraldry, some from the waters and the sky and the fields about, but all, down to the smallest shrew mouse, had come to help on account of love. Wart felt his power grow. . . .

A Snake, slipping easily along the coping which bounded the holy earth, said, '. . . Fold your powers together, with the spirit of your mind, and it will come out like butter. Come along, homo sapiens, for all we humble friends of yours are waiting here to cheer.'

The Wart walked up to the great sword for the third time. He put out his right hand softly and drew it out as gently as from a scabbard. (pp. 331–2)

T. H. White showed considerable temerity in undertaking to write of the childhood of Arthur, Britain's greatest folk hero. In spite of its generally light-hearted tone, the book contains some profound lessons in the nature of kingship, and in particular the kind of

kingship for which Arthur stands. In depicting the education of
Arthur through the lessons of the rocks and trees, and through the
traditional wisdom and natural gifts of the animals, T. H. White has
found a form which harmonizes completely with the nature and
traditions of Arthur. The book also reveals the future king's fatal
flaw – he is too gentle, too selfless, too compassionate to be a
successful king in a ruthless world. He is eternally vulnerable. This
flaw in his nature – a flaw in a king which nevertheless makes him the
most human of heroes – brought Arthur to a tragic end, but it won
for him a place in the hearts of his people for ever. So tradition holds
that one day he will come again: Arthurus Rex Quondam Et Futurus.

The traditional symbolic use of the animal in literature lends itself
very easily to adaptation in the form of the personal quest – the
search of the individual for personal freedom or fulfilment, the
achievement of a scheme of personal integrity or morality. Sometimes this takes the form of an individual pursuing a dream or
an ideal; sometimes a small band of companions, usually outcasts
from society, achieve their goal through mutual self-help. A few
animals living threatened and precarious lives on the fringes of
human society, as do the cats in *Jennie*, may turn to each other for
help in the fight for survival or in the pursuit of a better life. To such
animals, humans may be the providers of food, sometimes even of
comfort and friendship, but they may also pose a threat to life
itself. In E. B. White's *Charlotte's Web* and in George Selden's *The
Cricket in Times Square* small groups of animals band together for
self-protection against a largely hostile world. Virtually the only
marvellous elements are Charlotte's ability to spin words into her
web and Chester's to imitate classical music in his chirping. In both
books the interest lies in the highly developed characterization of the
animals and also in the satire directed against the human society
amidst which they live and which they both reflect and react against.
White's rat, Templeton, is a masterpiece of the egotistical and
amoral parasite who lives on the pickings of the affluent society. (He
has a good deal in common with another American rat, Hoban's
Manny Rat, although he is not actively evil.) The unnatural friendship between the mouse Tucker and the cat Harry, in Selden's book,
is used to direct much cheerful mockery against the unnatural lives
of the humans in large cities. Chester the cricket does manage to
establish an understanding, if wordless, relationship with the small
Italian boy in the subway station news-stand, but his freedom-

loving, artistic soul cannot endure the crowds and concrete of New York, and he flees from the material wealth and squalor of the city to the beauty and integrity of life in the country.

In these last two books, the animals use their talents to help their friends, but in the quest-tale it is the pursuit of an ideal which is central. The primary theme of Walter de la Mare's *The Three Mulla-Mulgars*, the ideal which drives the three brothers on in the face of danger and disaster, is the dream of the Valleys of Tishnar, where their father has gone before them. They attain their goal, but only after much suffering. The inborn magical gifts of the youngest, Ummanodda, and his precious heirloom, the Wonderstone, help them to overcome many dangers, but so too do his own simple resourcefulness, his elder brothers' strength and courage, and the generous help of the Mountain Mulgars who join them. The book was written too early (1910) to be considered in detail within the scope of this study, but it is probably the finest animal quest-tale ever written.

Very different in form and tone, but not in its underlying intent, is Russell Hoban's *The Mouse and His Child*. This is the story of a personal quest, but as the tale unrolls the theme of friendship takes on an equal importance. Like the title, the nature of the quest is two-fold. The mechanical mouse father is in search of independence and freedom, which for him is represented by self-winding. He is relieved when the tramp who finds them thrown away repairs them so that he and his child walk straight ahead instead of dancing in a circle. The father has little trust in the help of others, but patiently forges ahead into the unknown future and endures all the adversities which befall him, while he clings to his dream of self-winding, which Hoban uses with great aptness as a symbol for personal independence. The mouse child, forced to walk backwards, fills the hollow space within himself with grander dreams. He too wants to become self-winding, but he also treasures the memory of the plush-covered elephant whom he saw briefly in the toyshop and has longed for ever since, to be his mother. He wants the wind-up seal for a sister, and the elegant dolls' house for his home. The father tells him his dreams are impossible, but nothing will quench the child's indomitable spirit.

So powerful are the personalities of these fragile mechanical toys, the father's dogged courage and the child's passionate dreams, that they change the lives of many whom they meet. The villainous

Manny Rat, whose one desire is to smash them, finds himself track-
ing them across the wide countryside, curiously reluctant to deal
the fatal blow. The Frog, a charlatan fortune-teller and quack,
reminiscent of Selah Tarrant in Henry James's *The Bostonians*, finds
himself forced against his will to prophesy the truth. The misan-
thropic Bittern is moved to compassion; Miss Mudd, the nervous
dragonfly larva, exerts all her strength to aid their escape from the
pond, and in so doing discards her old and ugly form, becoming an
iridescent dragonfly: 'Glittering above the pond she flew away,
lilting on the warm wind like a song in the sunlight, like a sigh in the
summer air' (p. 129). This is typical of Hoban's use of natural
phenomena with a double level of meaning. Everywhere the mice go,
their determination, idealism, and a radiant quality of integrity affect
all they encounter, except the bloodthirsty shrews and the supreme
egoists, Muskrat and Serpentina.

   The individual heroism in this book is set against a multi-faceted
piece of social satire. The American obsolescent society, in which
everything, including the people, is expendable, is personified in the
cast-off toys, once so bright and lovely, which are thrown out to rot
on the town dump, and in the tramp, the human cast-off. Only the
tramp feels any compassion for the broken mouse and his child. It is
he who rescues them from the town dump, where he sleeps amongst
the material cast-offs. Hoban juxtaposes the wrecked cars, the
broken toys, the stray dog and the tramp in a ragged kaleidoscope
framed by the Christmas snow. The tramp, by mending the mice and
setting them on their way, asserts the right of the individual to
independence and dignity, even outside the social norms.

   Many types in contemporary American society are attacked in the
book – the sham artist in the Caws of Art Experimental Theatre
Group; the commercial prophet or evangelist in the Frog; the philosopher of nihilism in Serpentina, so strongly contrasted with the ugly
little Miss Mudd, whose inner conviction of beauty is fulfilled; the
introverted and narrow-minded scientist in the Muskrat, who is no
more than a cruel egoist, blind to the troubles of his fellow creatures
and filled with petty professional jealousies; the superficial and noisy
journalist, given to distorting facts for maximum effect, in the Blue-
jay. The theme of war and territorial rights is treated with bitter
irony.[7]

   The life of the dump is a sharp parody of the corrupt and vicious
life which threatens so many American cities. Ruled by the Boss

figure, Manny Rat, life in the dump is dirty, dangerous and empty, without hope. Cast-off wind-ups are converted into slaves. If they complain, they are murdered by dissection or smashing. Manny Rat runs a gang of thieves and scavengers, plans crimes, lives in sleazy luxury, and exacts protection money from surrounding businesses, which are themselves designed to trick money out of the unwilling or unwary:

> 'Hurry, hurry! Step right up!' shouted a red and black sexton beetle at the entrance of an orange-crate theatre. The guttering flames of birthday-candle stubs behind him threw his frisking shadow on the snow ahead. The beetle wore a cape made from the fur of a woolly bear caterpillar, but he shivered nonetheless.
>
> 'A scientific exhibit!' he announced to passersby. 'An education for the whole family!' He drew aside a ragged curtain to disclose, lit by the fitful candles, a headless pink celluloid hula doll wearing the faded remains of a cellophane grass skirt. Two cricket musicians, barely kept from freezing by a nest of dead grass in a glass jar, huddled together, too cold to chirp. . . .
>
> 'How much have you taken in this evening?' asked Manny Rat.
>
> 'Very slow tonight,' said the sexton beetle. He showed him the small end of a salami and a dead sparrow half buried in the snow.
>
> 'We haven't been burying anything on the sly, have we?' said Manny Rat, taking the salami. 'We make sure Manny always gets his cut?' (pp. 30–1)

Despite the horror and fear of so much which surrounds them, the courageous spirit of the mouse and his child make this an optimistic book. Gathering their small band of friends about them, the mice finally defeat corruption and tyranny and establish their territory in the old and damaged dolls' house. The book ends in an idyll of self-fulfilment. The explicit social satire will be examined in more detail later.

The animal tale is thus a powerful form for the personal quest story. The small protagonists must be truly heroic to face the large and hostile world. The significance of the personal quest and the ideals for which it stands, as of the comradeship which may help it to fulfilment, are highlighted by the social framework against which it is set. Such a quest by an individual is often seen by the writers of

fantasy as a reaction against his social environment and a search for
some new situation – a new society, or a new place for himself within
the existing society – in which he can realize his ideals or live at
peace.

The search for the ideal society, where the stress is on the morality
of social systems rather than on the morality of the individual, forms
the last category of animal fantasy to be examined in this chapter.
Two major animal fantasies have been written on this theme in
recent years, and one rather less well known: *Watership Down, Mrs
Frisby and the Rats of NIMH,* and *Breed to Come.* The individual
quest, if it succeeds, leads to a final and static closing point for a tale.
Thus, at the end of *The Mouse and His Child*, there is no more to be
told, no further for the wanderers to go. In the quest for the ideal
community, there is never any true ending. Although a happy and
stable community may be established, its members will always be
changing as the years pass; the ideal must constantly be defended if it
is not to be lost. Where the individual quest has a sense of completeness and finality, the search for the social ideal must always look to
the future. The end of any such story must itself be a beginning.

Andre Norton's *Breed to Come* is itself set in the future and, at first
glance, might seem to fall into the category of science fiction rather
than fantasy. It certainly has many of the outward trappings of
science fiction – advanced technology, space travel – but otherwise
the point of view and tone are those of the animal fantasy. Men
(Demons) have performed biological experiments on cats (People),
dog (Barkers), pigs (Tuskers) and rats (Rattons) which have produced mutations – all have grown larger and more skilled, all have
developed articulate language, although each race has difficulty in
communicating with the others except by signs. The People are at
war with the Barkers, but have a peace treaty with the Tuskers. All
other races fear and hate the Rattons, who still linger in the 'lairs', the
old homes of the Demons. Years before, a particularly gifted cat,
Gammage, has gone to the lairs to search out the secrets of the
Demons, who are now all dead as a result of their own experiments
and wars, except for a few who fled to the stars.

Events are precipitated by the arrival of a space ship containing
a scouting party of Demons, come for two purposes: to discover
why their ancestors left earth, and to try to find amongst the old
scientific records some means of combating a cloud of poisonous gas
which has developed on their own planet. However, little of Andre

Norton's attention is given to the operation of the scientific devices, exept in setting the scene. She is more concerned with the effects of the crisis on the various characters, so that the resulting novel is a characteristic use of the animal fantasy to probe the human condition.

The arrival on earth begins to affect the personalities of the Demons almost at once. One, Tan, who already has a ruthless streak, is fascinated by the possibility of watching the 'animals' at war; he captures and cooks two of the young Tuskers, and eventually joins the Rattons. Ayana, the medical member of the crew, finds herself revolted by the cooking of the Tuskers – even before she learns that they can speak – as if she were called upon to participate in cannibalism. It is she who, after rescuing three People and a Barker who have been tortured and maimed by the Rattons, persuades the other two members of the crew to join the alliance of the People, Barkers and Tuskers against the Rattons. The creatures of the wild and those of the lairs find that both are needed to defeat the evil: both the learning of the lair-people and the natural instincts and training of the People of the wild are essential to the community. Gammage himself is killed in the struggle, and, as Ayana points out, he was mistaken in some of his aims, but right in others:

> 'In a way he was wrong. He wanted you to be stronger, more intelligent with every generation. He wanted you to, as he thought, be like us. So he sought out our knowledge for you. He did it, wanting the best for his people. But in a way he gave them the worst. He wanted you to have all we once had – but that was not the answer. You know what happened here to us. Our knowledge killed, or drove us out. . . .
>
> 'One thing Gammage did for you which is right and which you must save more than you save anything you have taken from the lairs: He taught you that against a common enemy you can speak with Barkers under a truce flag, and gather and unite tribes and clans. Remember that above all else, for if he had only done that much, Gammage would be the greatest of your race.'
> (pp. 283–4)

The story of the animals thus becomes a parable for our own times, and, in keeping with the theme of the search for an ideal society, the close of the book looks to the future of the People.

The animal fantasy has gone almost as far as it can, in *Breed to Come*, in the direction of identifying humans and animals. Physically, the cats especially have come more and more to resemble humans. In some ways this actually makes them less acceptable as symbols for the human condition than the natural animal – their very strangeness alienates the reader from them. Although the characters of Furtig, Eu-La, Liliha, Gammage and the rest are well drawn and sympathetic, there is something faintly repugnant about cats with fingers and almost no fur.

The rats in Robert O'Brien's *Mrs Frisby and the Rats of NIMH* have also been the subjects of biological experiments, to lengthen their life expectancy and increase their learning ability – innocent-seeming experiments until the scientists start teaching the rats to read. Their appearance, however, is still that of normal rats. The power of developed mental capacity and of literacy is one of the central themes of the book. The rats are able to read the instructions for opening their cages and escape, taking with them two mice who have undergone the same treatment, but the return to their former life is not enough to satisfy the mental hunger of these rats who are no longer simply rats. They are exiles from their own kind, hated and feared, just as they are hated and feared by the humans who have made them what they are. Spending the winter in an empty country house, the rats satisfy their eagerness for knowledge in the large library, studying astronomy, electricity, biology, mathematics, music, art, poetry and history. Their first move is to the neighbour-hood of a farm, where there is a plentiful food supply, and where they construct an elaborate home, with electricity and water laid on, using a toy maker's tools which they have found. Most of the rats are content with the luxurious, even idle, life, but Nicodemus, the leader, is a visionary. During the winter in the library the seeds of a dream were sown, when he read of the self-sufficient monastic communities of the Middle Ages, and of the evidence that once prehistoric rats seemed to be evolving a civilization of their own.

Nicodemus dreams of building just such an independent civil-ization. The rats are on the point of moving out to a hidden valley in a forest nature reserve, with stores of grain and a few agricultural tools, in the hope of starting a new and independent life, no longer as scavangers from men. Some of the community rebel at the thought of deliberately destroying the luxurious home they have worked so hard to build at the farm and beginning a rough pioneering life in the wilderness. They leave to found their own parasite community. When they are discovered electrocuted in trying to steal an electric motor, the hunt closes in around the other rats. Two of the rearguard are killed, but the rest escape to found what they hope will be an ideal community – the sort of dream which drove the first settlers to America, and then ever westwards. It is a dream which has never lost its hold over the American imagination, and perhaps asserts itself so strongly in contemporary fantasy by American writers because it is more than ever before difficult to realize in life.

Mrs Frisby and the Rats of NIMH is an acute fable of modern life, posing two fundamental questions: first, what may be the results of tampering not only with inanimate, chemical and inorganic nature about us, but with the living creatures who, like us, have intelligence and sentient feelings; and, secondly, what will be the effect on the human mind and body of too much parasitical living, too much dependence on machinery and material luxury – may it not lead, in the end, to actual damage, to the degeneration of the mind and the spirit, and the collapse of civilization? These are, indeed, very much the questions Andre Norton poses in *Breed to Come*, but *Mrs Frisby and the Rats of NIMH* makes a greater impact on the reader through its greater immediacy. The setting is very much here and now, and the rats led by Nicodemus are probably very little different from the rats now in the medical research laboratories; indeed, Robert O'Brien himself said that stories he had heard of the exploits of such rats were the inspiration for the book.[8] As with all major fantasies, the links with primary world reality are close, and the issues confronted are those which cannot be shirked.

Certainly the best-known fantasy to have been published in recent years is an animal fantasy, *Watership Down*. A complex book, it draws on all the traditions outlined at the start of this chapter – folklore, animal fable, animal satire, the work of naturalists, and earlier fantasies. It is also almost Eliotesque in the oblique and direct references it makes to the whole range of European literature. As just one example, at the end of the Tale of El-ahrairah and the Black Rabbit, when the patriarchal folk-hero has sacrificed himself and suffered mutilation for his people, there is a recasting of one of Blake's prophetic writings:

As the light began to fail, [El-ahrairah] suddenly realized that Lord Frith was close beside him, among the leaves.

'Are you angry, El-ahrairah?' asked Lord Frith.

'No, my lord,' replied El-ahrairah, 'I am not angry. But I have learned that with creatures one loves, suffering is not the only thing for which one may pity them. A rabbit who does not know when a gift has made him safe is poorer than a slug, even though he may think otherwise himself.'

'Wisdom is found on the desolate hillside, El-ahrairah, where none comes to feed, and the stony bank where the rabbit scratches a hole in vain.' (p. 287)[9]

The episode as a whole is a parable of the ingratitude of children and grandchildren for the sacrifices made by their elders in time of war.

Within the scope of this study it is not possible to undertake a full assessment of *Watership Down*. The political criticism which forms one of its main themes will be considered in detail in Chapter 8; here we will outline the ways in which the rabbits are used to model human society. One point should be stressed at the outset. Richard Adams does not use the rabbit communities as simple mechanical allegories: there are clear parallels with their human counterparts, but they are also communities in their own right.

In the description of any community there are two distinct aspects – the physical or outer manifestation, and the mental or inner life of the inhabitants. The culture of a community, which originates in the inner life, may of course take outward form as painting, architecture and the like. In his study of the rabbit civilization, Richard Adams freely acknowledges his debt to R. M. Lockley's *Private Life of the Rabbit*. Every action which the rabbits perform in *Watership Down* is physically possible, and most are part of their regular behaviour. Certain deductions about the mental life of rabbits are made in Lockley's book, on the basis of his observations of their behaviour, and Adams uses these as the starting-point for his depiction of the characters and culture of his rabbits. The *Watership Down* rabbits are, of course, also given the power of speech, with all that implies, and so Adams sets out to create a secondary world of rabbits within the primary world of the Berkshire Downs of the present day.

This creation of the rabbits' world involves the evocation of a primitive community, very like a primitive human community. The characteristics of this primitive society are partly based on Lockley's observation of rabbits, partly linked with human communities: the vital, central issue of survival; the attitude towards the does, at once practical and protective; the importance of the warren as a whole rather than the individual; the indifference of most of the rabbits to any other creatures which are not *elil* (enemies), even if they are in danger or in pain; the practice of founding new communities to relieve overcrowding.

The characters of most of the protagonists can be seen against this background of a primitive civilization. Bigwig is a tribal hero, endlessly courageous and enduring, blunt, tactless, and not greatly imaginative. Holly is of the tribal warrior class, skilful, loyal, and obedient to his leader. General Woundwort is a Bigwig corrupted by absolute rule; he too possesses enormous courage, but he enjoys fighting to the point of bloodlust, and is filled with a desire to dominate and terrorize. Fiver is the visionary or prophet, again a figure from early civilization: sensitive, physically weak, with curious powers which he himself does not understand. Hazel is the exceptional leader, with capacities for foresight and compassion beyond his immediate society. Like El-ahrairah, he is prepared to sacrifice himself for his people, while General Woundwort would sacrifice his people for himself. The characterization of Adams's rabbits thus has much in common with that of Homer's protagonists, and we shall find further abundant evidence of the attraction the Bronze Age heroic civilization has for the writers of fantasy.

Adams gives his rabbits a language of their own, lapine, which is used so naturally that one almost expects documentary evidence for it, while they communicate with other animals and birds in a hedgerow patois. In addition to language, the rabbits have a developed culture. Like all primitive peoples, their concept of history is dark and but dimly grasped; there is little sense of anything clearly defined beyond the horizon of living memory or 'my mother told me'. On the other hand, they have a highly developed mythology and religion: the Lord Frith, Frithrah (the sun god), created the world and all its animals, and walked and talked among them in the early days. Inlé is the moon, and the Black Rabbit of Inlé is the death-bringer. There is a complex folklore centring on the folk hero El-ahrairah, the Prince of the Thousand Enemies, the first and archetypal rabbit king. The emphasis in these folk-tales, as is universally true of primitive folk-tales, is on survival, living by one's wits – all strongly laced with humour, usually coarse. El-ahrairah is a hero in the same tradition as Odysseus, the type discussed earlier in this chapter – the crafty trickster who outwits his enemies and saves his people. Like any body of folklore clustered about a popular hero, the tales of El-ahrairah confuse ancient and modern times, and may use words like 'camel' which have been handed down by word of mouth, but are no longer understood.

Within this overall picture of rabbit civilization, Adams creates a series of individual communities, as the saga unfolds, and these communities form the dystopias and utopias which embody the political theme, to be examined more fully in Chapter 8. The most fully documented community encountered by Hazel and his band, and the worst dystopia, is Efrafa, a military dictatorship strongly reminiscent of Hitler's Germany, Stalin's Russia, and other modern totalitarian states. Hazel's band are treated by the Efrafans like any other 'bunch of hlessil' (wanderers), they are bullied and threatened, and later their new warren on Watership Down is attacked viciously. Woundwort, Efrafa's dictator, is courageous, clever, and has a genius for organization, but he fails to rise to the challenge to accomplish something really worthwhile, to convert his dystopia into a utopia. Hazel, now crippled, has come out alone and incognito to parley with the attacking Efrafans; he offers Woundwort not war, but peaceful partnership:

> At that moment, in the sunset on Watership Down, there was offered to General Woundwort the opportunity to show whether he was really the leader of vision and genius which he believed himself to be, or whether he was no more than a tyrant with the courage and cunning of a pirate. For one beat of his pulse the lame rabbit's idea shone clearly before him. He grasped it and realized what it meant. The next, he had pushed it away from him. The sun dipped into the cloud-bank and now he could see clearly the track along the ridge, leading to the beech hanger and the bloodshed for which he had prepared with so much energy and care. (p. 425)

In the end Woundwort is defeated by the superior courage of Thlayli (Bigwig), the prophetic power of Fiver, and the outstanding heroism and leadership of Hazel. Yet he is also defeated by his own failure to respond to the higher demands of leadership. For Woundwort it represents only superior strength and ruthlessness, and his own crisis of leadership comes when he discovers that Thlayli, the biggest and strongest of the Watership Down rabbits whom he has seen, is not the leader. Thlayli is defending the one entrance to the warren:

With a sort of wary, dull surprise, Woundwort realized that he was afraid. He did not want to attack Thlayli again. He knew, with flinching certainty, that he was not up to it. . . . No, they would have to get in by some other way and everyone would know why.

'Thlayli,' he said, 'we've unblocked a run out here. I can bring in enough rabbits to pull down this wall in four places. Why don't you come out?'

Thlayli's reply, when it came, was low and gasping, but perfectly clear.

'My Chief Rabbit has told me to defend this run and until he says otherwise I shall stay here.'

'His Chief Rabbit?' said Vervain, staring.

It had never occurred to Woundwort or any of his officers that Thlayli was not the Chief Rabbit of his warren. Yet what he said carried immediate conviction. He was speaking the truth. And if he was not the Chief Rabbit, then somewhere close by there must be another, stronger rabbit who was. (p. 454)

It is beyond Woundwort's comprehension that the crippled rabbit whom he has scorned is the real Chief Rabbit. Hazel possesses the true attributes of kingship, not the brute strength of the brigand and pirate, and he leads his people to victory over Efafra. Adams thus uses his animals to examine the nature of leadership, as well as the characteristics of human communities.

There is much to *Watership Down* besides the quest for the ideal community, but this is clearly one of the most important themes. Like other animal fantasies which involve a quest for a social ideal, *Watership Down* ends not so much with the death of Hazel as with a sense that life will continue. In the Epilogue Hazel, his task completed, leaves to join the Owsla, the *comitatus* band, of El-ahrairah:

Then he saw that in the darkness of the burrow, the stranger's ears were shining with a faint, silver light. 'Yes, my lord,' he said. 'Yes, I know you.'

'You've been feeling tired,' said the stranger, 'but I can do something about that. I've come to ask whether you'd care to join my Owsla. We shall be glad to have you and you'll enjoy it. If you're ready, we might go along now.'

They went out past the young sentry, who paid the visitor no attention. The sun was shining and in spite of the cold there were a few bucks and does at silflay, keeping out of the wind as they nibbled the shoots of spring grass. It seemed to Hazel that he would not be needing his body any more, so he left it lying on the edge of the ditch, but stopped for a moment to watch his rabbits and to try to get used to the extraordinary feeling that strength and speed were flowing inexhaustibly out of him into their sleek young bodies and healthy senses.

'You needn't worry about them,' said his companion. 'They'll be all right – and thousands like them. If you'll come along, I'll show you what I mean.'

He reached the top of the bank in a single, powerful leap. Hazel followed; and together they slipped away, running easily down through the wood, where the first primroses were beginning to bloom. (p. 478)

Watership Down manages to fuse most of the elements of the animal tale tradition with great success. Animal fables are told amongst the rabbits, as part of their inherited culture; folk-tale, animal satire, and the detailed naturalist's study are all woven into the fabric of the novel. The use of the closely observed primary world setting, viewed from the rabbits' eye-level, is especially notable: Richard Adams has a keen awareness of the natural world, and walked over every yard of the actual ground covered by the rabbits when he was writing the book. The fine observation of the countryside in its changing weathers and seasons constitutes one of the outstanding and most attractive qualities of the work. The development of individual characters is not explored in any depth, and constitutes one area of weakness in the novel, but the relationships between the characters form the basis for the study of the community.

We have seen that the animal tale now, as in the remote past, can be used for many purposes, humorous or profound, and frequently didactic or moral. The closeness of the animals to ourselves, and yet their severance from us, establish the basic parameters of the animal tale. Given the powers of articulate thought and speech, the animals at once command our sympathy and understanding. Their emotions and beliefs, their moral and social structures, can be made to mirror those of the human world, and yet they are not human. Where they attempt to ape the ways of humans, as do Stuart Little or Andre

Norton's cats (or, indeed, even in the scenes involving humans and animals together in *The Wind in the Willows*), the reader feels a sense of disquiet. The animals lose their dignity and integrity by attempting to imitate the material trappings of human life. Either by leading their own true animal lives, as in *Jennie* or *Watership Down*, or by building their own ideal but secret communities, as in *The Mouse and His Child* or *Mrs Frisby and the Rats of NIMH*, they retain that integrity and our respect.

The best animal fantasies thus always operate on two levels: the animals serve as mirrors or models for human behaviour, but at the same time they are also true animals in their own right. The proportions between the two may vary, but both are always there. Man in general, like the young King Arthur, has much to learn from the birds, beasts and fish. The animal fantasy helps to remind us that we are, after all, only dressed animals, shielded by a few flimsy mechanical devices from the often harsh, but more natural life of our cousins. The strength of the animal fantasy lies in the closeness of this link. As R. M. Lockley says, after his years of close observation of the ways of wild rabbits:

> Rabbits are so human. Or is it the other way round – humans are so rabbit?[10]

· 3 ·
Worlds in Parallel

As the last chapter has shown, one of the commonest forms of fantasy, the animal fantasy, involves the exploration of certain occurrences of the marvellous within an otherwise normal primary world framework of experience. The next stage in abstraction beyond the primary world continuum is the tentative exploration of otherworlds, while the real world remains the basis and starting-point of experience. The fantasies to be considered in the present chapter are neither set entirely in the primary world, where the marvellous occurs exceptionally, nor are they set, entirely or completely, in a totally conceived secondary world, with all the imaginative complexity which that entails. They belong, rather, to an intermediate area of imaginative experience, where an often precarious balance must be maintained between two distinct worlds, and where the awareness of one world is constantly coloured by awareness of the other. Such fantasies involve the movement of characters in and out of some form of secondary world, but the perception of this world is often indistinct and dreamlike, in strong contrast with the secondary worlds to be considered in the next chapter, worlds whose tangible secondary reality is evoked in powerfully sensuous detail. While perception of the secondary worlds may be dreamlike, movement from world to world and the constant cross-reference between them creates a sense of parallelism between the two. Their structures are inevitably thrown into sharp juxta-position, while action in the secondary world may parallel hidden tensions and desires in the primary world.

One distinct type of secondary world in such fantasies of double experience is the world of time displacement. Such a secondary world is itself a true realization of the primary world, but with the additional disturbing perspective of a disruption in the normal perception of the time dimension. The parallels established are thus between different eras of the same physical world. On the other hand, the secondary world may indeed be a separate world, but when such dual worlds occur an apparently independent secondary world tends often to be a mirror of the inner mind. It may become an arena of intense experience for one central character, or for a group of characters linked by some close relationship. It may also present a visionary world of metaphysical reality.

The time fantasy, unlike most types of modern fantasy, is a comparatively recent development, and the evolution of the modern form needs to be related both to earlier literary forms and to philosophical problems involving the concept of time. Two traditional forms are akin to modern time fantasy, but are not strictly of the same genre: the dream vision and the magic sleep. In the majority of the dream vision poems the poet or dreamer visits the world of the dead or is guided to some other secondary world by a spirit, so that the time barrier is crossed in the sense that inhabitants of different periods of time meet and converse. However, the writers are primarily interested in the place visited or the advice given to the dreamer, rather than in the problems of time. The spirits of the dead are regarded as still existing in primary time, but in a secondary world. The magic sleep is a common folk- or fairy-tale element, often associated with heroes who will wake when help is needed in time of national disaster; traditionally such a magic sleeper can be woken only by the sound of a particular drum, horn or bell, or by the drawing of his sword.

It will be observed that in neither of these two traditional forms is there any real sense of movement through time. The spirit guide of the visionary dreamer moves, as it were, 'sideways' through space barriers, but not back and forth through time barriers. The magic sleepers continue to live in a suspended existence through the linear continuum of primary time, and after their awakening there is never any question of their being able to move backwards to their former time. The modern time fantasy, on the other hand, is concerned above all with time movement. It may be movement backwards or forwards through time, where time is envisaged as a linear continuum. More daringly, it may attempt to portray different times as coexistent layers, through which the characters of the fantasy may move, possibly experiencing more than one time at once.

Despite the interest of numerous philosophers, from Aristotle onwards, in the concept of time, the idea of moving outside primary time in the way described seems hardly to have entered fiction until the later nineteenth century.[1] The characteristic features of the modern time fantasy involve the relationship of time to the space dimensions, the concept of eternity, and some of the simpler problems and paradoxes in philosophical definitions of time. In turn, these raise problems of predestination and free will, as well as demanding an imaginative understanding of the past.

If time is conceived as a fourth dimension analogous to the three space dimensions of the primary world, then linear movement along the axis of this fourth dimension is generally regarded as possible in only one direction, and at a fixed rate. If neither of these two limitations of movement is imposed, the characters of a time fantasy can move either back into the past or forward into future time.

Time need not, however, be regarded as a fixed and isolated linear dimension, along which the present moment moves while irrevocable changes occur in the nature and condition of the primary world. There can be other freedoms in the time fantasy besides the freedom to move back and forth along the linear time dimension. The view from a moving railway carriage is continually changing, but the entire composite view exists both at the beginning and end of the journey, and more closely resembles the view from a high-flying aircraft. If time is considered in this way, the present moment is like the brief glimpse from the train window, but all time, like the whole scene, exists eternally. Thus time and the space dimensions form a composite, eternally existing, four-dimensional world. In *Flatland*, E. A. Abbott shows how the three-dimensional sphere, passing through a two-dimensional world, appears to a two-dimensional observer to be a point which grows into an ever larger circle, and then shrinks to a point again before disappearing. The sphere itself is whole and unaltered, but the two-dimensional observer perceives it as a time-changing phenomenon.[2] If time change is understood in this way, as an imperfectly comprehended movement in a further space dimension, then all time coexists, past and future events exist 'now', but in our limited capacity as observers we cannot perceive them. Such a concept of time is, of course, inextricably bound up with the issue of predestination: is there only one fixed future or are there many possible futures?

Mathematically, there is no reason to limit the number of dimensions in which fantasy may work. In order to escape from the restrictions of space–time as four-dimensional, Madeleine L'Engle in *A Wrinkle in Time* moves her action outside the primary space–time barriers by invoking a fifth dimension. The concept is worked out with some care – the characters experience a feeling of disintegration and then a sense of being pushed hard through a barrier as the normal dimensions are re-entered. On one occasion after 'tessering' Meg suffers from temporary paralysis as her body fails to function again in the normal space–time dimensions. The author introduces another vivid analogy when the characters are accidentally taken into two dimensions for a few moments, which produces a sensation of being squeezed flat, and an inability to breathe, since breathing involves three-dimensional motion.

A further problem in the consideration of time is that there may be not one but an infinite number of times. If the present moment is moving through time T_1, how 'fast' is it moving? This can only be deduced by introducing another time T_2 by which to measure the rate of movement through time T_1. To measure movement through time T_2, time T_3 must be postulated, and so on *ad infinitum*. When Milo in Norton Juster's *The Phantom Tollbooth* decides to conduct the dawn without telling anyone, he loses control and the sun rises and sets seven times in rapid succession. 'In just a few minutes a whole week had gone by' (p. 130). So it had, if time is determined by the rising and setting of the sun – but how are the minutes to be counted? What time is timing Time itself?

A different time problem arises in *The Starlight Barking* by Dodie Smith, when all the dogs in the world awake one morning to find that every other creature is 'asleep'. They are eventually told by Sirius the Dog Star that they have been granted twenty-four hours during which they will feel neither hunger nor thirst, and will possess extraordinary powers of movement and telepathic thought. The rest of the world will remain totally unaware of this day. The clocks, it should be noted, continue to function. But what 'time' are they measuring? Are the dogs in fact living through twenty-four hours of time in the primary world, while given other exceptional powers? If so, after the awakening it will be evident to astronomers that primary time has elapsed. Instead it appears that the dogs are living in a parallel, secondary time, with powers appropriate to a secondary world, even though the action takes place within the framework of the primary world.

The possibilities of different times occurring either in series or in parallel, or totally disconnected, simplifies the task of the 'magic door' fantasist. A character may pass from primary to secondary world and back again, and find that the rates at which primary and secondary time pass are quite unrelated. This is characteristic also of traditional tales which treat of visits to otherworlds. In *The*

Chronicles of Narnia, however much secondary time visitors from
the primary world spend in Narnia, on their return they find that no
time at all has passed in the primary world. On the other hand, after
they have spent some time in the primary world and then revisit
Narnia, they find that varying amounts of secondary time have
elapsed during their absence – on one occasion it is centuries, on another several years, on yet another just a few minutes.[3]

This question of differing rates of time is treated by writers of
fantasy in a variety of ways. The visit to a secondary world may
lie within specified limits in the primary world, while expanding
indefinitely in the secondary world, as in *Tom's Midnight Garden*,
when the visits to the past fall in the few moments after the striking of
thirteen instead of twelve on the old grandfather clock at midnight.
The two times may run parallel, as in Penelope Farmer's *Charlotte
Sometimes*, where there is the additional link that the dates and days
of the week coincide, and only the years are different. In *The
Diamond in the Window* the visits to both past and future, as well as
to other secondary worlds, lie within the span of a night, or a dream.
However, if all time is coexistent, the problem of differing rates of
time need not arise, nor need it arise if visitors from the past are
regarded as 'ghosts', and thus outside their own time for ever.

In addition to the exploration of its more serious philosophical
implications, time can be examined from a light-hearted standpoint
in linguistics or logic. This literary inheritance from Lewis Carroll is
particularly popular amongst American writers. In *Where the Wild
Things Are* by Maurice Sendak, Max sails off 'through night and day
and in and out of weeks and almost over a year'. On his return
journey from otherworld he reverses the process and sails 'back over
a year and in and out of weeks and through a day and into the night
of his very own room'.[4] In *The Time Garden*, Edward Eager takes a
whole series of time phrases and aphorisms, and interprets them
literally, with hilarious results: all the time in the world, wild time,
time will tell, all in good time, the time is out of joint, time flies,
old time's sake. Throughout time is symbolized by thyme. In *The
Phantom Tollbooth* Norton Juster considers the question of 'spending time' and 'wasting time', in a literal sense. In James Thurber's
The Thirteen Clocks the wicked Duke has 'murdered' time, or
believes that he has, so that all the thirteen clocks in the castle have
stopped, frozen:

Even the hands of his watch and the hands of all the thirteen clocks were frozen. They had all frozen at the same time, on a snowy night, seven years before, and after that it was always ten minutes to five in the castle. Travelers and mariners would look up at the gloomy castle on the lonely hill and say, 'Time lies frozen there. It's always Then. It's never Now.' (p. 18)

The task of the young hero, a prince in disguise, is to defeat the villain and, with the help of the Golux and the Princess, to free time once again. After the starting of the clocks

> Something like a vulture spread its wings and left the castle. 'That was Then,' the Golux said.
> 'It's Now!' cried Saralinda.
> A morning glory that had never opened, opened in the court-yard. A cock that never crowed, began to crow. The light of morning stained the windows, and in the walls the cold Duke moaned, 'I hear the sound of time. And yet I slew it, and wiped my bloody sword upon its beard.' ... 'No mortal man can murder time,' [Hark] said, 'and even if he could, there's something else: a clockwork in a maiden's heart, that strikes the hours of youth and love, and knows the southward swan from winter snow, and summer afternoons from tulip time.' (pp. 107–8, 110)

There are thus many possibilities open to the time fantasist, but on the whole most have confined themselves to the concepts of linear displacement through time and the coexistence of all time. Occasionally the distinction between the two may become blurred, particularly when the movement is from the past into the present. Are people transposed into the present from the past, who are dead in primary time, to be regarded as ghosts or as time travellers? Thomas Kempe, in Penelope Lively's *The Ghost of Thomas Kempe*, is undoubtedly a troubled spirit, an unlaid ghost, unseen and possessing the attributes of a poltergeist. Yet his personality is clearly unchanged from what it was when he was alive. On the other hand, although Toby, Alexander and Linnet in Lucy Boston's *The Children of Green Knowe* are at first unseen by Tolly and continue to vanish when it pleases them, they later look and behave like children in primary time. They have experienced illness and death, but they live again at Green Knowe as they did in their own lifetimes. Moreover, Tolly experiences past events with them, so that the coexistence of all time is stressed, as Tolly is conscious of living in both periods of time at once. Both books, like most time fantasies, are rooted in a very strongly realized sense of place. A consciousness of past time is closely associated with old buildings, old towns, old farmland, all of which bear the impress of many generations. This widely shared sense of the past which permeates places long inhabited is perhaps the major reason why most time fantasies link present and past in some kind of time change; very few attempt to link present and future. It also helps to account for their popularity with both writers and readers. One of the few time fantasies to explore the future is *The Diamond in the Window*, chapter 13, when Eleanor and Edward discover the possible futures which lie ahead of them. Here the power of the will to shape the future for good or evil is the theme, and there is no question of surveying a fixed, predestined future.

Time fantasy is based in the primary world, and when a time shift takes place many writers associate it with some form of material talisman. In *The Time Garden*, the characters crush and smell the thyme plants in order to move back through time, and the different varieties of thyme provide the clue to the sorts of time they experience. The thyme garden itself is old, planted in American pioneering days, and contains additional time talismans in the form of a sundial and an immortal Natterjack, an adviser and guide with a taste for heavy sarcasm. This is a fantasy of verbal wit as well as of time, and the apparatus for time shift is more elaborate than in most other cases. In *The Ghost of Thomas Kempe*, the ghost is released by the accidental breaking of a bottle in which he has been sealed. Charlotte and Clare change places in time in *Charlotte Sometimes* through the coincidence of dates and through both sleeping in a particular bed, but also because of certain similarities in their characters and circumstances. The grandfather clock with its erratic striking habits and its quotation from Revelation X, 'Time No Longer', is the main talisman in *Tom's Midnight Garden*, while in *The Whistling Boy* the appearances of the boy are linked with the room in an old farmhouse where he once lived, a tune he whistled, and a causeway to a lost village drowned by the sea.

Time shift does not always require a talisman or other material device. In many cases the pervading atmosphere of a particular place merges gradually into a sense of time change, and there may also be a strong thread of dreaming, memory, or lonely introspection. In the Green Knowe books the feeling of all time eternally present in the old house is built up through the accumulated details of past lives and the memories of Mrs Oldknowe and Boggis. The solitary, unhappy Anna in *When Marnie Was There* broods over the old house on the creek which seems strangely familiar, and when Marnie appears she is unaware for a long while that there has been any time change. Apart from two occasions – the ball and the visit to the mill – the two lonely children belong neither to past nor present, and after Anna's near-drowning they are parted for ever. Later it is discovered that Marnie was Anna's own grandmother who died when Anna was two, and that as a small child in the orphanage Anna had treasured a picture of the old house, her grandmother's childhood home, until the picture fell apart. The relationship between past and present is brought full circle as the submerged memory of the photograph is linked with the time shift experience. Similarly, the dreams of old Mrs Bartholomew, recalling her childhood and youth, are as important as the clock in opening the door to the past for Tom in *Tom's Midnight Garden*. The leap across the abyss of time is thus more often associated, in serious fantasy, with the power of the mind and the strength of the memory than with superficial devices.

Certain types of detail are of particular importance in the time fantasy. In the first place, any aspect of time itself must be made part of a logical pattern: the movement of clocks, the rising and setting of the sun, the phases of the moon and the seasons of the year. In *The Fellowship of the Ring*, when the companions emerge from Lothlórien after their period of rest, they are puzzled by the appearance of the moon, which seems to have moved out of phase. Legolas the Elf explains that the passage of time in Lothlórien differs from that in the rest of Middle-earth, because the Elves do not count time in the same way as mortals. The travellers think they have spent only a few days in the kingdom of Galadriel, but in fact a whole month has passed by. Similarly, Tom notices that his visits to the midnight garden are always on perfect spring or summer days, or later in sparkling skating weather. He realizes finally that he is visiting the memories of Hatty's times of happiness, which are enshrined by the memory in ideal seasons. The timing of the visits thus has a logic, although not the logic of normal chronology.

Secondly, there arises in time fantasy the problem of the physical appearance of the time travellers. Would such a time traveller appear normally solid and 'real' in the three dimensions of the world in which he finds himself? Or would he have a transparent 'ghostly' look? In most cases the fantasist prefers the former: in *The Whistling*

Boy, Earthfasts, Charlotte Sometimes, When Marnie Was There and many others, the time travellers seem to have the same spatial properties as the people they encounter. However, the children from the past in the Green Knowe books are elusive, sometimes invisible, and only occasionally appear in full bodily form. The child in *The Ghost Downstairs* is accepted as normal by all but Mr Fast, yet he has a 'fragile [and] unearthly pallor' (pp. 56 and 48). On the other hand, Tom, in *Tom's Midnight Garden*, who moves back into the past, is seen only by Hatty and by Abel, the gardener. He is invisible to everyone else, and becomes gradually 'thinner' for Hatty as she grows older. Tom cannot move physical objects in the past world, and instead of opening doors must force his way through them. These experiences lead to a frightening crisis for Tom, when he begins to doubt his own reality, and in panic accuses Hatty of being a ghost. The children finally agree that they are both real, yet privately neither believes the other, and Philippa Pearce's analysis of Tom's predicament is logically consistent – a displacement in the time dimension may well mean an inability to move normally in the space dimensions of another time.

The time fantasy may explore a number of themes particularly related to the idea of movement through time. At the simplest level, such a story may use a humorous or menacing ghost figure, but the serious fantasist probes further beneath the surface and – as in *The Ghost of Thomas Kempe* – may examine the complex and some-times painful relationship between past and present. Thomas's inability to cope with the modern world, and his final unhappy plea for help and release, is a kind of parable of the confusions and sufferings of the elderly in a violently changing technological age. Penelope Lively thus establishes a parallel between the experience of the time traveller and the normal experience of aging within the primary world. One of the earliest time fantasies, Rudyard Kipling's *Puck of Pook's Hill* (1906), was an evocative survey of British history, and some time fantasies, like those of Edward Eager, are still used as a device for exploring the past in its own terms. However, with the growth of the serious and imaginatively written historical novel, the time fantasy has become more concerned not with an objective view of the past, but with the vital interrelationship between past and present.

The time traveller, who is usually solitary, rarely remains a dis-passionate observer, but forms deep and abiding relationships with the people he meets. In *A Traveller in Time* (1939) by Alison Uttley, one of the best time fantasies but outside the strict limits of our period, Penelope falls deeply in love with Francis Babington, whom she meets in the past. The sense of coming separation is more poignant than in any star-crossed love affair in the primary world, for the ultimately unbridgeable gulf of time lies between the lovers, as irrevocable as death. The time fantasy frequently stresses this double quality: the enduring nature of the basic human relationships of love, friendship, loyalty and trust, amongst all people of all time, set against the changes which the relentless passage of time renders in places and individuals. Most people only experience the pathos of changing human relationships and the sense of loss through time as they grow through maturity to old age. In the time fantasy an intense lifetime of the emotions can be compressed into a short period, as it is in *Tom's Midnight Garden, Earthfasts* and *Charlotte Sometimes*.

The intellectual basis of the time fantasy is closely related to the philosophical problems of time mentioned earlier, as to whether all time is coexistent, whether displacement in the time dimension is possible, and whether multiple times exist. Hence if a time traveller is displaced into the past, there arises the additional problem of the outcome of his actions. Can he change the course of events and remake the past? Penelope knows that she cannot rescue her friends from the disaster of the Babington plot, in *A Traveller in Time*. Tom cannot physically move objects in his midnight garden, but he directs Hatty's building of the tree house from which she falls, and she carves his private sign on a tree. Both actions are a direct result of the visit to the past. Further problems arise for the visitor to the future. When Charlotte and Clare change places in *Charlotte Sometimes*, Clare is displaced some forty-five years into the future. It would be perfectly possible for her still to be alive in primary time (as indeed her sister Emily is). Would Clare then be alive twice over, as child and as adult? Or would the adult Clare really be Charlotte, who has become permanently displaced in time and grown up as Clare? If so, what would happen when the time came for Charlotte to be born – would she exist in double form? In fact, as Charlotte eventually discovers, Clare died in the influenza epidemic of 1918, shortly after their last time exchange, and she realizes that only thus would it have been logically possible. (This is true if time is seen as linear, but the concept of coexistent time makes no such demand.)

The question of creating or affecting past and future is closely bound up with moral responsibility and the growth of personality. A sense of personal identity can be achieved only through a fully realized relationship with time and space. Disruption to the individual's frame of reference may lead to the fragmentation of the emotional self. Time travellers frequently lose their sense of identity and have to grope their way back to a conscious personality, which may have been altered by their experiences. The search for a future identity is symbolized by Jane Langton in *The Diamond in the Window* by multiple mirror images of Edward and Eleanor. As they pass through the series of reflections, they observe that the images of themselves are growing older. One wrong choice of personality leads to more and more wrong choices until they find themselves forced to follow a single sequence of ever more evil images. Frightened by the experience, they grope their way back in darkness through the mirror images and begin the search again. As they select their future selves more carefully, the choices widen out instead of narrowing:

> Instead of two choices, there were many. . . . And beyond that choice lay a hundred, and beyond the next a thousand. Just as the other maze had led them down a narrowing path until there was no choice left, this one opened out into wide and shining worlds of possibility. (p. 111)

The possibility of remaking the past of one's own personality, instead of creating the future, is most searchingly examined in Leon Garfield's inversion of the Faust legend, *The Ghost Downstairs*, which will be considered in detail later.

It is clear from the preceding discussion of the predominant qualities of the modern time fantasy that it has moved very far away from any earlier types with which it has links. The time fantasy is probably the most intellectually demanding of all the different types of modern fantasy, both for the writer and for the reader. A writer who has the necessary logical capacity may lack the imaginative gift for evoking other times, while the writer of poetic and descriptive talent may construct the time relation loosely and illogically.

To what extent do writers succeed in reconciling the sometimes conflicting demands of time fantasy? Where the treatment of time change is predominantly humorous, little difficulty seems to arise. Norton Juster in *The Phantom Tollbooth*, Edward Eager in *The Time Garden*, and James Thurber in *The Thirteen Clocks* all use the element of time fantasy as an opportunity for verbal humour, although there is an underlying seriousness of intent in Juster's book.[5] These three American writers are some of the heirs of the Lewis Carroll tradition, mentioned above – the fantasy of word-play and logic, whose chief delight lies in mental gymnastics. In this type of treatment, the time fantasy need only have logical consistency. Any relationship with primary world experience is purely coincidental.

Fantasies which treat the problem of time seriously range very widely in their approach. In *A Wrinkle in Time*, Madeleine L'Engle is deeply aware of the mathematical and philosophical nature of time, but as her time travellers pass into a distinct secondary world by disruption of the space dimensions also, she does not explore the parallelism between different eras of the same world. At the other extreme, in *The Ghost Downstairs*, Leon Garfield does not consider the process by which the seven-year-old phantom comes to be present in the world of the adult Mr Fast. Once the clerk has sold his childhood to Mr Fishbane it is no longer in the past, but present. Perhaps it would be more accurate to say that we all carry our own pasts within us – Dennis Fast's childhood is no longer contained within his mind and memories, but moves outside into the spatial world, and meets him face to face. Garfield is thus not interested in the mathematical aspects of time movement, but is concerned above all with the living past which is always present, with the personal past for which each individual is accountable, and in relation to which he shapes his future. He thus explores, through the medium of fantasy, the time-dimension of the individual personality. Susan Cooper, in her quintet, *The Dark is Rising*, uses many time shifts to explore the fundamental unity in human affairs. The external differences in clothes and material surroundings are portrayed as irrelevant by comparison with the larger moral issues. This group of novels is not primarily concerned with the parallelism between two worlds, however, and will be discussed later.

Three books which consider both the problems of time displacement and the parallelism between worlds are *The Children of Green Knowe* by Lucy Boston, *Charlotte Sometimes* by Penelope Farmer, and *Tom's Midnight Garden* by Philippa Pearce. The first of these reveals the tensions which exist between the need for a closely argued logical structure and a sensitivity to other times. Lucy Boston's setting of the old house and its rambling gardens with their hidden and unexpected corners, the long memories of Mrs Oldknowe, the children's voices and laughter, tantalizing and elusive, are all handled with great fidelity to a sincere vision of time past. However, it is in nature of time fantasy that even one error stands out in sharp relief, and causes the imagination to stumble and hesitate in accepting the whole. In *The Children of Green Knowe* there are many errors. Awkward questions spring to mind. Would the chaffinches remember nesting in a cage after an interval of three hundred years? Could Toby's fish possibly have lived the same length of time? Could the same wooden platform, repeatedly submerged by the river, have survived without rotting for three centuries? These things are part of time present, not time past. The garden rose was not a new discovery in the seventeenth century, nor were voyages to Japan common then. The rocking horse is clearly Victorian. Despite the fine poetic quality in much of *The Children of Green Knowe*, these and other flaws in historical accuracy or in basic credibility mar the book, and enforce the lesson that fantasy must have a firm basis in realism. In the case of the time fantasy, historical realism and a credible presentation of the effects of primary time, either in preserving or destroying material objects, are essential.

By contrast, *Charlotte Sometimes* is planned with meticulous accuracy. With the use of a perpetual calendar it is possible to calculate that the two parallel years are 1918 and 1963, and to construct a table of dates. The 1918 portions of the story are presented with the same calm realism as those set in 1963. The parallels and the sense of the fundamental unity of all periods of time are further enhanced by the setting: the rather old-fashioned girls' boarding school has changed very little, even the uniform is almost the same. The similarity is emphasized by the small changes which have occurred: Charlotte is always first made aware that she is in 1918 again when she hears the rustling in the branches of a large cedar tree outside the dormitory window, where in her own time there is a new wing of the building. Small incidentals of life are different too – 1918 wartime food, lawns converted into vegetable patches, the teachers' high-piled hair, no sound of aeroplanes – but the overall pattern of school life, lessons, walks, prayers, discipline, remain the same. Charlotte finds herself in a sense becoming Clare, losing her own identity as she fills Clare's place in the past:

> Clare had always been a kind of skin about her, Charlotte thought, containing what she did and said and was; but the skin

had thickened imperceptibly the longer she stayed in the past. After the night-time expedition it began to thicken more rapidly than ever, pressing that part of her which still thought of itself as Charlotte tighter and smaller, until it lay deep down in her, like a small stone inside a large plum. (p. 119)

For a brief, disturbing time, she slips even out of Clare's identity. Moved into lodgings with Clare's younger sister, Emily, Charlotte finds herself sleeping in a bed formerly occupied by Miss Agnes, the spinster daughter of the house whose younger brother, Arthur, has recently been killed at the front. Like Clare, like Miss Agnes, Charlotte is a responsible elder sister with a naughty, but sometimes insecure younger child to care for. She begins to dream about Arthur as a small boy – Arthur who played at soldiers and forced himself to be brave, even when he was terrified:

> She thought she heard someone laughing and someone else crying. Then, without seeming to move she found herself standing beside a boy who beat the drum. Its gold and green stripes were bright, its soft top vibrated, it sounded not only like a drum, but also like a roaring aeroplane, and it made lights as well as sounds, beams like searchlights dazzling at every stroke. She was begging the boy to stop. 'Oh, please, Arthur, please, you'll wake everyone up, Papa will hear you, oh, please.'
>   The boy wore bandages on his head under a cricketer's hat, and he laughed and went on beating the drum. (p. 135)

Charlotte wakes from this terrifying dream, in which Arthur the child and Arthur the soldier have become merged, into what she thinks is still Clare's time. When she becomes aware of movement in the dark bedroom her time sense is that of 1918, but another time slip has thrust her back into the childhood of Agnes and Arthur, the Arthur whose bravado was all on the surface and who was really gentle and easily frightened. Arthur, who has been killed in the trenches, calls out to her as a small boy to his sister, and Charlotte's sense of identity slips perilously through her fingers:

> 'I'm not Aggie. Go away! I'm not her. I'm Clare, I'm Clare. No, I'm not. I'm Charlotte. I'm Charlotte, I'm Charlotte.' She was screaming it at last, again and again. 'I'm Charlotte.' (p. 137)

Moving in this way into other people's pasts and personalities,

Charlotte finds herself understanding and sharing a whole range of emotions and relationships beyond her own personal experience. Penelope Farmer, through her use of time fantasy, thus makes both Charlotte and the reader aware of the dissolving of barriers between apparently dissimilar people, of different ages and different periods, when the deep springs of human emotion are touched. The double nature of time change – its immediacy and its remoteness – are brought curiously home to Charlotte when she realizes that an elderly geography teacher who works part-time at the school in 1963 is the same Miss Wilkin whose fiancé had been killed in 1918:

> Charlotte stared at this Miss Wilkin, stared and stared and stared. The Miss Wilkin she had known in 1918 must surely be too old now to teach, even part-time like this. . . . But then she remembered seeing her skip upstairs like a schoolgirl, not like a grown-up woman. Bunty and Emily had thought it funny and giggled afterwards, but it made Charlotte think now that Miss Wilkin must have been very young as teachers went, perhaps no more than ten years older than Emily herself.
>
> Gradually she began to see in this old Miss Wilkin the younger one; the way she batted her head about and smiled, the jolly eyes, the inappropriately nipped-in waist. On her left hand there was an engagement ring. What would Emily look like now, Charlotte wondered sadly. In a way she wished, as she had wished before, that Clare and Emily had lived long enough ago to be quite safely dead. (p. 174)

Past and present are linked through Miss Wilkin, and yet there remains the finally uncrossable divide between them. Charlotte learns from Emily's youngest daughter, Sarah, a senior girl at the school in 1963, that Clare had died in 1918, only a few days after they had last changed places. She cannot contain her grief:

> On that bleak track, the sun almost gone again, tears were pouring down her face. She was crying and crying for a girl who had died more than forty years before, whom, in any normal world, to any normal way of thinking, she could not possibly have known; whom she had never even seen, though she had lived as her. She was crying for herself, perhaps, and for Emily. (p. 178)

In *Tom's Midnight Garden*, Tom does not take on another personality, but he does find his own sense of identity threatened when he moves, ghostlike, into the past, visible only to the sensitive eyes of the lonely Hatty and to Abel the gardener, a religious man with a deep feeling for the natural world. Like Charlotte, Tom experiences a range of unfamiliar emotions. Unhappy and neglected, Hatty reaches out for love and companionship across the gulf of the years, and Tom, who is unaware that he is responding to her need for him as much as to his own curiosity about the lost garden, steps in and out of the past. Time does not stand still in Hatty's world. Over a few weeks of his own life, Tom experiences the whole span of Hatty's life from the time she arrives at the Melbourne's house, a small unwanted orphan, to the night before her marriage to Barty. The experience is not always chronological. Although for most of the time Hatty grows up from an age slightly younger than Tom's to early womanhood, there are two events out of sequence, both events which are etched sharply on Hatty's memory, and so shared with Tom – her first arrival at the Melbournes', dressed in mourning, and the destruction of the great fir tree by lightning, the night before her wedding.

Apart from these dislocations, Tom finds himself living at a different rate from Hatty. He believes he visits the garden every night, as he does in his own time, but she tells him that sometimes he does not return for months. Philippa Pearce uses these incompatible time scales to explore the pain of changing relationships. Hatty grows at last perceptibly older, but Tom remains wilfully blind to this until a crisis forces him into awareness. As her kindest cousin tries to interest Hatty in life outside the garden and in other friends, she finds Tom growing thinner and thinner to her sight, until finally, driving home with Barty after she and Tom have skated together to Ely, she ignores him altogether.

Tension mounts in the story as it moves towards what seems to be an inevitably tragic end. On his last night in the present day of the old house, Tom cannot find his way back into the garden. Separated for ever from it and from Hatty, he runs 'like a rat with the dogs after it' and screams for Hatty. 'Tom's call, sharp like a bird's warning, reached up even to the topmost flat and woke Mrs Bartholomew from a dream of her wedding one Midsummer Day some sixty-odd years before' (p. 212). The next morning Tom, stunned with grief, climbs up to the top flat to apologize, and then comes what Tolkien called the 'eucatastrophe' of fantasy, the 'sudden and miraculous grace. . . . Joy beyond the walls of the world, poignant as grief' (*TL*, p. 60):

> 'Oh, Tom,' [Mrs Bartholomew] was saying, 'don't you under-
> stand? You called me: I'm Hatty.'
>   The words of the little old woman were meaningless to Tom;
> only her black eyes compelled him. . . .
>   Tom listened as she began her tale; but at first he listened less
> to what she was saying than to the way she was saying it, and he
> studied closely her appearance and her movements. Her bright
> black eyes were certainly like Hatty's; and now he began to
> notice, again and again, a gesture, a tone of the voice, a way of
> laughing that reminded him of the little girl in the garden.
>   Quite early in Mrs Bartholomew's story, Tom suddenly
> leaned forward and whispered: 'You were Hatty – you *are*
> Hatty! You're really *Hatty*!' She only interrupted what she was
> saying to smile at him, and nod. (pp. 217, 219)

Throughout his visit to the garden, Tom is obsessed with time and how it functions. On the pendulum of the grandfather clock is inscribed 'Time No Longer' and on its face the reference Rev. X, 1–6. Hatty and Tom consult Abel's Bible:

> And the angel which I saw stand upon the sea and upon the
> earth lifted up his hand to heaven, and sware by him that liveth
> for ever and ever, who created heaven, and the things that
> therein are, and the sea, and the things which are therein, that
> there should be time no longer.

Tom believes that he can 'dodge' time: 'if Time is ever to end, that means that, here and now, Time itself is only a temporary thing' (p. 168). In his struggles to understand the theory of time, he interrupts his uncle's dry scientific explanations with the angel's vow that there will be time no longer:

> 'What on earth have angels to do with scientific theories?' Tom
> trembled, and dared not explain that this was more than a
> theory: it was a blazing, angelic certitude. (p. 169)

As Philippa Pearce shows in her denouement, it is not so easy for ordinary mortals to side-step time. When he fails to re-enter the garden on his last night, Tom realizes that he has not been able to circumvent time in the way he had hoped. He cannot 'Exchange

Time for Eternity'. Instead, on his last visit, the hurrying pace of Hatty's time overwhelms him: he cannot find time to tell her of his plan; the tower-keeper at Ely hurries them along, crying 'Time'; 'It's late,' cries Hatty. . . . 'we must hurry.' Yet after the horror of being cut off for ever from the world of the garden, Tom finds unexpectedly that time past is not altogether lost:

> 'I called to you, but I never really thought you could hear me.'
>
> 'You woke me,' said Mrs Bartholomew. 'I knew it was Tom calling to me for help, although I didn't understand, then. I couldn't believe you were real, until I saw you this morning.'
>
> Tom said: 'We're both real; Then and Now. It's as the angel said: Time No Longer.' (p. 226)

In *Tom's Midnight Garden* the abstract theory of time, and the effects of time on temporal, aging humans and their ever-changing relationships with each other, are welded together into an artistic unit. Here there are none of the tensions which exist between imagination and logic in *The Children of Green Knowe*. To succeed as a whole, a time fantasy must reconcile its different temporal worlds and also its abstract with its human qualities. This is done in *Charlotte Sometimes*, and especially in *Tom's Midnight Garden*, by setting the mutable nature of an individual's life against the enduring traits of humanity, by setting the present, fleeting moment against the long span of history. By exchanging Time for Eternity.

In other fantasies of dual worlds, where there is no time shift, two types in particular have attracted a number of writers: that in which the secondary world embodies the mental landscape of the characters, and that in which it represents a visionary world. When writers use the concept of dual worlds in order to mirror the landscape of the inner mind, the fantasies they produce are, of course, not unaffected by the researches of Freud and Jung, and their successors. William Mayne in *A Game of Dark* uses the secondary world to explore the terrors of a sick mind; *Marianne Dreams*, by Catherine Storr, probes the inner world of the heroine during a period of physical illness; Penelope Farmer's *A Castle of Bone* is concerned with the relationships between four teenagers, with all their suppressed tensions and affections.

In *Marianne Dreams* the heroine, a normally active girl, suffers a prolonged bout of illness which leaves her weakened and confined to bed for several months. Through a shared tutor, Marianne learns of

Mark, whose slow recovery from polio is hampered by his loss of the will to live. Although she never meets Mark in the primary world, Marianne encounters him in the secondary world created by her drawings, which she enters in her dreams. Parallels between the two worlds are immediately established. Not only is the secondary world actively created by Marianne's drawings in the primary world; the emotions she experiences in the primary world influence events in the secondary world. Moreover, actions and moods in the secondary world affect the primary world: when, in her dream world in the house she has drawn, Marianne yields to a fit of jealous rage and threatens Mark, she finds that the primary world Mark becomes more seriously ill. Similarly, anger, fear, jealousy or cruelty in the primary world produce dangerous or threatening elements in the secondary world. The house in the drawing becomes less of a sanctuary and more of a prison, shut in by the high fence and iron bars which Marianne has drawn, and surrounded by the one-eyed stones which watch the children's every move. Mark and Marianne must circumvent the dangers partly by means of Marianne's drawings in the primary world, and partly through actions in the secondary world; the two parallel worlds are thus more closely linked than in many other cases.

The special pencil cannot be erased; so Marianne finds that the secondary world she creates is, like the world of our past actions, ineradicable. Errors and sins cannot be wiped out, they can only be regretted, and compensated for. Thus the angry scribbling-out of Mark's face at the window and the drawing of the eyes on the formerly harmless stones cannot be altered, any more than Marianne's brief, bitter wish that Mark were dead, and her vow that she will stop dreaming about him. When the real Mark is in hospital, and dying, Marianne faces up to her possible guilt and tries to atone for her actions. The barred window and the monstrous seeing stones remain, but through her help Mark regains his strength in the secondary world. In the primary world his recovery is slower, less compressed in time, but it follows the same course as in the secondary world.

The world of the pictures becomes a map of Marianne's mental state, her frustrations and depressions in her illness, her dawning sympathy and understanding for another person. Like the image of an individual's past life, the drawing grows ever more complicated; it contains horror and fear, but also moments of peace and happiness, and the hopeful beam of the lighthouse. Through her experiences in the secondary world, Marianne moves, sometimes painfully, away from the egotistical world of childhood towards a more mature comprehension of herself and of others.

William Mayne's *A Game of Dark*, like *Marianne Dreams*, presents the secondary world as the inner world of the central character. Unlike the world of Marianne's drawings, however, Donald Jackson's inner world is shared by no one else from his primary world. *A Game of Dark* is a fantasy of deliberate escapism for a disturbed mind, 'fantasy' in the psychologist's sense, unlike any other literary fantasy considered in this study. Although it is primarily a conscious flight from everyday reality to a world 'with less shame and guilt to it' (p. 52), it is not a reassuring escapism. Donald Jackson's feudal secondary world is filled with horror and stench, the physical manifestation of his suppressed feelings.

Donald's need to escape arises from his situation in the primary world. Mr Jackson is crippled, and tyrannical in his pain, yet Donald is haunted by memories of his father playing car games with his wheelchair when his son was small. Mrs Jackson, who teaches at Donald's school, has become a cold, unsympathetic mother in her grief and bereavement. Her attitude to her son is epitomized by Mayne in her language. Forgetfully, she addresses him even at home by his surname, and uses pedantic impersonal constructions in their casual conversations. Both parents are harsh Nonconformists, combining a self-righteous attitude towards religion with an element of masochism.

Donald has grown up in the shadow of a much-loved elder sister, killed in the train crash which crippled his father, just before Donald was born. Confined within the barriers of their own grief, his parents have never fully explained the events to him, and it is not until nearly the end of the book that he learns the facts from 'Berry', the Anglican vicar who was responsible for Cecily and Mr Jackson being on the train. Donald follows Berry about, joins his youth group, visits his house, grateful even for his shallow kindness, but Mayne's analysis of this character is if anything even more damning than the portraits of the parents. They at least feel deeply, although their grief has worked inwards, destroying humanity and sympathy just as the dragon or 'worm' of Donald's secondary world destroys everything it touches. Berry constantly acts the part of the hearty, broad-minded, modern clergyman, while at heart he is totally insensitive to those with whom he feigns a warm relationship. Donald wishes that 'Berry was not another empty person in a sharply-seen but fragile world' (p. 110) – it is the primary world he is referring to. Berry is leaving the village to go to another parish, and pays his last visit to the youth group – this substitute father, on whom Donald focuses all his emotions:

> Berry took Donald's hand and put something in it, then closed the hand over the thing and squeezed it. It was the warm Wilbert toffee Jacqueline had given him.
>
> When he got home the house was still empty. He made the fire blaze harder and sat beside it. The toffee was still in his hand. It smelt of snails from being Jacqueline Wilbert's, he thought, but Berry had touched it. He unwrapped it sticky from its paper, ate it, and folded the paper up to keep it, putting it with the note in Berry's writing about his address. These were the only things that Berry had ever given him. (pp. 72–3)

It is in this kind of detail – the intimate, affectionate gesture accompanying the worthless gift passed on from someone else – that Mayne displays his shrewd eye for the subtleties of personality and personal relationships. Significantly, Berry has no children of his own, just two adopted babies, chosen because they have brown eyes, both of whom he calls indiscriminantly 'Toby'. For Berry, the people he encounters have no individual significance. In his own way he is as egotistical as Donald's parents. Caught in this situation, Donald's personality has become twisted and cramped, shying away from normal human contact. Outwardly he is obedient, even conciliatory, to his parents, while inwardly he is torn by rebellion and the tumult of his emotions. Deepest of all is his sense of guilt – guilt for being unable to love his father, and guilt for being alive at all instead of Cecily.

In the secondary world under the obsessive threat of the monstrous worm, 'Jackson', as he calls himself, becomes first page, then squire, to the lord, and forms a natural and friendly relationship with a village girl, Carrica. The worm, with its freezing, deadly touch, embodies the 'shame and guilt' of Donald's primary world existence. Despite its overwhelming power, the lord and Jackson devise a means for keeping the worm regularly fed and pacified for several years, just as Donald has suppressed and hidden his emotional life, but eventually, partly through Jackson's carelessness, the worm breaks into the village, killing and destroying. The lord must fight the worm and is killed, leaving Jackson to assume the leadership. He fails to kill the monster in honourable combat and runs away, just as Donald in the primary world runs away from the crisis in his emotional life as his father lies babbling and dying in hospital. Later, hiding in a hollowed-out hole in the stinking ice of the monster's cave, Jackson kills it by stabbing it from below. The village is freed from the nightmare curse which hung over it, but Jackson is permanently dishonoured.

Mayne thus makes the actions of Jackson in the secondary world parallel the course of Donald's inner life in the primary world. He never overcomes his hatred of his father while Mr Jackson is alive, and he deliberately blinds himself to Berry's faults, despite his own moments of clear insight and the vicar's occasional efforts to be more emotionally honest. Donald does struggle, however, to make some sense of his life and his relationships with other people:

> He thought he could see all the people around him and found they were all in the wrong places. He needed a place to see them from so that they were all in their right order. Somewhere, he thought, there is a place that is right for me, there is a way of looking at things, and a time when the world will run smoothly again. But he could not see that time coming. (pp. 122–3)

When Jackson kills the worm – dishonourably – in the secondary world, it is the night Donald's father has come home and is dying in the next room:

> Half of him watched the house in Hales Hill. Half looked at the girl, Carrica, the girl in the photograph, Carrica was not his. She was his mother or his sister, and of those two he knew which was which, and he knew that the man in the other room was his father, whom he knew now how to love. Carrica was a phantom if he wanted her to be, and the house in Hales Hill was another, and he had the choice of which to remain with.
>
> In Hales Hill the sick man said 'Open the curtains. I want to see the day.' The curtains rattled open on their runners.
>
> 'I must go,' said Jackson. 'I shall start again in another place. I have not done well in this one.'
>
> Mr Jackson spoke. 'Lord, now lettest thou thy servant,' he said, and then was silent.

'I am going too,' said Jackson, and he withdrew from the presence of Carrica, so that there was no more the sight of the lord's fields or the town beyond or that golden morning but only the golden morning at Hales Hill, where reality was.

In the other room the curtains were closed again. Mrs Jackson came out of the room and closed the door and went into the kitchen. There was no more breathing. Donald lay and listened to the quiet, and went to sleep, consolate. (pp. 125–6)

In the end, then, Donald chooses the primary world of reality and rejects his secondary world. *A Game of Dark* is a sober and often disturbing book, which analyses with great honesty and no concessions the effects on a child of living always in the shadow of adult pain and grief. *Marianne Dreams* and *A Game of Dark* are thus structurally very similar – in each case the central character deliberately creates a secondary world which provides an escape from the pressure of primary world realities, only to find that in the secondary world the suppressed emotions explode into concrete forms and events. Both books take, initially, a somewhat depressing view of a small will struggling against apparently overwhelming odds. The tone of *Marianne Dreams* differs widely, however, from that of *A Game of Dark*. Marianne is a normally happy child, experiencing an unexpected period of illness and frustration, which produces uncharacteristic bursts of jealousy and anger. The mood of the book moves from claustrophobia and depression towards an optimistic sense of release and freedom as Marianne gropes, both in her dream world and in the primary world, towards greater self-knowledge, a sympathetic understanding of the feelings of others, and the recovery of health. On the other hand, Donald Jackson is a disturbed boy living constantly under great tension. The whole quality of the book is sick and oppressive, although it truly catches the atmosphere of the life which it intends to convey. Both secondary worlds have an inner, dream-like quality, but while Marianne learns to cope with and conquer hers, Donald's world remains, almost to the end, filled with horror and bitterness. Although he kills the worm, its significance as a symbol is never fully realized in the primary world, despite Mayne's careful parallelism of action. Donald never really solves his own problems. Only in the concluding paragraphs of the book, the extract just quoted, is there some kind of resolution, when Jackson determines to leave the secondary world as Mr Jackson leaves the primary world. Boy and man become in a sense fused, and Donald learns to understand his father by realizing that he too has 'not done well in this place'. But if a kindly fate had not killed off his father, could Donald have learned to love him? After such a scarred childhood, is the sick soul truly cured?

Penelope Farmer's *A Castle of Bone* initially presents the inner secondary world of one individual: Hugh's daytime thoughts become dominated by the strange cupboard he has bought, while in dreams he visits a remote, and dream-like, secondary world. Yet this secondary world is not simply one of dreams. It has a tangible reality, for Hugh finds his slippers soaking wet in the morning, and leaves are caught up among the bedclothes. Gradually Hugh's sister Jean, and their friends Penn and Anna, are drawn into the world, until all finally enter the cupboard and its secondary world in full consciousness.

This secondary world shifts and changes. The castle of bone is ruined at one time, and later is seen whole. As in *Tom's Midnight Garden*, the time dimension is distorted. A lake appears and disappears, woods change: at one time they are of willow, at another oak, at yet another overgrown apple trees. The trees seem somehow significant to Hugh, but their significance eludes him: they are, in fact, all part of the ancient sacred tree alphabets.[6]

The meaning of the secondary world and its effects on primary world objects and people appear inexplicable and frightening to Hugh and the others:

> But if it had not been a dream, the reality he had experienced had been of a different kind. It was as if everything he knew had been taken apart and then put together in a different way, in a pattern just as agreeable yet apparently wayward, because it was not the pattern in which he normally lived. He might follow it in time but it would take him time to do that; as eyes take time to adjust from light to dark. (p. 38)

In one sense the secondary world is a kind of distorting mirror of the primary world, composed of refracted images which are confused and constantly changing. The lake appears in the secondary world after the expedition on the lake in the primary world; glimpses of the woods recall fleeting impressions from the primary world. On his visits to the secondary world, Hugh is constantly aware of a haunting but elusive familiarity. In another sense, this is a novel of time fantasy. Objects placed in the cupboard move backwards through time towards their original form. In an incident partly comic and partly horrifying, a leather wallet bursts out of the cupboard as a full-grown sow, which runs amok in the town. Yet the rate at which objects change is variable and unpredictable, as Hugh finds when he experiments with old brass buttons: one becomes a shining new button, another a molten puddle of brass, another reverts to two lumps of ore-bearing rock. The primary time during which they have been left in the cupboard is no reliable measure of the changes.

The molten brass lies forgotten in the cupboard, and, when a brass button is later found there in its place, it goes unnoticed in the serious crisis the others face when Penn has been pushed into the cupboard and turned back into a baby. The significance of this reversal of the time change is thus ignored. The sense of unpredictable and uncontrollable change makes the element of time much more menacing in this book than in most time fantasies. It eats away at the individual's fundamental relationship with the surrounding world. The author considered this undermining effect of a disturbance in the time continuum in *Charlotte Sometimes*, but there the two time schemes did move forward in parallel. Here there is no recognizable relationship:

> If time as he knew it, running in a straight line, from the past through the present to the future, had related to the cupboard, even in reverse, it would have been something to cling to, to make him feel safe. It must be orthodox time, he thought, which made life seem relatively stable and ordinary. If time melted, had no force, then space, the whole physical world would easily melt as well. Hugh longed for one aspect of the cupboard to be controllable. (p. 60)

The cupboard and the mysterious world it conceals both attract and repel Hugh. Jean is filled with horrified repulsion, and only enters the cupboard in the hope of saving Penn. Alone of the four, the secretive Anna senses its real significance. When Hugh, Jean and Anna visit the old man from whom the cupboard was bought, hoping to find some help for the now infant Penn, it is Anna who points out to Hugh the meaning of the faces in the antique shop, which have worried him obscurely before:

'Didn't you see all those faces?' Anna asked. . . .

'They were all the same face. They were all of him only younger, some younger than others.'

'In the prime of life,' Hugh said. He tested Anna. 'But they all came from different periods. There was a Roman head and an eighteenth-century print and a mediaeval . . .'

'He had the cupboard,' Anna said, 'or whatever it was. Perhaps it wasn't a cupboard always.' (p. 132)

The cupboard brings perpetual renewal and rebirth for those who submit to it and share in its powers – constant change within an overall pattern of continuity. The old man who seems, to the powers of reason, to be so extraordinary, is in appearance and by superficial standards quite unremarkable:

'Everything is ordinary – dying, loving, being born – it's dirty sheets and bowls of water, and what to get for breakfast and what for supper, and eating breakfast and eating supper. It always was, it always is; except sometimes, occasionally, the looking and hearing and feeling.' (p. 131)

This secondary world is terrifying at first because it is uncontrollable, incomprehensible. When, on reluctant and obscure advice from the old man, Hugh and the others enter it willingly, they can to some extent control events. If they have the strength of will, Penn can be rescued from the ritual of sacrifice and resurrection, and restored to his proper age. The powers of the cupboard, and of the land beyond, are thus partly innate, and partly a result of the response of those who encounter them. The parallel world can draw Hugh in against his will, can render violent changes in people and objects, or it can be recognized for what it is, faced courageously, and so controlled.

The world of the castle of bone forms a three-fold image in paralleling the primary world. In the first place, actions in the secondary world show an intensifying of relationships, especially between brothers and sisters. In the primary world Hugh and Jean are easy-going, rarely make physical contact, and tend to ignore each other. Yet they find, in the frightening experiences they undergo, that they depend upon each other more than they had realized, a fact which is brought out briefly but significantly when Hugh takes Jean's hand in the terrifying darkness of the cupboard. Penn and Anna have a much more tense relationship, each acutely aware of the other. Anna, quiet, intense, always watching and rarely speaking, appears to be dominated by her good-looking and socially successful elder brother. When they argue, they dispute with a bitterness and violence totally alien to Hugh and Jean. Yet Anna, as her mother points out, is obsessed with Penn, and the obsession is a mixture of love and hate. This culminates in the final crisis in the secondary world, when Hugh and Jean find Anna, caught up in the ritual part she is forced to play, about to burn the infant Penn in the sacrificial fire. Penn and Anna are rescued from the ordeal only after Hugh has undergone a severe inner struggle, in which he has 'to hold tight to his own identity. He felt that if he did not he too would be lost, he too would be shifting shape from second to second' (p. 144).

A second parallelism is found in the way in which the changing images of the secondary world correspond to the changing experiences and ages of the individual. Through the changing images of Penn at different ages, Hugh gains a sense of his own mutable body and personality. This awareness is carried back into the primary world when Penn is changed first into a toddler, and then into a newborn baby:

> Its nails looked papery but were surprisingly long and sharp.... That these minute fingers now clutching him could ever hold the bat or the rackets was nearly inconceivable. Compared to the baby they looked grotesquely huge. He thought of Gulliver in Brobdingnag, for looked at from the baby's size the graining of willow on the cricket bat, of oak on the bookshelves, looked crude and coarse and the gut strings of the racket, swollen, positively disgusting; even the books and the silver cup might have been made for giants to read and to display.
>
> Hugh shook himself roughly and made his eyes see from his own proper adolescent size and not from the minuteness of the baby's. (pp. 121–2)

This heightening of perception is a characteristic quality of fantasy, used with some skill by Penelope Farmer throughout the novel.

Finally, the castle of bone itself, seen from different angles, from inside and outside, whole and decayed, is a symbol of the individual: young and old, changing, maturing, dying, being reborn. For Hugh at first it is something external, part of the landscape. Only gradually does he realize its significance for him, as he returns for the last time from the secondary world: 'The void had gone. Walls had closed round Hugh, confining him, imprisoning him in the narrowest of castles; a castle of bone, he thought. But this castle of bone was himself' (p. 148).

In *A Castle of Bone* Penelope Farmer develops the inner world of the individual into the shared world of a closely linked group of people. It is both a study of Hugh's growing awareness of himself, as an individual subject to time and to the cycle of existence continually repeated for all men, and an exposure, through the actions in the parallel world, of the tensions which exist between the characters. It is not only Anna who has been overshadowed by Penn, but Hugh also. He nearly yields to the temptation to stand idle at the sacrificial fire, but by taking positive, if hesitant, action to save Penn, he also asserts the positive qualities of his own character. Hugh turns his back on further direct experience of the secondary world, with its magic and dangers, its mysteries and its movement outside time. He confines himself willingly to his own 'castle of bone'. Yet the castle of bone is, by its very nature, a part of the whole landscape of the human awareness – not only the immediate primary world awareness, but the deeper, more elusive awareness of worlds within, beyond, and parallel to this world. In a sense Hugh no longer needs to enter the secondary world, because he now holds it within his own inner consciousness.

One final type of parallel world remains to be considered: the visionary world, which, as a literary form, has close links with the traditional form of the dream vision. Unlike the cases just discussed, where parallels between the two worlds arise mainly from a subconscious level of the mind, the vision is at least a partly conscious realization of a paradisal or eternal world. In relation to this eternal world the primary world must seem either an imperfect copy, or else the anteroom of a much vaster and more complex palace of existence. Occasionally the visionary world may also be a symbolic representation of what is attainable at a mental or spiritual level in this life. Two notable post-war examples of this visionary quality in the fantasy of parallel worlds are Theresa Whistler's *The River Boy* and Helen Cresswell's *The Outlanders*.

In *The River Boy*, Nat moves between the world of contemporary but unspoilt English country life, and a secondary world which in landscape and physical details is a closely similar but enriched and idealized version of the primary world. In this book the parallel world has a double function. On the one hand, it symbolizes, through the river imagery, Nat's passage from childhood to adolescence. On the other, in the transformation of the old horse and in the image of the shadowless farm, it presents a vision of transcendental reality. As in most of the fantasies considered in this chapter, the secondary world can be affected by actions and emotions in the primary world; it is not an isolated vision. The world of the river is more vivid, more intense, more richly sensuous, as well as more idealized, than the primary world, but greed, impatience or folly can destroy the vision. The river boy, Nathaniel's mirror image, is, within the visionary world of the river valley, an idealized version of himself, and yet he also possesses a secret inner life which Nat is never able fully to fathom. In thus uniting the vivid realization of physical beauty and pleasure with the piercing vision of a transcendent otherworld, and the simple but intense joys of childhood with spiritual joy, *The River Boy* 'rends indeed the very web of story, and lets a gleam come through' (*TL*, p. 61). This exceptionally fine fantasy will be discussed in greater detail in Chapter 5.

The River Boy presents what is essentially a vision of a world of ideals. *The Outlanders*, on the other hand, is concerned more with achievements within this world. Strictly speaking, the initial setting of *The Outlanders* is not, in any case, the normal primary world. All of Helen Cresswell's books have this suggestive, secondary world atmosphere, even when her characters have such apparently mundane occupations as that of master pie-maker. In *The Outlanders* the different qualities of existence overlap; there is no sharp transition from primary to secondary world – the worlds ripple outwards from each other like the concentric circles of waves on a pond. At the centre is Bray, the smug, comfortable, narrow-minded town where Tam Rhymer lives with his family. Bray is the symbol of limited primary world awareness, rather than the primary world itself. Its inhabitants, with few exceptions, fear the world beyond, and hear a wolf in every wind which blows from outside. As with many puritanical and unimaginative people, their sense of security is only a thin veneer, and when life is disturbed by unknown forces they turn, as other similar societies have done, to witch-hunting. Bray is encircled by mountains and then by the Mid-lands, believed to be wild, savage country, but in fact prosperous farming land. Beyond this lie the outlands, which fill Tam's son Piers with terror whenever he wanders to the edge of the town 'where the cobbles yielded to the greedy grasses, whose seeds invisibly invaded the town whenever the wind blew from the hills' (p. 21).

The grasses which blow into the town from the lands beyond are the key to the outlands. There are indeed wolves to be found there, but, as Piers discovers when he has to face them during one long night alone, they are not as frightening as his own irrational fears. The outlands are also the source of all that raises life above the mere humdrum existence of Bray. The seeds of more than grass are to be found there. The book is a quest by Tam, his wife Sary, his son Piers, and Emily, the indomitable daughter of the town washerwoman, in following a changeling fairy boy to the outlands. At the end they are joined by Olemary, Emily's half-mad grandmother, who wears sprigged muslin and ribbons so that the townsfolk will not suspect her of being a witch, and yet is too afraid of death by burning to realize her innate magical powers. The quest is one for artistic and individual freedom, an escape from the stultifying existence in a cramped and small-minded society. Tam Rhymer is a hereditary poet who cannot rhyme, although his son Piers finds to his distress that the Rhymer talent is beginning to appear in himself instead of his father. With the arrival of the fairy boy, Tam begins, apparently unconsciously, to compose rhymes.

The conventional world of Bray cannot tolerate an incursion from the outlands, however, and when the boy disappears from Bray, after the superstitious townspeople have attacked the Rhymers' house, Tam knows he must follow, even if it means searching for the rest of his life. For Tam the goal is clear-cut, and Sary, who believes in her husband's innate poetic gifts, swallows down her element of Bray common-sense and goes with him. Emily also has a passionate faith that life must hold something for her beyond the washtubs, while Olemary, half fascinated and half terrified, follows the boy until she achieves in the outlands the power to be herself, to cast off her madness and her fears, and use her magic at last. For Piers the quest is very different. His vivid imagination is possessed by fear, and he is largely responsible for the difficulties and delays which endanger the quest. At last, however, in facing the wolves and so bringing his hidden terrors out into the open, Piers unexpectedly achieves his own goal.

The world of the outlands, its shores washed by the sea, with its promise of even wider horizons beyond, is used by Helen Cresswell as a vision of personal and artistic freedom. Bray embodies the narrow limitations of most lives in the primary world. Only by climbing the surrounding mountains and facing both the mysteries and the fears of the outlands can one achieve one's true potential.

The Outlanders is particularly successful in combining its visionary world with a quality which is noticeably lacking in many of the books considered in this chapter: a rich sense of humour. Olemary is a tragi-comic figure, but the inhabitants of Bray, with their confused prejudices and their hackneyed proverbs, are a comic interpretation of the blindness of the majority to the artistic gifts of the few. Where Russell Hoban, in *The Mouse and His Child*, attacks the cramping conventions of the materialist society with savage satire, Helen Cresswell makes many of the same points with a light-hearted mockery.

The fantasy of worlds in parallel clearly involves many different aims and techniques. It is, moreover, a particularly difficult type of fantasy to present convincingly. It has neither the firm underpinning of realism found in the fantasy set entirely in the primary world, nor the combination of imaginative freedom and logical discipline which shapes the creation of the pure secondary world fantasy. Two worlds seen in parallel tend to clash, to contrast too strongly, to work against each other – making one or the other less credible, or undermining the relationship between the two. The time fantasy, in addition, makes considerable intellectual demands of both writer and reader. Complex ideas of time displacement must be linked with a sensitive feeling for other eras. Movement to and from the secondary world, if there is no clear structural link, tends to disrupt the attention and undermine belief. Thus, greatest artistic success in the parallelism between the primary world and a secondary world of mental landscape seems to result where there are clear symbolic parallels, and when both worlds are fully realized. The problems in presenting two worlds in parallel are, above all, those of balancing the conflicting tensions and of uniting what must be, of its nature, a centrifugal structure. Such problems do not arise in fantasies which are set entirely, or almost entirely, in a total independent secondary world. These are the subject of the next chapter

· 4 ·
Secondary Worlds

Otherworlds are as old as literature itself: Humbaba's Forest occurs in the ancient Sumerian *Epic of Gilgamesh*; the Underworld and Scheria, magical land of the Phaeacians, in *The Odyssey*. Although modern secondary worlds share with traditional fairy-lands and enchanged forests a quality of otherness, of strangeness and wonder woven into their fabric, they also differ very widely from their literary predecessors. Strangeness and wonder are still present, but the modern concern with precision of detail and coherent scientific data has had its effect on the creation and depiction of the secondary world. Such a world now has a precise geography, often including maps, which is quite foreign to the shadowy and imprecise journeyings of Spenser's knights in the realm of Gloriana.[1] The particular culture portrayed is not isolated, but set in a long context of mythology, legend and history. No other writer has produced the vast frame of reference which Tolkien created in his texts and his appendices, but the same process is to be found at work in others who have devised secondary worlds, such as C. S. Lewis, Ursula Le Guin, Lloyd Alexander, Carol Kendall, John Christopher, Joy Chant and Keith Claire. The religion and beliefs of the inhabitants of the secondary world are at least implicit, and frequently become explicit and central, notably in Lewis's Narnia and Le Guin's Earthsea. The existence of a literature is established, and sometimes complex languages. When the marvellous occurs in a secondary world it may appear marvellous to the inhabitants themselves, but more often the marvellous becomes part of the natural law of the secondary world.

It is not, however, sufficient simply to postulate a series of conditions and hope that it will constitute a basis for a secondary world. Such a world, in order to command belief on the part of the reader, must have 'the inner consistency of reality'. Its nature and laws must be self-consistent, and must be seen to operate consistently, of themselves. An external narrator, looking down and commenting on the secondary world, as it were, from without, destroys the illusion of secondary reality. Thus the somewhat intrusive narrator in C. S. Lewis's Narnia books is less successful than either the internal narra-

75

tor of Ursula Le Guin's *Earthsea Trilogy,* who refers to the varying
traditions and old lays of his own world, or Tolkien's ancient hobbit
records collated by a scholarly translator in *The Lord of the Rings.*

In addition to its own essential inner consistency, the secondary
world, like all fantasy, requires a firm basis in primary world reality.
The inhabitants and affairs of a secondary world will awaken an
interest in the reader only if he can feel some underlying comprehension of and sympathy for them. Perhaps the most outlandish of all
secondary worlds, the Flatland of Edwin Abbott's mathematical
fantasy, is full of domestic minutiae, and appeals both to our social
prejudices and to our sense of humour. Our immediate point of
contact with Middle-earth is through that very conventional and
down-to-earth creature, the hobbit, while the inhabitants of Prydain,
Earthsea, and John Christopher's Winchester are – in the main –
human beings like ourselves.

Although there is always some common ground between the
primary world and any secondary world, the secondary world
fantasy is clearly the furthest removed from everyday experience.
Such distancing involves both advantages and disadvantages. The
secondary world conceived and constructed with skill will command
complete secondary belief on the part of the committed reader to a
far greater degree than any irruption of the marvellous into a
primary world reality. Other readers, however, find the concept of a
secondary world irritating – too remote from experience and too
contrived. Where this is the reaction there is clearly a failure, either
on the part of the author in his sub-creative art, or on the part of the
reader in his capacity for imaginative sensitivity and freedom. Provided the secondary world does induce secondary belief, the advantages of the genre are obvious. The author has complete artistic
freedom, within his self-constructed framework. The society and
characters he depicts have no essential and given background of
culture, history or belief, so that he is free to construct them as he
will. For the author who wishes to start from a *tabula rasa*, it is the
ideal form.

Some of the characteristics which are involved in the construction
of a secondary world have been mentioned above. The remainder of
this chapter will discuss in more detail the technical aspects of
secondary worlds, the purposes for which some modern writers have
used the concept of the secondary world, and the success, or lack of
it, with which they have employed this complex and demanding

medium. The main secondary worlds to be considered are J. R. R. Tolkien's Middle-earth, C. S. Lewis's Narnia, Carol Kendall's Valley of the Minnipins, Ursula Le Guin's Earthsea, and Lloyd Alexander's Prydain.

The first essential in making a secondary world acceptable to readers is that its physical nature should seem comprehensible and logical. The physical laws of nature and the vegetation need not be the same as those of the primary world, but they should have a similarity of structure, and a reasonable cause-and-effect relationship. None of these secondary world fantasies move into the remote physical settings of some science fiction. The fundamental physical laws of gravity, heat and cold, dark and light, are the same. Plants grow, wither and die. Few, if any, creatures are immortal, though life-spans may differ radically. The seasons move in their regular cycle of spring, summer, autumn, winter. The sun, moon and stars have their appointed stations in the sky. Compass directions are preserved and, for these northern hemisphere writers, north implies cold lands and south warm ones. Certain differences from the natural laws of the primary world may occur, but these are rarely arbitrary. They are physical manifestations of the author's underlying ideas, as the dust and desolation of the world of Charn, with its dark red and dying sun, embody the concept of a world exhausted by evil and violence.[2]

Some secondary worlds are themselves a kind of reinterpretation of the primary world. Lloyd Alexander, in discussing the setting of his books, writes:

> This chronicle of the Land of Prydain is not a retelling or retranslation of Welsh mythology. Prydain is not Wales – not entirely, at least. The inspiration for it comes from that magnificent land and its legends; but, essentially, Prydain is a country existing only in the imagination. . . . The geography of Prydain is peculiar to itself. Any resemblance between it and Wales is perhaps not coincidental – but not to be used as a guide for tourists. (*CP*, I, p. 7)

Certainly the geography of Prydain is somewhat difficult to follow, and even appears inconsistent at times, but Alexander does not have the desire for topographical accuracy which characterizes most writers of secondary world fantasies:

> Prydain itself . . . is entirely imaginary. Mona, background for

The Castle of Llyr, is the ancient Welsh name of the island of Anglesey. But this background is not drawn with a mapmaker's accuracy. My hope, instead, is to create the feeling, not the fact, of the land of Wales and its legends. (*CP*, III, p. 8)

However, his descriptions of the individual areas which make up his world are often powerful: the golden castle of Caer Dathyl on the eve of destruction; the Free Commots; the secret valley of Medwyn, with its grass-grown ruin of the Ark; the abandoned castle of Caer Colur, ancient home of the enchantresses of Llyr; Annuvin, realm of the Death Lord. The inhabitants of Prydain are mainly men and dwarfs. Notable exceptions are the comical half-man, half-beast, Gurgi,[3] the three fatal sisters of Morva, and the terrible warriors of Annuvin, both the Cauldron-Born and the Huntsmen. There are no fully articulate beasts, but Medwyn, a Celtic Noah, understands the speech of the animals, while Hen Wen the oracular pig and Kaw the crow communicate at least partially with the human characters.

It is not clear whether Carol Kendall's Valley of the Minnipins is intended to be some remote part of the primary world, as the lands visited by Gulliver were, but it seems likely. It is, however, fully self-contained – a peaceful valley surrounded by impassable mountains, which are themselves encircled by desert. The setting is miniature, but precisely detailed. The twelve Minnipin villages are built along the course of the Watercress River, the street plan of the main village is described in detail, and maps are provided.

Tolkien's Middle-earth has the most complex topography of all secondary worlds. The mountains, valleys, rivers, farmlands, forests and desolate wastes are not those of the primary world, but they correspond to similar areas in the primary world. The stars appear to be those of our skies.[4] The journeys undertaken by travellers in *The Hobbit* and *The Lord of the Rings* are long and arduous, and the terrain covered is described with meticulous care. The temperate zone is narrower than it is on this earth, however, the distance from the semi-tropical lands of Haradwaith to the frozen Ice Bay of Forochel being only some thirteen hundred miles. It should, of course, be remembered that during some eras on this planet the temperate zones were also narrower.[5] Middle-earth is inhabited by a great variety of peoples – men, hobbits, elves, dwarfs, orcs, wargs, wizards, ents and others. Animals are mainly those of the primary world, and some have speech for those who can understand it.

Earthsea, the setting for Ursula Le Guin's trilogy, is a complex archipelago, extending approximately two thousand miles from east to west, and the same from north to south. The islands are mainly independent or united in small groups under a prince. Only the Kargad lands form a large, and aggressive, empire. The people of the central archipelago are described as bronze or copper skinned, while those of the East Reach are dark skinned. The Kargads are tall, fair, and warlike, falling upon the other lands in sea-going raids, to plunder and burn. A little-known race of the far Western Reach is the Raft People. Thin and tall, they live most of their lives on great floating raft villages. The animals of Earthsea are mainly those of the primary world, with some additions such as the small wild animal, the otak, which Ged befriends. These animals are not articulate, but the dragons have the gift of the Old Speech, the language of all power and magic, which the mages spend their lives studying.[6] Many trees, flowers and herbs are described, a number of them original to Earthsea. Maps also form an essential part of Earthsea geography, and the stars are described and named.[7]

In *The Chronicles of Narnia,* C. S. Lewis traces the creation, development and eventual destruction of an entire world, although the order in which the books were written does not correspond to the chronology of Narnia. The events of all seven books except *The Horse and His Boy* are precipitated by the arrival of characters from the primary world, but almost the whole of the *Chronicles* is set in the secondary world. A number of different lands constitute this world. Narnia, a country of woods, hills, rivers and valleys, is inhabited by talking beasts, dumb animals, and occasionally men. To the south, amongst the hills just north of the desert, lies Archenland, ruled by men. Beyond the desert is the land of the Calormenes, 'a wise, wealthy, courteous, cruel and ancient people' (*CN*, III, p. 61). Telmar, home of the Telmarines who later occupy Narnia, is west of Archenland. To the north of Narnia lie the Wild Lands of the North – Ettinsmoor and the mountains beyond – a country of giants, while in the Far West beyond Lantern Waste, on the top of a smooth green hill, is the paradisal garden of the Tree of Life.[8] Narnia faces the sea on the east, a sea dotted with islands and leading ultimately to sweet waters and Aslan's country.

Besides talking beasts and men, Narnia and the surrounding lands are inhabited by dwarfs, giants, centaurs, nymphs, dryads, naiads, fauns, satyrs, merpeople, earth gnomes, wargs, warlocks, monopods, unicorns, minotaurs, former stars, and a host of other creatures from the folk-tales, myths and legends of our own world. There is one original and delightful creation – the marshwiggle.

In any civilized and long-inhabited land, the geography is considerably affected by the history of the races which have held it, farmed it, built upon it, and perhaps deforested and mined it. All these writers give their secondary worlds a historical depth either through factual history or through myth and legend. Sometimes, as is often the case with the pre-scientific societies which they mostly depict, history is inextricably merged into myth and legend, just as the natural geography of the lands merges into the decaying ruins of man's past civilizations.

The long span of history is ignored, to their cost, by most of the Minnipins. They live a conventional life dominated by trivial and meaningless customs instituted in the days of Fooley the Balloonist, who once ventured outside the hidden valley, and since maintained by the authority of his descendants, the Periods. Only Walter the Earl studies the records of the ancient and heroic days of his people, and only a few unconventional friends help him to defy the narrow-minded society in which they live. Yet it is the knowledge of the old records and the use of the ancient weapons which is the salvation of the Minnipins.

The span of history provides an essential part of the context in which the Prydain stories are worked out. Throughout the boyhood and youth of Taran he is involved, with Gwydion and others, in struggles against the forces of evil led by Arawn the Death Lord, but these are a continuation of a prolonged struggle which began before he was born. Gwydion is the last of the Sons of Don who came to the relief of Prydain, and, when he departs, taking with him all enchanters, it is left to Taran and other mortal men to rule the country as best they can by human arts. The three sisters of the Marshes of Morva, Orddu, Orgoch and Orwen, weave the pattern of events into their tapestries, but the pattern is chosen by the actors themselves, not the fatal sisters (*CP*, V, pp. 286–7). History is shaped by men, not by the forces of destiny, and if those with the gifts of magic seem more powerful at first, it is human heroism and self-sacrifice which finally triumph.

The history of Middle-earth is a vast subject in itself, and can best be studied in the appendices to *The Return of the King*, the third part of *The Lord of the Rings*. A considerable amount of this history emerges in the course of the narrative in *The Hobbit* and *The Lord of the Rings,* particularly in explanations given to the hobbits by Gandalf, Elrond and Aragorn. Brief accounts are also included by the hobbit narrator and compiler of the tales. *The Silmarillion,* assembled by Christopher Tolkien after his father's death, from writings composed over some sixty years, presents an enormously enlarged picture of the earlier history of Middle-earth. Written in the style of a saga or chronicle, the various components of *The Silmarillion* show Tolkien the sub-creator enriching the complex portrayal of his secondary world, but they are not the work of Tolkien the novelist. Strong in the minutiae of secondary realism, and sharing the implicit themes of *The Lord of the Rings, The Silmarillion* lacks that even more essential quality for successful fantasy, a realism of life, felt and lived. It is an excellent appendix, but a poor novel or collection of tales – perhaps this is why Tolkien himself never published it.

The essential principle underlying the history of Middle-earth is that there is a constant struggle between creative Good and destructive or decreative Evil. All creatures in Middle-earth have free will in this struggle, and each race has a period of dominance. In the Third Age the trees and the ents are long past their prime, the elves and dwarfs are declining. Briefly and unexpectedly, the hobbits become heroes, but they too are doomed to diminish. The Fourth Age will be the age of Men. The sense of history in Middle-earth is considerably enriched by old tales and legends which each race hands down from generation to generation, whether they be of Tinúviel, the elf princess, or of Durin, ancestor of the dwarfs. In Middle-earth more than in any other of these secondary worlds every acre of ground is rich in history.[9]

The most interesting parts of the history of Narnia are contained in *The Magician's Nephew,* with its account of the Creation, and in *The Last Battle,* containing the Apocalypse. There are also a number of other historical digressions, yet the civilization of Narnia is remarkably static. At the coronation of the King and Queen in *The Magician's Nephew* there are suggestions of a medieval culture, yet after centuries upon centuries, through the winter of the White Witch and the whole dynasty of the Telmarines to Tirian the last king, the civilization remains hardly altered. Lewis is thus interested in ultimate beginnings and ultimate ends, but shows little concern with portraying the changing patterns of history and development amongst the human and Talking Beast inhabitants of Narnia.

The history of Earthsea does not cover such a long span as that of Narnia, but there are many references back to the beginning, when Segoy spoke the First Word, and raised the islands from the sea.[10] The end has not yet come, although a desperate death-in-life end is narrowly avoided in *The Farthest Shore*. The end will come, however, when the fatal Last Word, known only to the greatest mages, is spoken. The times of the old, blood-thirsty religion have passed, and even in Kargad the worship of the old gods is maintained only as long as it is politically expedient. Throughout most of Earthsea the accepted faith is in magic, the magic wielded by the mages, born with natural gifts and trained on the island of Roke. When this faith is threatened by the lapsed sorcerer Cob, who perverts magic to evil ends, the very fabric of society begins to crumble. The final great *Deed of Ged* is the destruction of the evil sorcerer, the healing of faith, and the restoration of the ancient line of kings. The history of the people of Earthsea is shot through with tales of ancient heroes – kings and wizards – and their struggles against evil enchanters and dragons. Thus the events of the present are seen to be inextricably bound up with those of the past and the future.

The historical dimension of a secondary world leads naturally to a definition of the period of culture against which the narrative is set. Just as the geography and the natural law must be self-consistent, so must the cultural background. It is no doubt possible to devise a culture which is totally alien to anything known in the primary world, and this is often attempted in science fiction, but authors of secondary world fantasies tend to base their cultures on those known to Western Europe between the Bronze and the Middle Ages.

As has been indicated, despite its long span of history Narnian culture is of a medieval type throughout. Weapons are swords, spears, knives, and bows and arrows. Light armour is worn, and battles are fought on foot or on horseback. The Calormenes use curved scimitars and ride war horses trained for battle. Dwarfs fight with axes or bows, giants with clubs, while the Talking Beasts use their natural weapons of claws, hooves or teeth. The ships are driven by sails and oars, and there is some discussion of sea-faring in *The Voyage of the 'Dawn Treader'*. Dwellings are rarely described. There are a few fairly brief descriptions of the Castle of Cair Paravel, King Lune's castle of Anvard in Archenland, and of the House of the Giants at Harfang. No Narnian town is ever described, although the capital of Calormen, Tashbaan, is evoked in some detail. The only fully realized interior is the house of the Beavers in *The Lion, the Witch and the Wardrobe*. The animals of Narnia presumably live their natural lives, although the predatory nature of some is glossed over. How the humans live is not clear. King Lune is seen out hunting purely for sport, and from the medieval frame of reference one must infer that there is an agricultural basis to the society, but farms and farmers are never glimpsed. There are curious anomalies, too. Clearly there is no manufacturing in Narnia beyond the ancient craft of the blacksmith and armourer. So where, one is inclined to ask, did Mrs Beaver get her sewing machine?[11]

There are no such inconsistencies in the culture of Earthsea. It is a Bronze Age civilization, with a mainly village economy. Some towns have grown up at the sites of harbours, and, as is natural in an archipelago, there is much sea-faring and inter-island trade. Villages have their own bronze-smiths, weavers, tanners, and farmers, although some areas specialize in their skills – Gont is famed for fleeces, Lorbanery for silks. All tools and weapons are bronze; the only known use of iron is as lodestone for navigation (*ET*, I, pp. 40, 42). Material possessions are the work of traditional handicrafts-men, and they are often rich and wrought with great skill. The people of Earthsea have a high level of civilization, cultured and artistic, although many are poor, and few are 'educated' in the modern sense. Those few who have received an education have attained a great depth and width of learning, particularly those who have been trained at the School of the Wise on Roke, which strongly resembles the rigorous and demanding training schools for Celtic bards.[12] The culture of the Earthsea world as a whole, however, is above all Homeric in concept – a civilized, sea-faring, Bronze Age culture.

The Minnipins have a similar economy, although much simpler. Each inhabitant of a village has a recognized trade – candlemaker, baker, thatcher or the like. There is an official village poet and an official painter, who come into conflict with the naturally artistic Curley Green and Gummy. The Minnipins make much use of herbs and other plants in their economy, and especially of a particular reed from which they derive flour, thatch, cloth and paper. Metal work-ing is virtually unknown and the only weapons have been hidden away for safety years before by Walter the Earl's ancestors.

Prydain, drawing on *The Mabinogion*, has the same cultural basis as its source – a mixture of ancient myth and primitive brutality with early medieval feudal and courtly society. Arawn, Achren, the sisters of Morva, the Hunters of Annuvin, the Cauldron-Born, the great cat Llyan, Medwyn, and the enchanter Dallben all stem from the magical and folk-tale elements of *The Mabinogion*. Gwydion and the Sons of Don, like Arthur and his court, are part human, part legendary heroes, part ancient Celtic gods. Hen Wen, of course, was a famous pig even in *The Mabinogion*. Taran, the foundling boy reared by the enchanter until his own heroism, not his birth, makes him worthy to be High King, is a sort of Arthur in reverse – a bridge from the old magical world to the realities of medieval life. The Free Commots, on the other hand, which acknowledge no king but govern themselves as a loose federation of craftsmen, have more than a suggestion about them of the myths of American pioneering society. Alexander's writing is a curious but interesting blend of this love for the ancient royal and courtly framework of medieval life and the very American ideals of the independent frontiersman.

Tolkien's Middle-earth, being larger and more varied than most of the other secondary worlds, also has more varied cultures. The hobbits form an agricultural community and do not 'understand or like machines more complicated than a forge-bellows, a water-mill, or a hand-loom, though they [are] skilful with tools' (*LOTR*, I, p. 11). By contrast the dwarfs are, *par excellence*, metal and gem workers, diggers of mines and builders of underground cities. They neither cultivate crops nor breed animals, but they love the beauty of craftsmanship, and bring light to the dark places of the earth. The elves are closer to the natural world even than the hobbits. They do not cultivate and use the growing things of the earth – rather they tend and care for them. They are light-footed, musical, and tellers of tales. The men of Middle-earth vary widely. The Woses or Wild Men of the Woods are descended from an ancient people who once erected cities and built roads, and who carved the Pukel-Men. Gondor has fallen from its days of greatness, the people are diminished, the city falling into neglect. The people of Rohan are horse breeders, heroic upholders of the honour of the *comitatus*. One can see here clear parallels with the early Dark Ages of Europe, the hobbits, the Riders of Rohan, and the people of Gondor corresponding, not politically or physically but culturally, to the British, the Teutonic peoples, and the late Romans respectively. The dwarfs and the elves have the characteristics they usually assume in early European folk-lore, but they have been purged of any late accretions of 'cuteness'. The orcs are an amalgam of goblins and other horrors of the dark underground of the world. Sauron and his imitator Saruman employ machinery and slaves to exploit and destroy nature, and to extend their power over other people. This use of materialism as a weapon of power is portrayed by Tolkien as the ultimate denial of civilization.

An essential element in the definition of culture is language, and its corollary, literature. Writers vary considerably in the extent to which they define the language and literature of their secondary worlds. The enemies of the Minnipins speak a different language (ch. 20), but the language of the Minnipins themselves is treated as English. As a result of official policy, the existence of literature is minimal, but amongst his old manuscripts Walter the Earl finds the records of an earlier society, including literature and painting as well as historical documents. The other arts, notably painting, have suffered the same fate as literature amongst recent generations.

The inhabitants of Prydain all speak one language, although the language of spells and enchantments is different, and important inscriptions are in the Old Writing. There is a great heritage of tales, songs and bardic lore, which must be mastered by any who would be accepted as bards. Besides the main library of bardic texts at Caer Dathyl, three books or writings play important parts in the chronicles: *The Book of Three*, which records Man's past, present and future (if certain conditions are fulfilled); the book of enchantments handed down through the princesses of the house of Llyr, the pages of which appear blank until the writing is revealed by magic light; and the manuscript containing the secrets of all arts, crafts and skills, which Gurgi salvages from the treasure house of Arawn the Death Lord, who has stolen these secrets from mankind.

C. S. Lewis did not construct new languages for the people of Narnia and the neighbouring lands, and the literature of this world is mainly in the form of oral tales, although records are kept and messages sent in writing. The most striking feature of the language in Lewis's tales is the varying speech styles of the different races, and the principal element of humour in the books is linguistic. There is the speech of the Calormenes, full of devious cunning and oblique aphorisms:

'Compose yourself, O my son,' said the Tisroc. 'For the departure of guests makes a wound that is easily healed in the heart of a judicious host.' . . . 'How well it was said by a gifted poet,' observed the Vizier, raising his face (in a somewhat dusty condition) from the carpet, 'that deep draughts from the fountain of reason are desirable in order to extinguish the fire of youthful love.' . . .

The Tisroc was apparently sunk in thought, but when, after a long pause, he noticed what was happening, he said tranquilly:

'My son, by all means desist from kicking the venerable and enlightened Vizier: for as a costly jewel retains its value even if hidden in a dung-hill, so old age and discretion are to be respected even in the vile persons of our subjects.' (*CN*, V, pp. 100–2)

Prince Rilian, who has long been under the spell of an enchantress, is true at heart, but his courtly speech is a parody of the medieval writing with which Lewis was familiar in his academic work:

'If you were not so young a warrior, Boy, you and I must have fought to the death on this quarrel. I can hear no words against my Lady's honour. But of this you may be assured, that whatever she said to you, she said of a good intent. You do not know her. She is a nosegay of all virtues, as truth, mercy, constancy, gentleness, courage, and the rest.' (*CN*, IV, p. 133)

Even after he is freed from the 'Lady's' enchantment, Rilian still employs the same style.

J. R. R. Tolkien once said that he invented his Middle-earth languages first, and then had to write his tales to accommodate them.[13] This has provided a convenient weapon for his detractors, but of course it was meant only half seriously. Tolkien's original interests as a scholar in both the old literatures and the languages of Western Europe grew up simultaneously, and it seems likely that his own creative writing and his invented languages did the same. As early as 1920 he was writing Father Christmas letters to his children, describing and drawing Father Christmas's country and his assistants, including an elf secretary called Ilbereth. Details of the characters emerged gradually in the annual letters, and special scripts seem to have begun to appear later, in the early 1930s.[14] In *The Hobbit* the runes on the maps and on the dust-jacket transliterate into English. It was only with *The Lord of the Rings* in the 1950s that he produced new languages. The best source of information on these is Tolkien's own set of appendices, where he discusses Quenya (High-elven), Sindarin (Grey-elven), various forms of Westron, the Black Speech, and other languages. The names of people, animals and objects in Middle-earth are consistent with the invented languages or, frequently, have a basis in Anglo-Saxon.[15] This complex linguistic compilation – like the geography and maps, the history and genealogies – adds considerably to the depth and completeness of Middle-earth. It also adds greatly to the fun.

In Earthsea a number of languages are spoken: Hardic is the lingua franca of the Inner Islands, although there are various accents and dialects. To the ears of the prince of Enlad, Ged has a noticeable Gontish accent. The Raft People speak a dialect which is almost incomprehensible. Kargish is the language of the Kargad lands, while Osskilian is used on Osskil. The Old Speech is the language of the dragons, and is still used for magic, the recording of ancient lore, and occasionally as a language between mages.[16] A number of chants, lays and songs are referred to, and quotations are sometimes included. The legends of Erreth-Akbe, greatest of mages, who slew and was slain by the dragon Orm, are widely known, as are the tragic tale of Morred and Elfarran and the heroic deeds of their son Serriadh. Here legend, history and literature intermingle to enrich the picture of the secondary world. Language is much more, however, in Earthsea than a means of communication or record. The power of words is the basis of philosophy and magic. Only by learning the true names of things does the mage slowly and laboriously gain wisdom and power. As simple a form of magic as weather-working is useless without this basis of knowledge. At the Isolate Tower the Master Namer tells the apprentices:

'The sea's name is *inien*, well and good. But what we call the Inmost Sea has its own name also in the Old Speech. Since no thing can have two true names, *inien* can mean only "all the sea except the Inmost Sea". . . . So if some Mage-Seamaster were mad enough to try to lay a spell of storm or calm over all the ocean, his spell must say not only the word *inien*, but the name of every stretch and bit and part of the sea through all the Archipelago and all the Outer Reaches and beyond to where names cease. Thus, that which gives us power to work magic, sets the limits of that power. A mage can control only what is near him, what he can name exactly and wholly. And this is

well. If it were not so, the wickedness of the powerful or the folly
of the wise would long ago have sought to change what cannot
be changed, and Equilibrium would fail. The unbalanced sea
would overwhelm the islands where we perilously dwell, and in
the old silence all voices and all names would be lost.' (*ET*, I, p.
60)

When the young Ged had earlier begun his training with Ogion, he
had not understood this lesson. Yet in the end it is his knowledge and
understanding of the true names of people, objects, places, of human
emotions and abstract ideas, of life and death, and of the relationships between them, which enable Ged to achieve his final victory.

Behind and beyond all the physical attributes of a secondary
world, the geography, history, habitations and arts, lies a basis of
philosophy, religion and belief. Some sort of assumptions about the
scale of values in human life, about forms of society, and about the
rational and marvellous aspects of their worlds must be made by the
inhabitants of all these secondary worlds. In some cases these beliefs
form a relatively small part of the writer's concerns, in others they
become virtually the centre of the action. Almost invariably, the
elements of the marvellous are used to illuminate this basis of belief;
that is, it is the essential fantasy which is most closely related to any
underlying system of values invoked by the writer.

The interweaving of the folklore elements of *The Mabinogion*
with the physical realities of Taran's youth in *The Chronicles of
Prydain* makes the marvellous a part of the natural law of the
secondary world. No one ever questions the reality of the Cauldron-
Born, or of Achren's magic before her fall. The traitorous Pryderi in
his arrogance doubts the powers of the enchanter Dallben – with
fatal consequences. There is no explicit element of religious faith in
the Prydain stories, but Taran gradually learns a philosophy of life.
In childhood his one dream is of attaining glory and of discovering
that he was born of noble or royal blood. The warrior's life seems
infinitely desirable, and he despises his life on the farm at Caer
Dallben with its domestic chores of gardening, pig-keeping and the
forging of horseshoes instead of swords. Bitter experience teaches
him that a warrior's life is far from glorious; from Coll, the former
hero turned farmer, and from the craftsmen of the Free Commots, he
learns that there is more honour in well-tilled soil or skilful work of
the hands than in killing one's enemies. Taran becomes a warrior, a

leader, and a high king, but he has discovered that it is more important to be a man.

In *The Minnipins* the question of belief is presented in a fairly low
key, and usually with humour, but the issues are important. Carol
Kendall is not concerned with spiritual values so much as with social
and artistic ones. She shows how social conventions can crush character and independence, how utterly meaningless customs, enforced
with sufficient authority or majority consent, can lead to artistic
deadness, complacency and witless conformity. It takes real heroism
to defy such social conventions and to pursue personal independence
of thought and artistic freedom – and even the unconventional
characters find that they need mutual help and support in order to
survive. There is little of the marvellous in the lives of the Minnipins,
but the glowing swords of their ancestors and the thrilling notes of
their war trumpets awaken a response in the Minnipins to something
beyond the narrow rationalistic confines of their lives.

Discussion of religious belief rarely if ever becomes explicit in
Middle-earth. This is partly the outcome of the style, which, in the
most successful parts of *The Lord of the Rings,* becomes the objective style of the historian and chronicler. The manifest battle between
light and dark, and the struggle between good and evil impulses
within the minds of the inhabitants of Middle-earth, is, however, the
essence of *The Lord of the Rings* and is already present in parts of
The Hobbit, notably in the development of Bilbo and in the Battle of
the Five Armies. The importance of free will, and the marvellous
presence of free will even in trees, mountains and rings of power, is
one of the distinguishing features of Middle-earth. Through the
exercise of a will towards good, the small and weak are able to defeat
the materially and physically stronger Dark Lord, Sauron. The final
struggle is enacted both between the armies before Minas Tirith, and
in the lonely and seemingly hopeless quest of Frodo and Sam. The
decisive victory over evil is achieved not on the battlefield, but by the
pathetic figures crawling painfully up the side of Mount Doom. The
marvellous in Middle-earth is part of the natural law, although some
aspects of it, particularly the powers of the elves, seem remarkable to
the hobbits, who, like us, have led sheltered lives, protected from the
wonderful and mysterious elements of life. There is hardly any
reference to spiritual ideas as part of a recognized religion amongst
the inhabitants of Middle-earth, although they are much concerned
with moral problems. The creation myths and the legends and

natures of the gods are to be found in the first part of *The Silmaril-lion*.

In Earthsea the belief in magic and the training of the mages is centred on a philosophy of life which holds that understanding of the world and some measure of control over it can come about only through much study, self-mastery, and the slow growth of wisdom: 'Manhood is patience. Mastery is nine times patience' (*ET*, I, p. 28). Ursula Le Guin may perhaps have been influenced by Hermetic philosophy, with its belief that magic is above religion, and indeed embraces all religions. Certainly there are links in Earthsea with many oriental philosophies which teach that learning, meditation and self-knowledge are the basis of spiritual growth. The prime importance of 'Balance' or 'Equilibrium' in the world is constantly stressed, a belief related to many of the main tenets of Zen Buddhism. Magic must always be exercised with discretion because it disturbs the Balance – the natural law and the right relationship between both physical and spiritual elements of the world. Man must face and understand the nature of evil in order fully to appreciate good. This philosophy, of setting goodness and light against evil and darkness, in order that both may be fully understood, is that of John I: 5, 'And the light shineth in darkness; and the darkness comprehended it not' – 'comprehended' being understood in both senses of the word. So in Earthsea darkness and death have their rightful place, for only set against them do light and life have meaning. In Earthsea nothing is marvellous in the sense that nothing is ultimately incomprehensible, but a man is limited by his own capacity, and understanding comes only after knowledge and suffering. What appears to us marvellous is given not simply a metaphysical but a physical reality.

The religious ideas behind C. S. Lewis's Narnia are somewhat different in character from those of the other secondary worlds, for overt Christian allegory runs through the whole of the Chronicles. The inhabitants of Narnia have a clearly stated religious faith in the Emperor-Across-the-Sea, the original Creator, and his son Aslan the Lion, his manifest agent on earth. There is a definite moral code, but not a great deal of theology or doctrine. Aslan is portrayed calling the world into life at the founding of Narnia, and presiding over the final destruction. He is, moreover, subject to his own laws, and those of the Emperor.[17] The moral code is sometimes a little dubious, parti-cularly with regard to the non-talking beasts. There is a good deal which is vicious and blood-thirsty: Peter's slaying of the wolf in *The*

Lion, the Witch and the Wardrobe and the many battle scenes are described with relish. There is an almost masochistic delight in Eustace's shedding of the dragon skin.[18]

Perhaps the difficulty in accepting some parts of *The Chronicles of Narnia* lies in the fact that they are partly allegory and partly a true secondary world. When Aslan is sacrificed to redeem Edmund, and after dying rises again, the Christian allegory is clear and acceptable. At other times, when allegory is replaced by secondary realism, doubts creep in. On the level of secondary realism, the Talking Beasts would seem to be rather less than Christian towards their less fortunate dumb cousins. On the level of allegory, the existence of talking and non-talking animals in Narnia suggests the most bigoted doctrine of predestination. Lewis is at his best in presenting the religion of Narnia when he portrays Aslan in action – the solemn, awful, yet joyous and gentle God incarnate. As willing sacrifice, as restorer of the creatures turned to stone, as the glowing albatross at the darkest moment of the 'Dawn Treader's' voyage, as the awakener of Narnia, and as presider at the Last Judgment, Aslan is a powerful figure. When he inflicts punishment on Aravis by viciously clawing her back and terrifies the innocent and humble Hwin, the identification with Christ is somewhat disturbing.

It is clear from the above discussion of the technical aspects of secondary world creation, involving the natural world, history and legend, culture, language and literature, religion and belief, that there are large areas of common ground between the different worlds. All the facets considered are to be found to some extent in each of these secondary worlds. There is a general desire for precise delineation of physical setting and civilization, and on the whole the societies depicted are pre-industrial, based on rural or village communities, and possess a considerable heritage of bardic lore. The marvellous is usually an element of the secondary world, sometimes as part of the natural law of that world, sometimes as a manifestation of the marvellous to the people themselves. The inhabitants of the worlds are faced with problems of social behaviour, and above all with spiritual and moral problems, which parallel those of the primary world. The problems tend to be more clearly posed, and to demand answers more insistently, than is normally the case in the primary world. Evil is present and manifest, and must be fought if it is not to triumph. In considering the question of religion and belief, we move closer to a study of the writers' intentions in creating their secondary worlds. Although the general issue of such intentions is the subject of later chapters, it is appropriate here to discuss what, if any, common purposes may be found amongst writers who choose to set their fantasies in secondary worlds.

Superficially at least, the secondary world fantasy is remote from everyday life. Such distancing may alienate the reader, or at any rate fail to involve him, may not awake that deeper level of sympathy which is necessary before a writer's more serious intentions can be conveyed. However, if the reader can be involved, if a basis of sympathy and identification can be established, the secondary world fantasy offers unique advantages to a writer whose aim is something beyond the painting of a realistic picture of the primary world, whose desire, rather, is to offer his own view of society or philosophy of life.

The main advantage of the secondary world for such writers is a freedom from the restricting assumptions and realities of the primary world. Any writer depicting the latter must take as a basis the many centuries of human history, the rise and fall of known civilizations, the many religious beliefs, social conventions and artistic canons which are established in our civilization. The creator of a secondary world is freed from these restrictions. A reader may be more easily convinced of the marvellous 'reality' of a secondary world than of the irruption of the marvellous into the everyday primary world. Moreover, in the context of an independent secondary world, a new corpus of values may more easily be presented.

The marvellous takes many forms in these fantasies: there are talking beasts in many; trees walk in Middle-earth; weather can be controlled in Earthsea; *draugrs* are created and fight for the Death Lord in Prydain; immortality is seen sometimes as a gift, sometimes as a curse. Other magical elements are here too: swords which glow at the approach of the enemy, rivers of fire, dragons, rings of invisibility, magic cauldrons and the like. It should be noted, however, that most writers are fairly sparing in their use of the marvellous in the secondary world. The most generous is probably C. S. Lewis, in his sheer abundance of creatures, but these are acceptable mainly because they are all so well known already to the reader from traditional literature. Tolkien's creatures also, apart from the species hobbit, are drawn from traditional material, although his conception is considerably more detailed and enlarged than the original. A prudent restraint seems to be essential in depicting a secondary world. A superabundance of marvels will strain the reader's credulity just as inconsistencies in the natural law or in the structure of civilization will do. First novels have a tendency to overindulge in the marvellous,[19] and even as experienced a writer as Lewis displays notably more control in his later Narnia books, after the *embarras de richesses* of *The Lion, the Witch and the Wardrobe*.

When a writer of fantasy is in full control of his imagination, and not simply soaring off into the void, he uses these marvellous elements for specific purposes – either for the imaginative enrichment derived from exploring an experience beyond everyday reality (such as understanding the language of the animals) or else for the realization of some serious intent which lies behind his fantasy. The secondary world fantasies discussed in this chapter achieve both aims, but the former is more often subordinate to the latter. Thus Carol Kendall's heroes wield the glowing swords only after they have achieved their own emancipation from stifling convention, and therefore earned the right to wear them. Similarly, the magic sword in *The Chronicles of Prydain* repulses and nearly destroys Taran when he is too young and inexperienced to draw it – later it reveals itself as his by right when he has come to his full powers. In *The Chronicles of Narnia* Lewis is intrigued by the idea of Talking Beasts – it was an idea which had interested him since childhood[20] – but he uses his Talking Beasts very much as he saw Kenneth Grahame using his in *The Wind in the Willows*.[21] For Lewis, the animals provided an acceptable way of presenting, not Grahame's social types, but religious ideas. The marvellous powers of the mages in Earthsea are not gratuitous – they furnish the starting-point for the whole analysis of the use and abuse of power.

Tolkien explores many of his ideas on the conflict between good and evil through the symbolism of light and dark, treating these not simply as symbols but as physical manifestations. 'God (or Good) is light' is realized literally.[22] The darkness of evil also implies limitation and ignorance: Sauron is unable to conceive that anyone possessing the Ring would not use it for his own advantage. Colin Manlove maintains[23] that good only succeeds by luck in *The Lord of the Rings* and that, throughout, Sauron and the forces of evil possess all the power and mystery in the book. This is missing the significance of one of Tolkien's central themes. Evil is physically stronger, but it is morally and intellectually weaker than good. It cannot comprehend good. The good creatures, however, recognize the nature of evil and so circumvent it, through dogged, unspectacular heroism.

The corrupting effects of materialism and the lust for power are realized by Tolkien in terms of the 'dragon sickness', in which the traditional magic hoarder of gold, the deadly dragon, assumes a powerful significance for men of the primary world. In *The Lord of the Rings* evil is, for the moment, defeated, but war always brings loss and many fair things are destroyed in the War of the Ring. The Elves must pass away into the West, and Gandalf, while the grievous wounds sustained by Frodo can never be healed in Middle-earth. Most of that which was marvellous in Middle-earth is drained away in the aftermath of war, leaving it not so very different from our own, greyer, primary world.

Given the freedom from our usual basic assumptions which is provided by secondary world fantasy, another issue which is often explored is the true nature of manhood, or of kingship. Lloyd Alexander is a writer who addresses himself to this matter. In *The Chronicles of Prydain*, a curious change of tone is observable between the earlier and the later books. Although there are some serious and poignant moments in the earlier parts, in particular the death of Adaon in *The Black Cauldron*, the general atmosphere is one of rollicking adventure and broad humour. Gradually the tone changes until in the final two volumes it is sombre and even tragic. This leads to some incongruities. The Princess Eilonwy, Taran's pert girl companion, never seems fully to mature, so that in the last book her character seems oddly undeveloped beside Taran's. On the other hand Gurgi, hairy, hungry and loyal, and the source of much simple fun in the early books, develops into a figure of pathos, humbly in quest of intellect and understanding, but still ready to lay down his life for his friends. It is as if the theme of *The Chronicles of Prydain* had grown upon the author as he worked, and altered their very nature as they progressed.

Alexander presents the training of his young hero from youthful dreams of warlike heroism through suffering and loss to compassion, patience and wisdom. There are many milestones on the way, even in the earlier books: the death of Adaon; the sacrifice of Taran's brooch (the gift of Adaon) which gave the wearer a piercing vision into the transcendent realities of the world; Taran's pity for the bitter, twisted Ellidyr, who rides with 'a black beast on his shoulders' but ultimately dies in order to destroy the *draugr*-creating Cauldron;

his tolerance towards the fallen evil enchantress Achren. Taran is sometimes depicted as a little too competent in these early books, assuming a leadership over, for example, the adult king and bard, Fflewddur Fflam, to which he hardly has a claim. The major turning-point in Taran's career comes in *Taran Wanderer* when he discovers (so he believes) that his parentage, far from being noble, is humble. Taran's humiliation and eventual acceptance, and his patient attempts to learn the skills of a craftsman, constitute the training in character which parallels his earlier battle-training in courage. In the final book, *The High King*, Taran sees the royal citadel of the Sons of Don destroyed, the most powerful king in Prydain turned traitor, and many of his friends slain. After the last desperate victory he is faced with a choice. As at the end of *The Lord of the Rings*, the wielders of enchantment are leaving the land for good, and with them all Taran's friends, including Eilonwy. He must choose between immortality in the Summer Country, where all is fair and good, and evil never comes, or mortality and kingship in Prydain, and the age of Men. Taran chooses the latter, preferring to keep faith with his dead friends and to complete their humble and mortal work on earth. In his future as king his training in manhood and citizen-ship will prove as vital as his training in war. Eilonwy also chooses to resign her powers of enchantment and remain with him.

As with the Prydain stories, *The Earthsea Trilogy* is framed by the growth and training of the hero Ged, but the period of his life is more extended. The three books depict him in boyhood and youth, in the prime of manhood, and in late middle age. Ged is a brilliant and gifted boy, but headstrong, impatient, and eager for power – a natural overreacher. Before he completes his training he misuses his innate power and his half-learned magic to turn loose a terrible shadow on the earth, which it costs him much suffering to overcome. The training of Ged as a mage leads to his eventual understanding of the nature of light and dark, and the balance between them. Throughout his youth and into his maturity Ged must learn power over two kinds of darkness – the darkness from without, and the darkness from within. By the climax of the final book, the wheel has come full circle, and Ged by understanding evil defeats it, by under-standing death restores beauty to life.

The secondary worlds we have been considering have thus each been created as the setting for a tale with some underlying serious purpose. Many of the issues are social ones, paralleling those of the primary world. The question of right social values, of damaging social structures, and of the possibility of creating societies which provide mutual support and yet permit a reasonable degree of individual freedom, is the central issue of *The Minnipins*. In Narnia and Prydain the responsibilities and burdens of kingship are considered, as well as the responsibilities of citizenship. Ursula Le Guin depicts the aggressive empire of the Kargads, torn by internecine struggles, and the loosely knit island communities of the Archipelago. Even in the relative peace and stability of the Archipelago after the restoration of the King's Rune, a need is still felt for a king over all the princes and small communities, a centre for loyalty, a shield in danger and a fount of justice. Middle-earth presents a complex picture containing many types of societies. None is upheld as the ultimate ideal, for a society is good or evil according to the men who live in it, but rule by a good king, uncorrupted by power, who dispenses justice but leaves much of the government in the hands of the citizens, is seen as the most desirable.

Closely connected with the problems of social structure and government is the destructive nature of power – destructive both to those who wield it and to those who are subject to it. The desire for power may arise initially for seemingly good reasons, as it does for Ged, Taran, Boromir, Denethor, even Cob and Saruman. But if the lust for power is not recognized for what it is, and controlled or laid aside, it destroys the man himself. It is a form of ultimately self-destructive egoism – the desire to make oneself the very centre of life, to which all else is subservient. The lust for power is linked with the lust for riches, the 'dragon sickness'. Tolkien and Lewis both use this ancient symbol of the all-devouring dragon and his doom-laden hoard to great effect. The dragons of Ursula Le Guin are more complex, and less clear-cut as symbols. The dragon of Pendor tries unsuccessfully to bribe Ged with gold, but his more dangerous weapon of temptation is the one to which Faust fell prey – the temptation of ancient wisdom. Knowledge, like wealth, can be used for good or for evil. In *The Farthest Shore* it is the combination of the dragon's ancient learning, Ged's mature and compassionate understanding of the true nature of life and death, and Arren's youthful strength and courage, which triumphs over the corrupt and corrupting misuse of power and knowledge by Cob.

A recognition of the self-destructive effects of wealth and power and knowledge turned to the wrong ends are an aspect of the moral code, which in turn is part of a religious or philosophic view of life. Some of the views presented by writers of secondary world fantasy have been briefly considered above, and this aspect of fantasy will be discussed in greater detail later. Here it is sufficient to note the similarity of overall intent, despite the differences of detail. Within the context of a secondary world, the exposition of the author's philosophic views may be made explicit, through the dialogue of the characters or the statements of the narrator, as for example in the Narnia, Prydain or Earthsea books, or may arise implicitly from the action, as in *The Lord of the Rings*.

From the discussion of secondary worlds in this chapter, it would seem that this form of fantasy is serious, effective and powerful. Naturally, in order to consider the construction and use of the secondary world it has been necessary to select examples which are, on the whole, successful. It would not be difficult to find other such fantasies which are considerably less so. Indeed, the form is a trap for the unwary, and the problems of convincing, self-consistent sub-creation are considerable. E. R. Eddison's *The Worm Ouroboros* is an immensely original book, which influenced both Tolkien and Lewis, but the circular nature of its theme and structure are curiously unsatisfying. In *The Tree Wakers* by Keith Claire, Maboria is too much distanced from primary world reality to permit the reader any easily identifiable points of contact. Nor does there seem to be any underlying purpose or theme to provide unity. This reinforces the lesson that secondary world fantasy not only permits the writer to expound serious ideas, but demands some kind of overall purpose to give it coherence. The exploration of imaginative experience without the controlling strength of the given framework of the primary world, or a specific conceptual framework in a secondary world, runs the risk of degenerating into misty romanticism and sentimentality, or at least of an incoherent and episodic structure.

In Joy Chant's *Red Moon and Black Mountain* there are all the technical features of secondary world creation – maps, languages, suggestions of history and culture. There is an impressive clash between forces of life and forces of destruction. Yet somehow as a whole it fails. Individual scenes and characters are often vivid and moving – the portrayal of the Khentorei, living on the wide plains with their herds of unicorns; Vir'Vachal the earth goddess, the irresistible force of creation and growth, but terrible in demanding sacrifice. Still the whole is less than the sum of its parts. The world remains shadowy. What it lacks, in fact, is an overall sense of realism, that essential element of all fantasy, which is of paramount importance in the secondary world. Moreover, there is little sense of how or why the struggle in Khendiol relates to experience in the primary world. The finest moment in the book occurs when Oliver offers himself as willing sacrifice to Vir'Vachal, yet neither he nor the other characters seem greatly changed by their experience in other-world. Indeed, apart from Eustace, C. S. Lewis's characters also are not profoundly altered by their Narnian adventures. Edmund repents of his treachery, but then we learn that he has only recently gone to the bad. More worrying, perhaps, is that Susan, after apparently completing her Narnian education, falls prey to small worldly vanities and is at least unredeemed, possibly damned – an outcome which seems inconsistent with Lewis's overall conception of Narnia.

Even the selected secondary worlds, then, are not flawless. The greatest difficulty lies in maintaining the inner consistency, particularly where the secondary world is the setting for several books. The geography of Prydain sometimes seems a little vague and inconsistent, although as we have seen, Alexander insists that he is not deeply concerned about this aspect of secondary world creation. Lewis has to work some odd details into *The Magician's Nephew* in order to explain anomalies like the lamp-post growing in the forest in *The Lion, the Witch and the Wardrobe*. In *The Hobbit* there is a reference to outlandish folk who 'have seldom even heard of the king' (p. 43). Later, when in *The Lord of the Rings* Tolkien decided to depict a Middle-earth without a king, since Aragorn is still living in exile and concealment, he had to devise an explanation for the phrase (I, p. 19).

A basis of serious themes helps to provide coherence in the secondary world, but overt didacticism will bore the reader. Humour, however, sugars the pill of didacticism; Carol Kendall has a particular talent in this direction, but Lloyd Alexander's humour in the early Prydain books is a little heavy-handed. There is more often a danger with these writers of over-seriousness. Ursula Le Guin permits herself only a few touches of humour: she might with advantage have allowed herself more. Tone and style are also difficult to manage successfully in books which deal with old-fashioned heroic virtues and overt spiritual conflicts, in the current literary climate which favours a bare, underwritten, and sometimes blatantly ugly style. Some writers seem untroubled by this. Although *The Hobbit* is occasionally painfully avuncular, as it nears its climax it assumes the tone of the heroic chronicle which dominates *The Lord of the Rings*. Ursula Le Guin also shows no diffidence in adopting a rhythmic but unadorned style throughout which gives the story its rich depth of feeling through implication and action. Lloyd Alexander's jocular tone is excellent for his humorous sections, but mars the moments of danger and tragedy in the early books. Towards the end of *The Chronicles of Prydain* his style moves towards much greater harmony with the content.

The initial task of the writer of a secondary world fantasy would thus seem to be to convince. Much time and effort must be expended in the initial stages to plan the technical framework of the secondary world in order to provide secondary realism. The secondary world must have considerable common ground with the primary world in order to provide a basis of understanding for the reader; there must be large areas of realism, and characters with whom he can identify. Not only the setting, but the nature of the tale, must be such that the reader can recognize some relevance for himself and for his experience. Usually, as we have seen, the most successful secondary world fantasies have as their basis a religious or philosophic view of life, which may present metaphysical concepts as physical realities.

Some secondary worlds are indeed so closely bound up with their underlying philosophic or religious purposes that they do not attempt normal primary world realism at all. Such was Bunyan's allegorical secondary world in *The Pilgrim's Progress*, and a similar type of allegorical sub-creation is adopted in Norton Juster's *The Phantom Tollbooth*. Other writers may cast over fantasy set in the primary world itself such a special quality of significance that it becomes completely symbolic, the primary world transformed into a secondary world, as Arthur Calder-Marshall does in *The Fair to Middling*. It is this explicit use of allegory and symbolism in fantasy which will be considered in the next chapter.

Layers of Meaning

Fantasy, being of its nature a form of multivalent writing, naturally makes considerable use of allegory and symbolism. Allegory is not popular, or at any rate it has not been so during the period of dominance of the realist novel. Moreover, modern writing in the allegorical mode, such as that of Kafka, Orwell, Huxley, or Mervyn Peake, tends to reflect the collapse of universal belief and the confusion and fragmentation of moral standards in modern Western society. Such allegories tend to be critical and destructive, rather than emulative and creative. Man is no longer seen as faced with a divinely ordered universe in which he may achieve salvation or damnation through his virtuous adaptation to or sinful rebellion against the God-given plan. Rather he is seen as an individualist who must discover his own morality and defy the man-made structures and hierarchies which are devised to destroy his individual integrity. This kind of modern allegorical writing occurs in modern fantasy; so also does traditional Christian allegory, and both will be considered later in this chapter.

In fantasy the symbolic element is in general closely related to the elements of the marvellous, and is used to provide that wider frame of reference which has already been illustrated as characteristic of the genre. Jonathan Raban discusses this quality with regard to the realist novel, but his remarks gain even more force in relation to the fantasy novel:

> a fabric of symbolism may enable the writer to create a moral and intellectual framework for the action of his novel. Symbolism allows an author to link the limited world of his characters to one of the great systems of values, so that we are made to compare the happenings in the novel with their mythological or historical parallels. Specific actions in the story illustrate general patterns of behaviour, and the private character acquires a new importance when he is seen in the light of his symbolic counterpart.[1]

Many writers of fantasy draw on traditional symbolism, from

mythology, folk-tale and Christian religion, or on the nature symbolism of the Romantics. One principal reason for using such established forms of imagery was discussed by Alan Garner:

> I begin to suspect that I use fantasy and mythology because I am
> not good enough to do without it. I need some kind of crutch,
> some kind of framework, I suspect. My most reputable reason
> for doing it is that myth is not an attempt to entertain, it is an
> attempt to explain something. Originally people did not sit
> around and cook up fairy stories to get through the long winter
> evenings. They were trying to come to terms with their environ-
> ment, so you find that over the millenia [sic] myth contains
> crystallized human experience and very powerful imagery. This
> imagery is useful for a writer if he uses it responsibly. It can
> work against him if he does not use it properly, but if he uses it
> correctly then he has very powerful cutting tools in his hand
> which work beneath the surface.[2]

A number of these 'very powerful cutting tools' are used by Lloyd
Alexander in *The Chronicles of Prydain*. Alexander himself is aware
of the danger of 'improvization' and an over-abundance of fantasy –
'Enchanted swords, wielded incautiously, cut both ways.'[3] The
marvellous elements of Prydain are closely linked with the symbolism. Cauldrons with magical properties are common in folklore,
one of the best known being that in *The Juniper Tree*, in which the
little boy is boiled up into soup for his unsuspecting father by a cruel
stepmother. His loving stepsister, however, buries the bones under
the juniper tree, and the boy is resurrected first as a bird, and
eventually as himself. The cauldron in *The Mabinogion*, from which
Alexander drew his inspiration, is also associated with rebirth after
death. The Irish throw into it the dead bodies of their warriors, 'and
on the morrow they would arise as good fighting men as before, save
that they were not able to speak' (Jones and Jones (trans.), *The
Mabinogion*, p. 37).

In *The Book of Three*, the first of Alexander's *Chronicles of
Prydain*, Arawn the Death-Lord has stolen the cauldron of rebirth
from the three fatal sisters of the marshes of Morva, and used it to
create fighters for his own evil cause by casting into it the bodies of
noble enemies, who emerge as the silent and deathless Cauldron-
Born. In the second book, *The Black Cauldron*, Arawn is no longer
content to rob graves: 'his servants dare to strike down the living and

bear them to Annuvin to swell the ranks of his deathless host. Thus, death begets death; evil begets evil' (p. 18).

It is the young hero Taran who finds the cauldron, once more in the possession of the fatal sisters:

> Though of iron, the cauldron seemed alive, grim and brooding with ancient evil. The empty mouth caught the chill breeze and a hushed muttering rose from the cauldron's depths, like the lost voices of the tormented dead. (p. 101)

To gain the cauldron, Taran exchanges for it his most precious possession, the brooch of Adaon. And he learns that to destroy the cauldron will cost not a brooch, but a life:

> 'A living person must climb into it,' Orddu said. 'When he does, the Crochan will shatter. . . . Not only that, but whoever gives up his life to the Crochan must give it willingly, knowing full well what he does.' (pp. 114–15)

In *The Mabinogion* the repentant traitor Efnisien feigns death in order to burst the cauldron from within. *The Black Cauldron* also contains an anti-hero, the bitter, twisted and occasionally traitorous Ellidyr. Ellidyr steals the Crochan from Taran in order to win the glory for himself, but both he and the cauldron fall into the hands of Morgant, would-be rival of Arawn. Repenting of his treachery at last, Ellidyr manages to leap willingly into the cauldron and his sacrifice destroys the Crochan, which robbed the dead of peace and turned good men to evil. Alexander has thus widened the reference of the symbolic cauldron on the moral level. Efnisien was thrown into the cauldron of *The Mabinogion* at his own desire, and destroyed it by physical strength. It is the strength of the willing sacrifice itself which shatters the Crochan of Prydain.

The sword Dyrnwyn has many predecessors – invincible swords of power which can only be drawn by their rightful owners, and which destroy any other who presumes to wield them. When the young Taran and Eilonwy first find Dyrnwyn in a barrow, Eilonwy has enough knowledge of magic inscriptions to realize the danger in using the sword (*CP*, I, pp. 64, 74–6). However, in a moment of extreme peril Taran does draw the sword to save his companions. His attempt results in his own severe wounding, and Eilonwy presents the sword to Gwydion, greatest hero of Prydain, and son of the house of Don. Even he does not fully know its history or power, although he has the capacity to wield it. After his long and painful growth to maturity, Taran is faced with the risk of drawing Dyrnwyn again at the climax of the final battle with Arawn and the Cauldron-Born:

> Once, long before, he had sought to draw Dyrnwyn and his life had been almost forfeit to his rashness. Now, heedless of the cost, seeing no more than a weapon come to his hand, he ripped the sword from its sheath. Dyrnwyn flamed with a white and blinding light. It was only then, in some distant corner of his mind, Taran dimly understood that Dyrnwyn was blazing in his grasp and that he was still alive. (*CP*, V, p. 262)

With Dyrnwyn Taran destroys the Cauldron-Born, and Arawn himself, and with that achievement the inscription on the sword glows clearly for the first time, before fading for ever:

> Draw Dyrnwyn, only thou of noble worth, to rule with justice, to strike down evil. Who wields it in good cause shall slay even the Lord of Death. (*Ibid.*, p. 275)

Dyrnwyn has passed on to Taran from Gwydion, for the leadership of Prydain has passed on also – as Gwydion says when Taran tries to return the sword to him: 'You have earned the right to draw it . . . and thus the right to wear it' (*ibid.*, p. 271). The attainment of Dyrnwyn is the culmination of Taran's training as the future High King, yet with the act of slaying Arawn, Dyrnwyn loses its magic powers. Just as in future Taran must rule without the help of the enchantments of Gwydion and Dallben, so Dyrnwyn will serve him only as a finely wrought weapon, and not as a sword of power.

C. S. Lewis also makes some use of mythological symbolism in *The Chronicles of Narnia,* but the Christian symbolism is much more prominent and central. The most potent and pervasive of these symbols is Aslan, the lion symbol of Christ. Dorothy Sayers, attacking a reviewer who complained that Aslan should have been given 'the shape as well as the nature and functions of an archangel',[4] pointed out the incorrect assumptions which lay behind this remark as well as the suitability of Aslan as a symbol for Christ:

> The Lion Aslan . . . has most emphatically *not* the 'nature and functions' of an archangel, and for that reason has not been given the form of one. In these tales of Absolutely Elsewhere,

Aslan is shown as creating the worlds (*The Magician's Nephew*), slain and risen again for the redemption of sin (*The Lion, the Witch and the Wardrobe*), incarnate as a Talking Beast among Talking Beasts (*passim*), and obedient to the laws he has made for his own creation (*The Voyage of the 'Dawn Treader'*, page 146). His august Archetype – higher than the angels and 'made a little lower' than they – is thus readily identified as the 'Lion of the Tribe of Judah'. Apart from a certain disturbance of the natural hierarchies occasioned by the presence of actual human beings, Professor Lewis's theology and pneumatology are as accurate and logical here as in his other writings.[5]

Aslan is both 'good and terrible at the same time' (CN, I, p. 117). Full of energy and creative power, he also has elements in his nature of the Old Testament Jehovah, god of vengeance.

In the figures of Jadis, priestess queen and White Witch, and of the Green Lady, Queen of the Underland and occasionally poisonous serpent, Lewis combines the folklore and medieval romance type of the beautiful but evil enchantress with elements from Christian mythology. Jadis attempts to gain her ends through threats of violence, and when that fails resorts to temptation – unsuccessfully with Digory under the Tree of Life in the paradisal Garden, successfully with Edmund, who is already partially corrupted. The Green Lady sometimes manifests herself openly as a poisonous serpent whose bite is deadly, but more often she works more subtly, undermining belief by dreamy enchantment and sweetly reasonable linguistic analysis. Underworld comes to symbolize this earth, full of unhappy, cowed, half-blind Earthmen, who either deny or fear the existence of Overworld – the transcendent heavenly reality. The Green Lady tries to destroy the belief of the children, Puddleglum and the disenchanted Rilian, in the very existence of Overworld, its sun, and Aslan, by arguing that they are only a game of make-believe.

Sometimes the Christian symbolism is used quite briefly, as when the stable takes on a new significance in *The Last Battle*, when believers and unbelievers are hurled through it:

'It seems, then,' said Tirian . . . 'that the Stable seen from within and the Stable seen from without are two different places.'

'Yes,' said the Lord Digory. 'Its inside is bigger than its outside.'

'Yes,' said Queen Lucy. 'In our world too, a Stable once had something inside it that was bigger than our whole.' (p. 143)

On the other hand, in a number of places *The Chronicles of Narnia* move into full allegory, and we will return to this below.

Unlike Alexander and Lewis, Russell Hoban tends to devise his own symbols in *The Mouse and His Child*. Much of this is figural symbolism, in which certain of the animals serve as types for humans. Moreover, in the incident of the shrew war, discussed in more detail in Chapter 8, Hoban treats symbolically the progressive destruction of war, as the wilfully blind are gobbled up by the more powerful.

A recurring symbol throughout the book is the Bonzo dog food can, with its various associations: Bonzo, the tramp's dog; Sirius, the dog star; and the Last Visible Dog. This complex symbol has both a negative and a positive pole. It is into a Bonzo dog food can that Manny Rat throws the dismembered parts of wind-ups which he has 'murdered' (pp. 34–5), and yet it is a canful of such parts which the mice and their friends use in their final successful attack on the rats (ch. 8). The mouse child throughout his long pilgrimage looks up to the stars for hope, and as the Frog's prophecy nears fulfilment – 'A dog shall rise; a rat shall fall' – Manny Rat is filled with unease; but fails to observe the triumphant rising of Sirius the Dog Star (pp. 154–5).

The label on the dog food can depicts pictures within pictures of dogs, a receding telescopic image of dogs passing almost beyond vision. The last visible dog of this image gives its name to the meaningless play written by Serpentina for performance by the crows, but it also gives its name to the renovated dolls' house, which becomes a sanctuary for the weary and homeless. Standing for months in the mud at the bottom of the pool, the mouse child searches for some meaning for life in the images on the dog food label. The Bonzo label becomes almost a symbol of a symbol – its significance depends on the minds and characters of those who study it. For Serpentina it leads to nothingness, a blank denial of all meaning, an infinity as featureless as the mud into which he sinks. For the mouse child it leads beyond nothingness to a vision of himself, and to a realization that an individual can 'swallow infinity'.

The extended use of a symbol or cluster of symbols is characteristic of a number of fantasies, and in some cases even the narrative structure takes on symbolic form. In *The Light Maze* by Joan North, the widely accepted identification of good with light and evil with darkness and stench are combined with the Yin-Yang symbol of balance. Ideas from Christian mysticism, Platonic Idealism and Zen are interwoven in the symbols of the Light Maze and of the Lightstone, which may enable one who holds it to pass safely through the Maze. The Light Maze can be entered only by some: 'If you hold in your hand the Lightstone and hear in the silence the true note which is yourself then you will be able to enter the Maze' (p. 124). Once entered, it is a place not only of mystic experience and visionary hope, but of darkness and danger.

The first impression of the Maze is one of 'wonder and glory', but in it there also lurks a shadow of darkness and corruption which for each traveller takes on an evil image of himself.[6] Mr Martin, the vicar, identifies this as the 'Guardian of the Threshold', linking the Light Maze with Jungian psychology and the probing of the inner recesses of the personality. Only by having the strength to repudiate this personal image of evil, while recognizing it as still a part, if a negative one, of his own personality, can the traveller escape from darkness into light, and only the truly pure in heart penetrate to the Well of Life at the centre of the Maze. The conception is very powerful, and the central symbolism is realized through the marvellous element of the fantasy. Unfortunately the characterization does not reach the same level of achievement as the imaginative conception.

Another uneven book which nevertheless makes occasional successful use of symbolism is Joy Chant's *Red Moon and Black Mountain*. Although as a secondary world Vandarei is not entirely convincing, this is perhaps more the fault of the sometimes over-elaborate style than of the underlying conception. The battle between light and dark is fought symbolically early in the book in the struggle between white and black eagles, but the encounter is indecisive, and the conflict continues until Fendarl, the corrupt Black Enchanter, has been defeated. Joy Chant employs a more interesting form of symbolism, approaching figural allegory, in depicting the outraged forces of nature after the battle has taken place, as the implacable nature goddess Vir'Vachal paces the desecrated battlefield:

> Yet it was not for the slain that she mourned; but for the injured earth itself. . . . as she moved she sank ankle-deep into the earth, and behind her green welled from the hollows her feet had pressed, welled up and overflowed and spread. Wherever she

passed the ground woke to life, and grass grew and flourished. The earth brushed by her skirt bore clover, and flowers bloomed where her poppies fell. A slow tide of verdure flowed out from her, and not one yard did she leave untrodden. The fire scars were thick with blossom; the graves were banks of scented growth; a vine wreathed Fendarl's cairn and twined his banner. Surely the dead would sleep more quietly under such a coverlet than in the cold naked earth. (p. 231)

Before Vir'Vachal can be appeased and the uneasy earth finally quietened, Li'vanh, who has been hurled from the primary world into the secondary world of Vandarei, must leap willingly into the abyss, not knowing whether he goes to his death or to some other fate. Vir'Vachal, this fiercely creative but ruthless embodiment of Nature, is more convincing and memorable than many other far better-known portrayals of the nature goddess.[7]

The structural pattern of *The Owl Service*, by Alan Garner, is not that of a symbolic quest for spiritual values and self-knowledge, as in *The Light Maze*, but a pattern arising from the legendary tale of Lleu Llaw Gyffes, Blodeuedd and Gronw Bebyr in *The Mabinogion*. In the legend Lleu is the incestuous child of Gwydion and his sister Aranrhod, who lays on her son the curse that he shall never take a mortal woman to wife. Gwydion with the help of Math makes for his son a wife out of flowers:

And then they took the flowers of the oak, and the flowers of the broom, and the flowers of the meadowsweet, and from those they called forth the very fairest and best endowed maiden that mortal ever saw, and baptized her with the baptism they used at that time, and named her Blodeuedd [Flowers]. (p. 68)

During the absence of her husband, Blodeuedd falls in love with Gronw Bebyr, and together they plot to kill Lleu. Although all the magical conditions for Lleu's death are fulfilled, when Gronw's spear strikes him he does not die but is transformed into an eagle. Later Lleu returns to seek his revenge; standing on Bryn Cyfergyr where Gronw had stood, he casts his spear at Gronw, who has taken Lleu's place on the river bank. The spear passes clean through a stone behind which Gronw has been allowed to shield himself, and kills the lover. Blodeuedd is turned by Gwydion into an owl – and 'the owl is still called Blodeuwedd' [Flower-face] (p. 74).

Ever since that day, as Garner chooses to expand on the legend in

The Owl Service, the power loosed on the valley has periodically built up, like water behind a dam or an electrical charge, until it can be released in another repetition of the tragic love story. The three young people in the book, Alison, Gwyn and Roger, find themselves forced to re-enact the ancient pattern. The twin symbols of flowers and owls are interwoven throughout the book, as are the varying recurrences of the love triangle. It is gradually revealed that Gwyn is the child of the apparently half-crazed gardener Huw and his sister Nancy, who, a generation earlier, has tried to escape her fate of reliving the legend by moving outside the valley after Gwyn was born. Her other lover was Bertram, the cousin of Alison's father, killed riding his motor bike after Huw had removed the brake blocks. Gwyn, like Huw, is the secretly acknowledged hereditary lord of the valley, descendant of Gwydion and Lleu. Like Huw, he is humiliated by the lover who is a stranger, in this case Roger, Alison's stepbrother. Other unhappy love affairs linger in the background. After the death of Alison's father, her mother has married Roger's father. Roger's own mother, whose case 'was in all the papers', had deserted her husband and child, and is referred to by Alison's mother as 'The Birmingham Belle'.

Alison begins to release the threatening power when she traces the flower pattern off old plates found in the attic of her house in the Welsh valley, and makes the tracings into paper owls, which disappear. An ancient painting of Blodeuedd seems to 'peck' its way out from behind the pebbledash which had concealed it. The missing paper owls are found in the room where Bertram's motor cycle is locked away, gathered around a stuffed owl, shot long before by Bertram and labelled 'The Bryn Ghost'. Gwyn, betrayed by Alison and derided by Roger, tries to escape from the valley, but is driven back by the sheep dogs and a vicious black sow.[8] Like his father, like all his Welsh ancestors, Gwyn cannot escape from the hereditary doom, at least not without help. But Gwyn is already partly alienated from his heritage by his education, and Roger, heroically resisting the shallow, easy prejudices of his own father and the deep wound inflicted by his mother, emerges from his cruelty towards Gwyn and rescues the three young people from the usual tragic end. Huw has said:

> 'We have the blood. . . . And we must bear it. A lord must look
> to his people, and they must not suffer for his wrong. When I

took the powers of the oak and the broom and the meadowsweet, and made them woman, that was a great wrong – to give
those powers a thinking mind.' (p. 81)

Huw himself thinks there is no escape, and yet he provides the clue to
one: 'She wants to be flowers, but you make her owls. You must not
complain, then, if she goes hunting' (p. 80). In the final scene Roger
takes charge and asserts that Alison, and Blodeuedd, and all the
power in the valley, are not owls, but flowers, not cruelty and lust,
but beauty. The air has been full of 'pouncing feathers', but Roger's
clear insight and laughter transform everything: 'And the room was
full of petals from skylight and rafters, and all about them a frag-
rance, and petals, flowers falling, broom, meadowsweet, falling,
flowers of the oak' (p. 173).

The tightly structured relationship between *The Owl Service* and
The Mabinogion story extends down to tiny details, easily over-
looked. For example, in the legend, Blodeuedd had retreated from
the valley, walking backwards so that she might watch for pursuers.
The following is Gwyn's last sight of his mother:

> She walked backwards up the road, shouting, and the rain
> washed the air clean of her words and dissolved her haunted
> face, broke the dark line of her into webs that left no stain, and
> Gwyn watched for a while the unmarked place where she had
> been, then climbed over the gate. (p. 164)

Nancy is both Blodeuedd and Aranrhod, and when the air is washed
clean of her, Gwyn is one step nearer being freed of the curse. This
quality of symbolism, both extended and detailed, the whole closely
interwoven with the structure and themes of the novel, together with
its shrewd characterization, social satire and humour, make this
easily Alan Garner's most notable book. Here he uses the 'very
powerful cutting tools' of Welsh legend to provide the marvellous
basis for his modern fantasy in a way which enhances not only the
modern fantasy, but our reading of the original legend itself.

A less well known but exceptional fantasy, Theresa Whistler's *The
River Boy,* was published in 1955, but was out of print for many
years until republished in 1976. Nat is a solitary boy, living with his
widowed mother and his grandfather in an old house in the country,
and much of the book is filled with a luminous, child's-eye view of
the countryside: snails crawling up grass stems, birds building their

nests, hazel nuts plopping into the river, a tiny water-wheel made of sycamore seeds. But Nat finds a river in a hidden valley which is not there in the primary world, and his reflection dives upwards out of the river to meet him. Together, from autumn through winter, spring and summer, and finally into winter again, the two boys explore the river, each time a little further down towards the sea. The river becomes a symbol of Nat's passage through childhood towards adolescence. As for the river boy, Nat asks: 'But are you just me – or partly me – or someone quite outside me?' (pp. 10–11). He never discovers the answer to this question, although he and the river boy are closely bound together. The river boy, however, can do all the things which Nat cannot quite achieve: he can climb far enough to count the eggs in a nest, make a perfect clay lamp, plait a basket and a horse's harness, tickle trout, work tirelessly at harvesting, and even walk upon the surface of the water. It seems that whatever Nat desires passionately enough, these things the river boy can do. While the river boy is primarily an ideal image of Nat, he has his own secret and inscrutable life which Nat can affect, although he cannot grasp its true essence. In this use of the marvellous element of fantasy there is some resemblance to the mental landscapes of *Marianne Dreams* and *A Game of Dark*, discussed in Chapter 3, but the visionary secondary world of *The River Boy* is a much richer construct.

Part of the vision is that death is a leap into a world of beauty and power. The creatures which in this life on earth are seen 'through a glass, darkly' are revealed in their inherent splendour. On one of his visits to the river world Nat follows the aged Old Rose, his mother's childhood pony. The pony and the boys are enticed by a haunting music through a forest where the animals perform strange, weaving dances. Nat, filled with some inexplicable foreboding, pursues Rose down a sheer rock face to a hidden water garden, where he makes a shelter and tries to keep her, but the impatient Rose goes on, down steps into the earth and through a waterfall to a grotto beyond.

> Her eyes were fixed on the waterfall, and seemed to burn with longing.
>
> Then he flung himself on her, to hold her back, but it was too late. She shook him off like a water-drop, and sprang full at the curtain of water, and passed through it, and landed in the dry grotto inside, and the waters closed behind her. . . . The pipes no longer played 'Come and rest!' but 'Come and dance!' . . .

> For a moment Nathaniel caught, through [the door], a
> glimpse of some unimaginable country, folded in a dazzling
> deep blue darkness. Then Old Rose, with a whinny of joy, had
> passed through, and the narrow door was softly closing. The
> music faded away, and though the waterfall still roared, it
> seemed to Nathaniel that a great unbearable silence had fallen
> on all things. (p. 33)

Nat tries to follow Rose through the waterfall to the paradisal
grotto, but is told by the river boy, 'Not yet! . . . It's not time for you
yet!' Waking in the morning in the primary world, he finds that the
old pony has died in the night, but his experiences in the secondary
world of the river have opened up for Nat a whole new perception of
the relationship between life and death.

This is not the last the boys see of Old Rose. Further down the river
they find her, gloriously transformed: 'at least twice as big and in the
full vigour of her prime. . . . Nathaniel had never seen any animal
with such clouds of rippling fine hair for mane and tail.' The white
pony who in life had become so old and bowed now appears in her
essential form, the horse of pure white, with its sacramental associations. 'Yet in spite of all the differences between them, there was
something which went on reminding him of the old mare. She held her
royal head as Old Rose had done, tucked in a little to her breast, with
neck arched. She pawed the ground with Rose's delicate impatience'
(p. 77). The eternal reality of the horse is revealed to Nat, as before it
has appeared only in daydreams. In a later episode, when he tries to
impose his selfish will on the river world and nearly loses the world
and all its visionary intensity, he glimpses Old Rose briefly, in her
diminished, distorted, primary world form: 'Over the tops of the
corn something white came floating – the wraith of a small white
pony with a magpie on her back' (p. 85). When he accepts the river
world with patience and joy, Nat experiences the underlying and
enduring reality of certain experiences, and perceives the essential,
unmarred quality of certain creatures. It is only his own impatience
and wilfulness which nearly rob him of this power of perception.

Another central focus in the book is the mill. In this the unifying
figure is the Miller, with all his attendant imagery of sowing and
reaping, flowing water and the grinding of corn. 'Everything comes
to the Mill,' says the Miller, as he paints a picture of Nathaniel on air,
with a brush 'made of the very first hairs that fell off your head' (p.

46). The Miller is a richly evocative figure: 'his clothes gave off flour as a puffball spurts brown dust when you stamp on it' (p. 44). He gives the boys a strange and fantastic supper, but for breakfast the boys eat fish and a loaf which is perpetually renewed. The Miller, in the more fantastic episodes, is overflowing with rich and varied creative energy, but he is also associated with the symbolism of Christ through the loaves and fishes, through his function as a link between fleeting time and eternity, and through the resurrection symbolism of the mill.

The Miller mills many strange kinds of grain besides the usual wheat, oats, barley, rye and maize. The 'tiny dark frame in which the Miller had so carefully painted a picture of airy nothing' falls through the hopper of the mill. Nat picks it up, expecting to find it crushed. Instead, it has been transformed, like everything else which passes through the mill, into a 'tiny likeness of himself, sitting at the round window in the upper room of the Mill. It was full of waving shadows and firelight, and through the round window appeared a dark landscape no bigger than a coin; and in it the silver thread of the river could just be seen' (p. 58).

There are many things at the mill which seem inexplicable to Nat. Who brings all the loads of grain to the mill? How many doors and windows are there really? How long can he stay? But the asking of questions immediately endangers the experience:

> Even as the words came out of Nathaniel's mouth a strange transparency had begun to steal through the solid shapes of things around him, as if thinning them away from behind. The Mill, the weir-pool, the very Miller himself, all quivered as reflections do when some current rises from below, but has not yet broken the surface into ripples. (p. 53)

The imaginative and spiritual experience too closely questioned, too deeply probed, begins to shiver and dissolve, as the innocence and wonder of childhood vision dissolve. For the moment Nat learns to accept his experience and not to destroy it with his anxious, restless queries, so that when he finds some strange objects in the mill loft, he remains silent, although he senses that the huge hour-glass and sharp sickle have some special significance. The flow of sand through the hour-glass, the grain through the mill and the water down the river all parallel the swift and inexorable movement of temporal life, just as the sickle embodies the sharp severance of its end.

Later Nat finds the symbolic sickle and hour-glass again, when he has run away from the river boy through the field of wheat they are harvesting with the help of the rediscovered Rose. Nat follows the maze-like path of cut corn through the field, trying to reach the strange, shadowless farm he has glimpsed in the distance, to the west. A church tower stands in the centre of a circle of twelve roofs, like a sundial, but the tower casts no shadow, for it lies beyond time. Nat's own shadow stretches out behind him. 'Yet the whole farm, and the ancient tower, and the flowering trees [myrtle amongst the yews], lay in a circle of untroubled radiance. Gazing at them long and silently, Nathaniel felt as though something he had always minded had been put right, as though he had found something he did not know he had lost' (p. 83).

The maze comes to a sudden stop in the uncut corn, and it is here that Nat finds the Miller's sickle and hour-glass. Seizing the sickle he tries to cut his own way through to the farm. Everything about him begins to fade, colour and light and vision, and he only has the presence of mind to right the hour-glass, which he has knocked over with the sickle. By his actions, even more dramatically than earlier by his questions, Nat has endangered his vision. He has tried to force his way ahead to an experience for which he is not yet ready, to cut his way through to the eternal world of the shadowless farm when his place is still in the temporal world of harvest and hour-glass. The swathe through the corn, like the river, thus serves as a symbol of Nat's life, which is endangered when the hour-glass falls.

When Nat at last returns to the river world, he himself is feverish after deliberate self-exposure in the snow, a rash and near-fatal attempt to force his way back to the river world. He finds the river boy in a coma, lying at the bottom of a bitterly cold chasm, into which the river plunges as 'an endless, terrible cascade of snow' (p. 96). Nat secures the help of a strange old woman pulling a handcart, who does not speak to him, but who shelters the river boy from the snow and feeds Nat on roast chestnuts and broth in a wooden bowl – 'It smelt of fungi and withered winter berries and mouldering seeds' (p. 98). Animals and birds, including a great white swan, also come to the woman for help, and she is constantly planting and tending the trees. Briefly, as he falls asleep, Nat catches an odd glimpse of her:

> He thought for a moment, when she went back to the fire without her cloak, that he saw her wearing a gown as green as a

leaf, with a hem as red and blue and gold as a June border. And for a moment she seemed to throw off her stoop and stand up as tall as a young tree. (p. 99)

Although Nat sees this archetypal figure of Nature in her winter guise of withered body clothed in rags, he thus catches a shadowy image of her youthful summer of strength and beauty. All through the second night in the chasm, Nat seems to hear the hammering of steel on stone. He wakes to find 'a great stone aqueduct, flung across from one side of the ravine to the other' (p. 101), carrying the waters of his river of life safely across the terrible chasm. The old woman disappears in a shower of tools. Nat climbs up to find the river boy riding the swan, and awakes to his own slow convalescence. In the river world the ancient healing powers of Nature have provided a way across the chasm for the real boy and the river boy. Reunited they can follow the river to the sea.

On Nat's final visit to the river world, the boys reach the floating city at the end of the river – it is garlanded as if for a festival, and is full of the chiming of clocks. Nat can no longer ignore the hurrying, insistent pressure of passing time. He runs after his ship, which is carried away through a cavern in the cliffs and out to the sea – and leaves the river boy behind for ever:

There was no return into that inner country – nor was there any way out from it to where he now stood on the brink of the sea. He could never now answer the river boy's good-bye. Since there was no help for it, he turned back again, between excitement and alarm, to face the ocean. (p. 113)

In *The River Boy* the symbolic mode and the allegorical mode are fully integrated. The symbolic journey down the river is, at another level, an allegory of the life of Everyman. Not only Nathaniel's own life is embodied in the river country. Old Rose's leap through the waterfall, and her re-emergence as the horse that Nat had always dreamed she might be, blends the concepts of baptism into immortal life and of the permanent transcendent reality behind the shadowy perceptions of the primary world. At the same time it enables Nat to face death calmly and thoughtfully. The river flowing through the mill-race, and the grain through the mill hopper, the ancient sickle and huge hour-glass are symbols of the Miller's functions, while he is himself a transformed but still recognizable allegorical figure, part Christ, part Father Time – a Father Time who creates as well as reaping and grinding, and a Christ-like provider of loaves and fishes. Nat cannot defy time, cannot leap too soon to the shadowless land, the eternity of peace and blessedness which Rose has inherited. He is rescued from his folly by Mother Nature, ancient crone and beautiful maiden, who restores his physical strength with the simple, if bitter, fruits of the earth, and casts the symbolic aqueduct across the chasm, to carry his river of life safely down to the sea of adulthood. The complex symbolic and allegorical levels of the book enhance the closely observed picture of a country childhood.

Theresa Whistler works with great skill, drawing together traditional symbolism and symbols of her own creation which are organically linked with them, and relating both to allegorical action and figural allegory – all within a novel which is a blend of fantasy and precise realism. C. S. Lewis's method is very different. His Christian symbolism is clear cut, his Christian allegories form set-pieces which can easily be isolated and discussed. The Creation, the Passion, the Apocalypse and Day of Judgment are presented by Lewis as straightforward allegories, although, with curious disingenuousness, he denied that the Narnia books *were* allegories.[9] A comparison of the two writers may reveal something about the ways in which symbolism and allegory may be used in fantasy to very different effect.

Although *The Lion, the Witch and the Wardrobe* may have had its very first genesis, as Lewis maintained, in a series of 'pictures' in the mind,[10] yet by the time he came to write it, many years later, he had much more clearly developed intentions. He had already written a number of works of Christian apologetics and his planetary romances with their strongly didactic element. Before embarking on his first Narnian novel, he was very much influenced by reading a manuscript novel by Roger Lancelyn Green.[11] Here, clearly, was an intriguing form, the fantasy novel, in which Lewis could express his views on Christianity. Unfortunately, the element of didacticism is so strong, the events allegorized of such cosmic importance, and Lewis's interest in them so much stronger than his interest in such aspects of his novels as the child heroes and heroines, that the allegorical elements are out of all proportion with the rest of the *Chronicles*. Moreover, the didacticism is too thinly disguised, and sometimes positively distasteful. The result is that the Narnia books are an uneasy and uneven mixture, and the passages of allegory float like stubborn lumps in a rather thin gruel.

On the other hand, Theresa Whistler's intentions are hardly didactic at all. What she presents to the reader is a fresh and arresting vision of childhood – clearly filled with memories from her own childhood, and with a deep sympathy for the childhood of others. Yet the whole is set within the framework of the adult's perception of childhood in the long voyage of life – something precious and lovely, but also shot through with sudden sorrows and fears, a brief passage of time in the long landscape of eternity. Once lost, it can never be revisited, except in visions or dreams. Thus the conception of the book is whole and integral from the start, not constructed from disparate pieces. She has no need to say, as Lewis does, 'It's all in Plato' (CN, VII, p. 171) – she simply presents the glorious white horse. As a result the symbolism and the allegory are as natural and acceptable as the freshly caught trout sizzling over the fire, or the child's eye view of a caterpillar climbing a grass stem.

Another writer who, like Lewis, uses allegory with a basis in Christian religion, ritual and tradition, is Leon Garfield in *The Ghost Downstairs*. The double-layered nature of the fantasy is explicit from the start: 'Two devils lived in Mr Fast: envy and loneliness. Together they gnawed him; drained the colour from his face, the lustre from his eyes and the charity from his heart' (p. 9). In this 'ghost' story, with its strong Dickensian flavour, Mr Fast sells seven years of his life, in exchange for a million pounds, to the mysterious Mr Fishbane, who seems at first to be a Mephistopheles figure. The theme is based on an inversion of the Faust legend: Mr Fast sells not the last years of his life, but the first years of his childhood. And unknown to the greedy clerk, the purchaser wants his soul not for damnation, but for salvation. The story is a psychomachia, acted out both within the soul of Mr Fast, and externally, as he and Mr Fishbane contend for possession of the uncorrupted seven-year-old phantom, who is Dennis Fast's childhood self. There are many echoes of Marlowe's *Dr Faustus* in the book, and a fundamental atmosphere of irony in that Mr Fast (and at first the reader also) believes that Mr Fishbane *is* the devil. The alert reader, however, soon realizes that the clerk and the strange old man are celebrating a form of Eucharist as the contract is signed, and that whenever Mr Fast suffers physical harm, it is not inflicted from without, but results from his attempts to injure the child, who is his innocent self. The final resolution is reached when Mr Fast throws himself in front of a train in order to prevent what he wrongly believes are the evilly inspired intentions of the child. But the child's character has become the mirror image of the man's – as Mr Fast turns towards goodness, the child is filled with joy. By the willing sacrifice of his twisted and corrupt adult life, Dennis Fast redeems his childhood soul.[12]

The Fair to Middling by Arthur Calder-Marshall also uses the Christian allegorical theme of temptation: the children of Alderman Winterbottome's School for Incapacitated Orphans are treated to a visit to the Bank Holiday Fair at Middling by Lady Charity Armstrong. During the afternoon some of the children and staff, and Lady Charity herself, undergo strange experiences which affect their whole lives and in particular their views of themselves. The fair, with its crowds, its confused noise, its odd miscellany of stalls, and its barkers calling 'Give us your money quick and go away! . . . in different dialects' (p. 17), makes the perfect setting for the stories. The children become separated or lost; some of the booths turn out to be rather different from the normal fairground ones; distorting mirrors suddenly take on a new significance. There are echoes here of John Bunyan's Vanity Fair, for most of the tempting wares which are offered are the treacherous ones of self-deception, and only in resisting them do the characters discover new inner strength.

The Fair to Middling is an interwoven fabric of individual allegories of temptation or assault by evil, and each of the characters emerges in some way strengthened by the experience, realizing that his disability need not be entirely fruitless and a source of bitterness. Mr Carruthers, whose experience at the fair is the last, and the most inward, frames this idea for Lawrie, the albino boy who comes to him to declare his wish to become a biologist:

> 'The point is,' he said, 'if you do this as your lifework, you've given your . . . your disability a meaning.'
> 'But I may fail.'
> 'Even if you fail, that won't matter. Not from your point of view. You'll have given your life up to something bigger than yourself. Perhaps you'll discover something that will be useful in some totally different way. Or make the first step towards a cure. In fact, you've already made the first step in thinking that albinism is a condition which might be cured.' He looked down at the boy who had so repelled him and saw him now not as an unfortunate who lacked the colouring of a normal human being but as an exceptional person whose physical appearance

marked his mision. He wore his whiteness as a priest his vest-
ments. (pp. 188–9)

Arthur Calder-Marshall stresses the moral lesson that everyone
has both abilities and disabilities – some may be clearly visible and
spectacular, others more hidden and private – but, as old Father
Doonan has pointed out to Lawrie: ' "There are worse things than
unhappiness and suffering," Father Doonan said. "Such as?" "Well,
evil," Father Doonan said. "Sin." ' Moreover, the individual who
accepts his disabilities and triumphs over them – even sometimes
transforming them into assets (as does the musical boy, Peter, with
the onset of his blindness) – is truly victorious, in moral and spiritual,
as well as in worldly terms.

Norton Juster's *The Phantom Tollbooth* is not an allegory of
temptation, but an allegory of the development of the mind. Milo is a
typical modern little boy: surrounded with a plentiful supply of toys
and mechanical gadgets, he has never learned to use either his mental
capacities or his physical senses. He rushes from home to school and
back again, locked in his boredom and blind to the world about him.
When he finds in his room a mysterious package labelled 'For Milo,
who has plenty of time', containing a tollbooth, he decides he might
as well play with it, for lack of anything better to do. Driving past the
tollbooth in his pedal car, Milo suddenly finds himself in the Kingdom of Wisdom.

The Phantom Tollbooth is unusual both in being an overt allegory
and in being openly and avowedly didactic. Yet the whole form and
style of the book are so witty that there is no sense of oppressive
didacticism. The reader, like Milo, is made aware of the beauty and
the fun of both words and numbers, as the verbal pyrotechnics carry
him forward through the Kingdom of Wisdom. In the prison of the
city of Dictionopolis, Faintly Macabre, the not-so-wicked Which
and great-aunt of King Azaz the Unabridged, explains the right use
of words to Milo and his companion, the Watchdog Tock. Faintly
Macabre was formerly the Official Which, in charge of choosing the
correct words to use on all occasions, until power made her miserly,
and she banned the use of all words. Repentant now, she tells Milo:
'they never appointed a new Which, and that explains why today
people use as many words as they can and think themselves very wise
for doing so. For always remember that while it is wrong to use too
few, it is often far worse to use too many' (p. 60).

Setting out later from the city of Digitopolis, ruled by the Mathe-magician, Milo, Tock and the Humbug struggle up the mountains of Ignorance in order to bring back the exiled Princesses Rhyme and Reason, and rescue the Kingdom of Wisdom from chaos. Their way is barred by the Terrible Trivium, 'demon of petty tasks and worth-less jobs, ogre of wasted effort and monster of habit' (p. 180). Milo recalls how much of his life has been spent doing unimportant things, and the Trivium urges them to stay with him: 'If you only do the easy and useless jobs, you'll never have to worry about the important ones which are so difficult. You just won't have the time. For there's always something to do to keep you from what you really should be doing, and if it weren't for that dreadful magic staff, you'd never know how much time you were wasting' (pp. 180–1). Here too they encounter the Senses Taker, who demands that they fill in endless forms, telling him: 'When you were born, where you were born, why you were born, how old you are now, how old you were then, how old you'll be in a little while, your mother's name, your father's name, your aunt's name, your uncle's name, your cousin's name, where you live, how long you've lived there, the schools you've attended, the schools you haven't attended . . .' (p. 192).

As his questions indicate, the Senses Taker epitomizes that aspect of modern life which destroys privacy and diminishes the worth of the individual. He is concerned to misdirect people's energies, so that they become hopelessly entangled in a web of trivia:

'I help people find what they're *not* looking for, hear what they're *not* listening for, run after what they're *not* chasing, and smell what isn't even there. And furthermore, . . . I'll steal your sense of purpose, take your sense of duty, destroy your sense of proportion – and, but for one thing, you'd be helpless yet.'

'What's that?' asked Milo fearfully.

'As long as you have the sound of laughter,' he groaned unhappily, 'I cannot take your sense of humour – and, with it, you've nothing to fear from me.' (pp. 194–5)

Not only is the stress on mental agility and the ability to dis-tinguish between words used to communicate ideas and words used to confuse. Milo is also brought to a keen sense of the world about him, mainly through sight and sound, but also through taste, touch and smell. Alec Bings, who can see 'whatever is inside, behind, around, covered by or subsequent to anything else' (p. 91), explains to Milo that 'it's just as bad to live in a place where what you do see isn't there as it is to live in one where what you don't see is' (p. 102). The capacity to perceive the physical world aright is thus linked with the power to distinguish between reality and illusion. 'Perhaps some day you can have one city as easy to see as Illusions and as hard to forget as Reality,' Milo answers (p. 102).

The subtle relationships between colours and moods are evoked in the scene with Chroma's orchestra, which is responsible for washing in all the colour in what would otherwise be a grey and featureless landscape. Having watched Chroma conduct the sunset, Milo decides to try to conduct the dawn:

> The 'cellos made the hills glow red, and the leaves and grass were tipped with a soft pale green as the violins began their song. Only the bass fiddles rested as the entire orchestra washed the forest in colour. (p. 110)

In the Valley of Sound, Milo discovers the results of the misuse of sound, in a sharply pointed allegory of modern life, where the senses are so often dulled to the world around. The Soundkeeper, who used to rule wisely and well, has grown disgusted at the behaviour of the people in the valley:

> 'She was generous to a fault and provided us with all the sound we could possibly use: for singing as we worked, for bubbling pots of stew, for the chop of an axe and the crash of a tree, for the creak of a hinge and the hoot of an owl, for the squish of a shoe in the mud and the friendly tapping of rain on the roof, and for the sweet music of pipes and the sharp snap of winter ice cracking on the ground. . . . Slowly at first, and then in a rush, more people came to settle here and brought with them new ways and new sounds, some very beautiful and some less so. But everyone was so busy with the things that had to be done that they scarcely had time to listen at all. And, as you know, a sound which is not heard disappears for ever and is not to be found again.
>
> 'People laughed less and grumbled more, sang less and shouted more, and the sounds they made grew louder and uglier. It became difficult to hear even the birds or the breeze, and soon everyone stopped listening for them.' (p. 126)

To punish the inhabitants of the valley, the Soundkeeper has locked up all the sounds in the filing cabinets in her fortress and refuses to release them until reconciled with the people of the valley by Milo's efforts.

What is eminently satisfying about *The Phantom Tollbooth* is that it requires of the reader exactly that mental alertness, both to the surface complexities and to the deeper levels of meaning, which is the theme of the allegory. With its insistence on the right use of words – neither hoarding them nor over-spending – and the right use of the reasoning and mathematical faculty of the mind, it becomes an almost archetypal allegory, an allegory of the way in which Rhyme and Reason together maintain the right balance in the realm of Wisdom.

The use of symbols and symbolism in the novels discussed in this chapter is closely related to their use of the marvellous, as we have seen. The symbolic element thus tends to stand out more clearly than in most realist novels. Allegory is rarely overt, as in the traditional allegories, but may often shape the structure of the action in the form of a life's journey, a psychomachia or a Faustian temptation. Occasional archetypal figural allegory is used – as in the embodiment of the forces of nature in both *Red Moon and Black Mountain* and *The River Boy* – but the allegorical figures are very individualized conceptions on the part of their creators, and can in no sense be regarded as naive personified abstractions. Only *The Phantom Tollbooth* is a full-dress allegory, and its outstanding quality is a freshness of perception and a zest in verbal wit which transforms what might have been a solemn lesson.

One quality is shared by all the books discussed here – a quality to be found in most fantasies, but especially strong in those which employ sustained symbolism or allegory. It is the desire to communicate to the reader a vision of some kind of transcendent reality. The primary world is seen as possessing an intense beauty of its own, which is too often neglected within the circumscribed boundaries of modern life. At the same time, the beauties of the primary world are in some sense, and in different ways and degrees for different writers, only a shadow, a temporal manifestation of a luminous and eternal reality. Milo is made aware of the first side of this vision:

> He noticed somehow that the sky was a lovely shade of blue and that one cloud had the shape of a sailing ship. The tips of the trees held pale, young buds and the leaves were a rich deep

green. Outside the window, there was so much to see, and hear, and touch – walks to take, hills to climb, caterpillars to watch as they strolled through the garden. There were voices to hear and conversations to listen to in wonder, and the special smell of each day.

And, in the very room in which he sat, there were books that could take you anywhere, and things to invent, and make, and build, and break, and all the puzzle and excitement of everything he didn't know – music to play, songs to sing, and worlds to imagine and then some day make real. His thoughts darted eagerly about as everything looked new – and worth trying. (pp. 217–18)

Nathaniel, in *The River Boy*, has two glimpses of the other side of the vision, first of the land beyond the waterfall, into which Old Rose leaps, and later of the shadowless farm. Both are glimpses of an eternal world beyond the river world which, although a world of ideal beauty, still shares with the primary world the insistent pressure of time. Nat is unable to cross under the waterfall or to cut his way through to the farm of the vision. For him it is still not yet time to move beyond this world to the one beyond, where the world of fantasy attempts to shadow forth a glimpse of eternity. First he must leave the river valley and face the sea of maturity in the primary world.

Nathaniel's experiences in otherworld – the journey down the river to the sea, and the sight of the shadowless farm and the land beyond the waterfall – link the essential elements of the multi-level fantasy: the vision of the individual's life within the primary world, seen with sharpness of detail, but set within a framework of continuity and wholeness, and the vision of a secondary world of metaphysical reality, unattainable in this life, but constantly enhancing the individual's perception and experience of primary world reality.

· 6 ·
Experience Liberated

In a sense, all fantasy is imaginative experience liberated, in that it surpasses the bounds of empirical reality. The framework of such experience may, however, be the normal primary world. It was of such types of extraordinary experience within a primary world setting (but without necessarily any implications of the marvellous) that Henry James was thinking when he wrote, of the romance:

> The only *general* attribute of projected romance that I can see, the only one that fits all its cases, is the fact of the kind of experience with which it deals – experience liberated, so to speak; experience disengaged, disembroiled, disencumbered, exempt from the conditions that we usually know to attach to it and, if we wish so to put the matter, drag upon it, and operating in a medium which relieves it, in a particular interest, of the inconvenience of a *related*, a measurable state, a state subject to all our vulgar communities.[1]

Fantasy operating within the primary world is even more 'disencumbered' than the type of romance which Henry James envisages here, but one of its prime functions appears to be to examine precisely the relationship between 'experience liberated' and the primary world itself, limited, as it is, by its 'measurable state' and 'vulgar communities'. In subsequent chapters the philosophical and the social uses of fantasy will be examined, with the particular view of experience which they present – a view which may often find its most effective expression through the creation of a secondary world. However, the kind of experience liberated to be discussed in the present chapter must be set in the primary world because it is, of its essence, an enhanced and marvellous experience of primary world reality.

Such fantasy within the primary world is a very specialized form: through marvellously augmented physical powers, or some form of metamorphosis in the fictional characters, the reader is led into a vivid and enriching imaginative exploration of primary world experience. The use of such marvellous powers leads to heightened

awareness and keener perceptions, a freeing of the normally limited
human capacity for exploring both the surface reality of the primary
world and also its inherently numinous qualities. Occasionally a
metamorphosis may be employed to investigate strange areas of
experience. One special kind of metamorphosis has already been
considered in Chapter 2, that of human into animal, and it is worth
recalling this particular aspect of animal fantasy in the present
context, as it is closely related to the other types of metamorphosis to
be considered here. In Paul Gallico's *Jennie*, the vision of the eyeless,
blind feet, which trample and kick him, is Peter's first experience of
the cat world. It awakens the reader to the terror which may be latent
in situations which to the human eye appear harmless. Throughout
the novel, Gallico builds on this initial scene, detailing the cat's world
– our own world but with a different perspective – with meticulous
accuracy.

T. H. White, in *The Sword in the Stone,* uses a series of animal
transformations to build up for the young King Arthur a complex
perception of the world, in microcosm and macrocosm. He learns to
experience a multifaceted primary world reality by means of succes-
sive metamorphoses. Each kind of creature imparts to him its own
traditional knowledge and view of the world, but he learns most by
simply becoming another creature and living within a new set of
primary world parameters. He must discover in turn how to live with
a different set of physical attributes, in a world of changed scale and
radically altered appearance. It is through these metamorphoses, and
other marvellous experiences within his own primary world (which
is, of course, not quite ours), that Arthur is trained by Merlyn for
kingship.

The subject of animal transformations and their implications have
already been discussed in some detail in Chapter 2. There are at least
three other main ways in which experience may be liberated through
types of fantasy which introduce the marvellous into the primary
world. One of these has a clearly identifiable literary predecessor in
Swift's *Gulliver's Travels*, and the use of Lilliputians as the marvellous element will be considered in relation to Mary Norton's
Borrowers Tetralogy, Pauline Clarke's *The Twelve and the Genii*
and T. H. White's *Mistress Masham's Repose*. The second marvellous element is the use of profound changes of scale, that is, those in
which the scale factor is markedly greater than that involved in
human to animal transformations, or in the usual 12:1 linear ratio

between normal humans and Lilliputians. In Madeleine L'Engle's *A Wind in the Door* the changes of scale are between the human and the galactic, and between the human and the microcosmic. Changes so profound in the perception of the world render it almost a secondary world. Finally, the novels of Penelope Farmer and Susan Cooper illuminate the ways in which marvellously enhanced physical powers may heighten human perception of the immediate primary world, which our normal senses observe and interpret so crudely.

The enlargement of human understanding through the use of Lilliputians was employed by Swift principally for the purposes of political and social satire. As a distancing technique it enables the reader, through Gulliver's eyes, to observe and assess the absurdity of the disputes between the Big-Enders and the Little-Enders and of a system of political promotion based on skill at leaping and creeping. While the depiction of Lilliput has its own charm, which has led to its being the most widely known and best-remembered section of the *Travels,* its real significance for Swift was in the parallelism, especially the doctrinal and political parallelism, with the primary world of human life in general and his own contemporary England and Europe in particular.

The use of Lilliputians by Norton, Clarke and White is somewhat different from Swift's, although there is a fair amount of satire in White's novel. In the first place, the juxtaposition of different scales – the human and the Lilliputian – is used to enlarge our perceptions of the physical world. The angle of vision may be Lilliputian (as in the case of *The Borrowers Tetralogy*) or human (as in *Mistress Masham's Repose* and *The Twelve and the Genii*). The former corresponds to Gulliver's experiences in Brobdingnag, the latter to his experience in Lilliput.

What precisely is the imaginative experience which the reader undergoes in these novels? In the first place, he is required to re-evaluate his concept of physical scale and the way in which it is used as a framework for his perceptions and experience. If this fundamental concept is disrupted, experience is indeed 'liberated', sometimes in quite a disturbing way. The reader is forced to realize, as Maria is in *Mistress Masham's Repose*, that tiny, quasi-human creatures no more than six inches high may be as intelligent as he is himself, and indeed more skilled, cultured and mature. Here White achieves much the same ends as Swift by reversing the means. Satiri-

cal fun is poked at most of the human characters, including Maria
herself, by making the modern descendants of the Lilliputians and
Blefuscans (captured and brought to England by Captain Biddel) not
a ridiculous parody of humankind, but intelligent and hard-working
citizens of a state which, though poor, is independent, artistic and
enlightened.

Despite the confusing perspective and the misleading outward
appearance of the Lilliputian characters, a mutual respect develops,
in *Mistress Masham's Repose*, between the human characters Maria,
the Professor and Cook on the one hand, and the inhabitants of
Lilliput in Exile on the other. Maria's governess, Miss Brown, and
the Vicar, Mr Hater, who 'were so repulsive that it is difficult to write
about them fairly' (p. 10), treat the Lilliputians as valuable vermin,
but this is merely an extension of the way they treat Maria, whom
they bully and exploit because she is a child, and the Professor,
whom they despise and underrate because he is poor. Thus, while the
experience of a change of scale becomes an illuminating one for
Maria, it only serves to emphasize more clearly the vices of Miss
Brown and Mr Hater. It is as if the presence of the Lilliputians, who
can be perceived clearly by the humans only with the aid of a
magnifying glass, itself serves as a magnifying glass in relation to the
moral qualities of the human characters.

Maria herself is obliged to face certain unpalatable truths in the
course of her occasionally stormy relationship with the People.
Moved, as she believes herself to be, only by a desire to help and
befriend them, she cannot understand their initial unfriendliness and
fear, and their subsequent coldness towards some of her schemes. On
being shown the first captive Lilliputian woman, the Professor
attempts to explain to Maria how benevolence can turn to despot-
ism:

'Think what may happen, for a minute. Suppose you managed
to tame her, suppose you even managed to tame all the other
people from the Island of Repose. No doubt there are several
more. You would be a Big Bug then, however kind you were,
and they would be little bugs, without the capitals. They would
come to depend on you, you would come to boss it over them.
They would get servile and you would get lordly. Do you think
that this would be good for either of you? I think that it would
only make them feeble, and make you a bully.' (p. 29)

Similarly, in *The Twelve and the Genii*, Max realizes quite soon that Branwell Brontë's wooden soldiers which he has found will only come fully alive and assume their complete and individual personalities if they are allowed total independence of action and thought. Throughout *The Borrowers Tetralogy*, Mary Norton makes the same point. Pod and Homily are obsessed with the fear of being 'seen' by humans, for they know that it will almost certainly lead to the annihilation of freedom, if not to death itself. Arrietty's incomprehensible urge to befriend humans is always viewed as an aberration by her parents (even when the human is the gentle and diffident Miss Menzies), and is always the prelude to another flight on the part of the Borrowers. It requires particularly acute and sensitive humans not to tyrannize over creatures one-twelfth their height, but all three writers are agreed in this, that power, however benevolent in its intentions, eventually corrupts, and is corrupted into tyranny, while personal independence and freedom are human values which must be respected in Lilliputians or in any vulnerable individuals, including children, as much as in full-size humans.

In all this it is clear that the juxtaposition of the Lilliputian and human scales is used to explore the kind of moral and political issues which will be dealt with more fully in the next two chapters. That is, the element of the marvellous in the primary world – the changed perspective of scale – is used to heighten our awareness of human dignity and the need for mutual respect regardless of outward appearances. Diminutive humans are also used to illuminate other aspects of primary world reality. The small soldiers in *The Twelve and the Genii* are not strictly Lilliputians, they are the wooden soldiers which inspired the first stories of the Brontë children, rediscovered after more than a hundred years under the floorboards of an attic in a Yorkshire farmhouse. Played with by another sensitive and imaginative boy, they come literally to life for Max as they had done (at least through the activity of an intense imagination) for Branwell Brontë. Some of their adventures curiously repeat those described in *The History of the Young Men* and other Brontë juvenilia, while other adventures are entirely new, under their new Genius, Max.

As he becomes better acquainted with them, Max realizes that he has a strange mental rapport with the soldiers. Thoughts which he has not voiced are spoken by Butter Crashey, the Patriarch of the Twelves, of whom Branwell said: 'Revere this man Crashey, he is entrusted with secrets which you can never know' (pp. 61 and 89).

By visualizing their actions in his mind, Max can discover what the soldiers have been doing – or is it that by imagining he creates their actions? The alternate 'freezing' and coming to life of the soldiers is another kind of metamorphosis, of wooden toy into sentient being, and touches on one of those deep springs of fantasy, so often sentimentalized and trivialized through overuse, and yet deeply moving in the hands of a master of serious fantasy like Hans Andersen. Pauline Clarke does the notion full justice – the soldiers are quarrelsome, rude, courageous and inventive.

There is something particularly persuasive in the notion that a toy, or a statue, in human or animal form, has a secret life of its own. Above all, in the case of a toy which has been invested with all the attributes of a complex personality by its owner, the assumption of the marvellous in the form of sentient life seems only a small step away from reality. Branwell Brontë's soldiers are a special case of a common phenomenon. All children pretend that favourite toys are alive. Few invest them with the passionate life with which Branwell and his sisters endowed the Twelves. These wooden soldiers were the originals of all the characters who peopled the imaginative worlds devised by the young Brontës, which formed the basis of a quite remarkable series of early literary compositions.[2] For Charlotte, Emily and Anne, this was the training ground for their mature literary talents. For Branwell, the literary achievement stopped here. It is entirely convincing, in Pauline Clarke's novel, that the Twelves, having been made so vibrant with life by the Brontë children, should be awoken from a 'living death' by another boy of vivid imagination and passionate feelings, who has an instinctive sympathy for Branwell, the boy who promised so much, and achieved so little. This use of the marvellous thus opens up a new perspective for the reader, both a sense that anthropomorphic objects, sub-created in man's likeness as man is said to be in God's, may have a secret sentient life, and a sense that an object, a toy, upon which deep human emotional resources have been expended by someone of imaginative genius, may hold within itself some key to that genius and that emotion.

Although Pauline Clarke, T. H. White and Mary Norton all relate the human to the Lilliputian scale, there are, as has been noticed, two different perspectives in viewing the relationship – are there essential differences in imaginative experience between the two? This does seem to be the case: where the viewpoint is human, the world is observed from the usual perspective; only the Lilliputians and their artefacts are seen to be on a different and alien scale. If the viewpoint is Lilliputian, this angle of vision virtually creates a secondary world out of the primary world. From the human viewpoint of *Mistress Masham's Repose*, the reader is made aware of the fineness and delicacy of the Lilliputians' persons and their possessions. Maria watches a Lilliputian woman thread an 'invisible' needle with an 'invisible' thread, which raises the question of what is meant by invisibility; although so often spoken of as if it were an absolute quality, it is usually only a relative one, based on the scale and precision of our perceptions. Moreover their skills make our handicrafts and manufactures look crude and coarse. Maria is given a scarf by the Lilliputians, and T. H. White uses this incident both to heighten the reader's awareness of the difference in scale, and to open his eyes to certain fine details of his primary world surroundings which normally pass unnoticed:

The silk was taken from the webs of the garden spider, the brown one with a white cross on its back, and it was treated with the juice of gorse blooms to get rid of the stickiness, which also made it yellow. Then it was knitted in thin strips by a team of volunteers, for they had no looms, and the strips were finally sewn together. . . .

It made a wonderful scarf, and the curious thing was that it was as strong as good linen, or stronger. It was resilient, like elastic, and she could stick her finger into it without breaking it, although she could see through. Many years later, she wore it as part of her wedding dress. (p. 80)

In addition to this mode of perception centred in the human view of the world, White also gives the reader a few glimpses from the Lilliputian angle. When the People set out to rescue Maria and the Professor from the dungeon of Malplaquet, the house is seen as 'a range of mountains':

The pavements of the colonnades were aerodromes. Even the smaller columns seemed to be two hundred feet in height; the greater columns, which held up the pediment, were half as much again. The basins of the fountains were great lakes. The statues were colossi. . . .

The obstacles which we should overlook were tedious to Lilliput. Gravel paths seemed bouldered beaches, which might turn an ankle in their desert strips. The long grass was a jungle of tripping roots. They moved, climbing and jumping, clambering and toiling, where we should stroll. . . . Now they had to carry [the ladders] round three sides of the Armoury, through an archway, across the Boilerhouse Yard, and down the basement to the cellar stairs. By their measurements, it was as if they had to march three miles; and it was not across easy country. (pp. 159–60)

In *The Borrowers Tetralogy*, a much closer examination is made of a miniature otherworld within the primary world, which is essentially human, not animal like those discussed in Chapter 2. Although the stories are concerned with the precarious existence of the Borrowers, living close to and dependent upon full-size humans while constantly threatened and persecuted by them, the most outstanding quality of the books is the precisely detailed picture of the Borrowers' domestic world, in which thimbles are tumblers, an onion ring is the size of a hoop, and a roast chestnut is sliced with a razor blade like a hot loaf of bread.

The plots of all four novels are, indeed, very simple, and the characters, with the exception of Arrietty, undergo little development. However, Mary Norton's exquisite eye for minute detail compensates for this, and the evocation of the little world enhances the central ideas.[3] In addition to the theme of persecution and escape, a strong contrast is presented between the traditional world of the older generation of Borrowers, under dusty floorboards, or in the dark crevices behind the lathe and plaster, and the wild and open world of garden and countryside where the more independent of the younger Borrowers find their natural home. The countryside is as full of dangers for a Borrower as the jungle is for humans, for rats are the size of horses, and cats are like carnivorous dinosaurs, but Arrietty finds there a liberation of the spirit which exceeds even the joyous physical liberation.

Arrietty's constant dread is that her parents may someday choose to return to the claustrophobic environment of her childhood, where she knows that her emotional and spiritual self will wither and die. One of the bogey tales of Arrietty's childhood has been the story of her cousin Eggletina, whose longing for fresh air and freedom led her to run away from home, and who is believed to have been eaten by a cat. It is revealed, however, in *The Borrowers Afield*, that Eggletina survived, and that for a time her family joined her in the fields, until

Aunt Lupy's smothering respectability drove the whole family back behind the plaster of the gamekeeper's cottage. Here Eggletina, denied the freedom of her father and brothers to go 'borrowing', is virtually kept prisoner. Apart from helping her mother with the housework, her one activity is painting *trompe-l'oeil* scenes for the blank, dark walls, all with views of mountains.

This theme of imprisonment is only lightly touched on, but in her cousin's fate Arrietty sees the danger to herself. Eggletina is silent, withdrawn, avoiding the painful awareness of her surroundings by maintaining a rigid self-control. Arrietty finds the experience of meeting her long-lost cousin not joyful, as she had anticipated, but deeply disturbing. The novels are set at the end of the nineteenth century, so that Mary Norton is here making an explicit point about the position of women at the time, but the constant juxtaposition of the stifling and constricted but relatively safe world in the dark corners of human houses, as against the dangerous but life-enhancing world outside, is implicitly related to the situation in any society which suppresses and stunts the growth of the human spirit, and to the individual's struggle to escape from such restrictions. Arrietty's own spiritual growth is linked with her increasing emotional involvement with Spiller, the wild orphan Borrower who lives an independent gypsy-like existence in the fields and on the river. Despite her gratitude to Spiller, Homily can never quite reconcile herself to him as a future husband for her daughter. He is the spirit of freedom, the ultimate threat to all Homily's notions of safety and gentility.

There are flaws in *The Borrowers Tetralogy* besides the oversimplification of plots and the undeveloped characters. Irritating inconsistencies of detail occur in the time structure (especially in the second part, *The Borrowers Afield*) and in the precise number of children of Uncle Hendreary's and Aunt Lupy's various marriages. The enclosed narrative, as a structural device, is taken up and then dropped for no apparent reason. However, few writers have ever matched Mary Norton's capacity for presenting the Lilliputian view of the primary world.

The adjustment of the reader's perceptions to the one-twelfth scale demanded by Lilliputian stories is difficult enough, but it leads to an increased awareness and appreciation of the minute details of the surrounding primary world which can, by a little effort, be perceived by the normal senses. Madeleine L'Engle, in *A Wind in the Door*, makes far greater demands. Although the primary senses are in part utilized to perceive the enhanced primary world of this novel, the scale involved, by turns galactic and microcosmic, forces the reader first to make an imaginative extension of the primary senses and then to augment them still further with the concept of 'kything', or silent mental communication, and with the concept of movement-without-movement in the episodes in the mitochondrion. Even the permanence and validity of perceptions through the normal senses are called into question. The cherubim Proginoskes is first described as 'a drive of dragons' by the immensely gifted small boy Charles Wallace, who is dying of a previously undiagnosed disease of the mitochondria. Later the cherubim appears to be all wings and eyes:[4]

> Merry eyes, wise eyes, ferocious eyes, kitten eyes, dragon eyes, opening and closing. . . . And wings, wings in constant motion, covering and uncovering the eyes. When the wings were spread out they had a span of at least ten feet, and when they were all folded in, the creature resembled a misty, feathery sphere. Little spurts of flame and smoke spouted up between the wings. (p. 56)

There is, at the start, some confusion even about whether Proginoskes is a single creature: ' "But cherubim is plural." The fire-spouting beast returned, "I am practically plural. The little boy thought I was a drive of dragons, didn't he? I am certainly not a cherub. I am a singular cherubim" ' (p. 58). So in the first place even such a basic concept as the difference between 'singular' and 'plural' is undermined. Moreover the cherubim speaks 'not in vocal words, but directly into their minds' (p. 57). By the power of his thought, he can also draw Meg, Calvin and the others in through the pupil of one of his eyes and convey them to otherworlds, where he is himself present. Finally, the physical appearance of this vivid, wild, but curiously comforting creature is shown to be merely an illusion, an outer shape assumed in order to console the limited and unadventurous perceptions of the humans. As Blajeny (referred to simply as the Teacher) says: 'Myself, I find him a little simpler when he's just a wind or a flame, but he was convinced he'd be more reassuring to earthlings if he enfleshed himself' (p. 65). By this Madeleine L'Engle does not mean anything as simple as to say that Proginoskes possesses a 'true' physical form but can become invisible. Rather, the reality of his personality sometimes becomes manifest in the biblical form of wings and eyes, and sometimes in the form of a wind or a flame. At the climax of the novel, Proginoskes apparently annihilates himself in order to save Charles Wallace's life by rescuing his micro-cosmic farondolae from the destructive Ecthroi (Greek for 'the enemy'). The humans believe that this is the tragic end of the cheru-bim until, at the very end of the novel, Meg and Calvin become aware of 'a wind in the door' – Proginoskes in another manifestation.

Behind the presence of the cherubim in the novel lie concepts of vast time and space, almost beyond imagining. From time to time Proginoskes sighs comically for some simple task to perform, one he is accustomed to, like learning the names of all the stars (not merely those visible to humans; *all* the stars).[5] He is, moreover, of an entirely different order of being: 'Age, for cherubim, is immaterial. It's only for time-bound creatures that age even exists (p. 58). . . . we have things to learn from each other. A cherubim is not a *higher* order than earthlings, you know, just different' (p. 64). This difference in order of being is illustrated by Madeleine L'Engle through an analy-sis of two different meanings of the word 'matter', which requires the reader to reconsider the significance of the very concept of emotion.

Similarly, the concept of time, which in human thinking is usually clearly defined (or presumed to be) and related to the normal frame-work of space dimensions, is irrelevant to Proginoskes. On the other hand, when Meg is inside Yadah, one of Charles Wallace's mito-chondria, she hears a thrumming sound which she believes to be her little brother's heart beat. Proginoskes enlightens her. It is not a heartbeat, the time scale is wrong. 'In farondolae time, Charles Wallace's heart beats something like once a decade' (p. 146). It is dislocations like this in the normal patterns of perceiving the world which make *A Wind in the Door* a particularly outstanding example of experience liberated through fantasy. No one who has carefully followed Madeleine L'Engle's imaginative exploration of different qualities of time, scale, and space can view the primary world with the same dulled perceptions as before.

For Madeleine L'Engle not only enlarges the reader's imaginative experience of time. One of the underlying functions of the book is to enlarge his imaginative experience of space and size. In order to lead the humans to understand what it means to be 'as small as a galaxy is huge', Blajeny takes them to Metron Ariston:[6] 'Where sizes don't matter' (p. 141). Metron Ariston is not strictly a 'place' at all, not even in the sense of an otherworld. It is, as Blajeny says, a postulatum, an imaginative and intellectual construct. This imaginative exploration of galactic and microcosmic scales is the central 'experience liberated' in the book, more important than the consideration of time. ' "Nothing is anywhere in Metron Ariston," Blajeny said. . . . "You must try to understand things not only with your little human minds, which are not a great deal of use in the problems which confront us. . . . You must understand with your hearts. With the whole of yourselves, not just a fragment" ' (pp. 125–7). The style at times is deliberately didactic, and assuredly the ideas are difficult, especially for the reader whose mathematical faculties of perception are weak, so that a certain amount of formal exposition is inescapable. The implications of the ideas are then developed imaginatively in the course of the action, particularly that part which is set in Charles Wallace's mitochondrion Yadah.

These violently disrupted senses of scale are much more disturbing than the juxtaposition of Lilliputians and humans. They go beyond what is physically perceivable by the eye to what can only be perceived by intellect and imagination. Thus the Lilliputian fantasies enlarge the reader's perspective of the normal primary world, while Madeleine L'Engle, by the use of these radically different scales, explores areas of primary world reality so remote from empirical experience that they must be approached as imaginatively as otherworlds.

Madeleine L'Engle is not, however, simply interested in imaginative exploration; as in her other novels, there is an underlying moral significance. The battle between good and evil which takes place only partly on the human scale is explicitly related outwards to the galactic scale (and so to the universal and eternal values) and inwards to the worlds within worlds of our own human bodies, each of which seems a galaxy to its inhabitants, as Yadah does to Sporos and the other farandolae. Thus this search for an understanding of how our own human scale is related by dilation and contraction to other frames of reference in the universe is linked to the literally universal importance of moral values. At the crux of the story, the body of the child Charles Wallace, a boy with both exceptional intellectual and spiritual gifts, becomes the battleground: 'Man. The mean point in the universe. And Charles Wallace – is that it? At this moment in time Charles Wallace is the point of equilibrium?' (p. 143). . . . 'One small child – why is he so important?' 'It is the pattern throughout Creation. [Proginoskes says] One child, one man, can swing the balance of the universe' (p. 173).

Moving outward from this 'mean point in the universe', Madeleine L'Engle has Blajeny show the human characters, the cherubim, and Sporos the farandola 'something to encourage' them before they enter one of Charles Wallace's mitochondria – they witness the birth of a star:

> Ahead of [Meg] was a tremendous rhythmic swirl of wind and flame, but it was wind and flame quite different from the cherubim's; this was a dance, a dance ordered and graceful, and yet giving an impression of complete and utter freedom, of ineffable joy. As the dance progressed, the movement accelerated, and the pattern became clearer, closer, wind and fire moving together, and there was joy, and song, melody soaring, gathering together as wind and fire united. . . . Meg looked in wonder at the star. It was indeed so small that she could have reached out and caught it in her hand, but its flaming was so intense that the song itself came out of the fire and was part of the burning. She thought in wonder, – I must be the size of a galaxy.
>
> And then all thoughts dissolved in the glory of the melody and dance. (p. 144)[7]

After this vision of light and creation on Metron Ariston, Meg, Proginoskes and the others find that Yadah is filled with darkness, pain and frustration. As they move inwards to the microcosmic scale in the mitochondrion, the human characters suffer the loss of all normal sense perceptions. It is now that they must develop their earlier attempts at 'kything' or communication through pure thought, without the need for speech. Speech is related to human size and physical characteristics which have been left behind, but the *essential* elements of Meg, Calvin and Mr Jenkins, as of Proginoskes – their permanent reality – survive the violent changes in scale and are thus linked to the spiritual concept of the immortality of the soul, the vital essence which is independent of any temporal or spatial manifestation.

At the final crisis of the book, Meg finds that she must combat the Echthroi, the powers of evil, by pure thought, so that at this point the novel moves beyond an enhancement of the sense experience of primary world reality to a purely intellectual and spiritual level of experience – one which is, however, still set in the primary world. Madeleine L'Engle does not here expound a Manichean concept of evil. Meg realizes that the Echthroi are not so much positively evil, as evil through the negation of all which is creative and life-enhancing. This is why they so nearly succeeded in making an agent of the petty and repressive headmaster, Mr Jenkins. Madeleine L'Engle discards straightforward prose at this spiritual crisis, and moves to a disjointed, stream-of-consciousness style:

> Cold.
> Cold beyond snow and ice and falling mercury.
> Cold beyond the absolute zero of outer space.
> Cold pulverizing her into nothingness.
> Cold and pain.
> She struggled.
> You are not to X me, Echthroi. I fill you.
> Cold.
> Darkness.
> Emptiness.
> Nothing.
> Naught.
> Nought.
> Echth.
> X.   (p. 194)

All through the struggle in the mitochondrion 'Charles Wallace was sharing in that anguish, his parents helpless as his small body convulsed in spasms of pain. They struggled to hold him, the Murrys, the Louises, to hold him during the convulsions, to give the racked frame support. . . .' (p. 194).

Proginoskes sacrifices himself by 'flinging his great cherubic self into the void of the Echthroi who were Xing Mr Jenkins and Calvin and Meg – and Charles Wallace' (p. 195). The only way to defeat the cold denial of existence is to fill it, to embrace it, and Meg throws out her vibrant personality in defiance of the Echthroi, in a lyrical passage which is surely one of the strangest ever written in a 'children's' novel:

> I Name you, Echthroi. I Name you Meg.
> I Name you Calvin.
> I Name you Mr. Jenkins.
> I Name you Proginoskes.
> I fill you with Naming.
> Be!
> Be, butterfly and behemoth,

be galaxy and grasshopper,
star and sparrow,
you matter,
you are,
be!
Be, caterpillar and comet,
be porcupine and planet,
sea sand and solar system,
sing with us,
dance with us,
rejoice with us,
for the glory of creation,
sea gulls and seraphim,
angle worms and angel host,
chrysanthemum and cherubim
(O cherubim)
Be! . . .
Echthroi! You are Named! My arms surround you. You
are no longer nothing. You are. You are filled. You are me.
You are
Meg.
'Meg!'
Her encircling arms were around Charles Wallace.
'Where –'
(Where doesn't matter.)
Here.   (pp. 195–7)[8]

After this peak of spiritual experience, mirrored in the stylistic
change in the writing, Charles Wallace recovers, but the cherubim
Proginoskes can never again be perceived through direct visual and
aural experience. His presence is only made known to Calvin's and
Meg's heightened senses through a curious and unexplained primary
worlds phenomenon – 'a wind in the door'.

The use of Lilliputians by the first group of writers considered in
this chapter and the use of radical changes of scale by Madeleine
L'Engle both serve to explore 'experience liberated' in a variety of
forms, but both are also means to other ends. By contrast, several
novels by Penelope Farmer are concerned almost exclusively with the
experience of enhanced perception itself. Penelope Farmer has
written a number of fantasies of different types, two of which –
Charlotte Sometimes and *A Castle of Bone* – are considered else-

where in this study. Three others, *The Summer Birds, William and Mary* and *The Magic Stone,* examine, respectively, the power of flight, life under water, and a general heightening of all the physical senses. In each case the plot is of the slightest, little more than a series of episodes illustrating the marvellous power in question. Two of the novels do hint at a further theme: in *William and Mary* the quest for the pair to the magic shell is connected, by implication at least, with the reuniting of William's estranged parents; in *The Magic Stone* two girls of opposed social backgrounds are brought to mutual tolerance and understanding through their shared experiences. However, these themes are not developed in any detail, and Penelope Farmer's real talent lies in her imaginative exploration of the marvellous.

As we have seen earlier, fantasy operates largely through an extension of the creative and empathic faculties, and in the enhancement of primary sense perceptions empathy is the dominant mode. Writers considered earlier in this chapter united their use of empathy with some thematic purpose, but in these three novels Penelope Farmer employs it almost in pure form, in its intrinsic magical and mystical quality, thus raising to the level of the marvellous a common mental experience which has powerful physical associations.

The nature of empathy, and its strongly physical quality, is expounded by Clarence DeWitt Thorpe. It is noteworthy that one of his specific examples, the flight of a gull, is also the basis of the most vivid realization of flight in *The Summer Birds*:

> The theory of empathy essays to explain imaginative experience in which there is an involuntary projection of ourselves into the object. More specifically, empathy is response to imagery that is produced by shapes, bodies, and movements, and in which, though more purely intellectual elements are present, dynamic or motor content is prominent; it owes its quality and force to accumulated and integrated experience brought into focus by an appropriate stimulus, with an instant and unconscious attribution of this experience to the thing perceived. Thus one's sense of firmness and weight, of solidity and strength and durability in observing a Norman arch is the result not only of the mind's comprehension of facts about materials and structure, but even more of the tactile and muscular impressions, of tensions and other organic sensations, gained through experience with strongly poised, substantial objects throughout our lives. Likewise the easy flight of a sea gull sets off a complex of

remembered motions and unconscious recognitions, all the store of hidden connotations that have centred in our being, through real or imagined experience, in connection with our idea of effortlessly soaring in space. And presently we soar with the gull, attribute to him the well-being and pleasure we ourselves experience.[9]

As explored in a fantasy, of course, such experience is not usually 'an involuntary projection'. The subject, whether voluntarily or involuntarily, is assumed *literally* to have acquired the marvellous power of physical movement, or to have undergone metamorphosis, and not simply to be experiencing it imaginatively. The reader, however, does precisely that. By projecting himself into the consciousness of the fictional figure, he experiences vicariously all that the latter experiences. Thus the experience of the fictional character is not normally empathy, but some partial or total physical metamorphosis, while the experience of the reader is indeed a kind of empathy.

The problems seen by R. H. Fogle[10] in some of the definitions of empathy given by earlier writers, as a union or merging of oneself with other objects or orders of being, do not arise in the use in fantasy of the empathic mode. Fogle points out that if true merging of subject and object occurs, self-consciousness is lost, so that the experience is ultimately unverifiable and undescribable. The method in fantasy is to deal with two separate consciousnesses. The consciousness of the fictional figure is fully aware of the experience being undergone, and it is described by both character and narrator. The reader may identify himself empathically with the metamorphosed character, but he is constantly having the experience explained to him. That is why, for example, a human who becomes a cat is better able to interpret a cat's view of the world for the human reader than a cat character could – he is more self-aware, more conscious of differences and anomalies in this new experience of the primary world.

Easily the most successful of Penelope Farmer's three novels which explore enhanced primary world perception is *The Magic Stone*. The plot is minimal, but the imaginative realization of heightened sense perception is very powerful. Alice and Caroline find that the magic stone with its fragment of sword which they can only draw out together, never separately, gives them, occasionally and unpredictably, extraordinary powers of sight and hearing. The quality and duration of these perceptions do not remain static, however. Sometimes they occur only 'between footfalls' (p. 135), sometimes they last much longer. Moreover, the experience develops from heightened sense perception of the primary world to a sense of union with other parts of objective reality. On the ferry the girls are conscious of becoming one with the sea gulls, and then with the clouds: 'they were the clouds themselves, wispy and light and flying in the wind; and the wind sounded not just inside their battered ears but inside their bodies, sounding in and out of their legs and arms, their ribs and stomachs and shoulder blades. Everything was wind; they themselves were wind; their limbs shifted and changed shape as the wind demanded' (p. 108).

In the episodes involving this heightened awareness and empathy with creatures and objects of the surrounding primary world, Penelope Farmer produces the effect of the marvellous by direct development from a type of imaginative experience which is common to most people, particularly in childhood. However, a more penetrating awareness of the true reality of the primary world is not always pleasant or reassuring. In the London episodes, an acute consciousness of the true meaning of the great, multi-layered city forces into the reader's awareness aspects of reality which are normally forgotten or deliberately ignored. Caroline has such an experience in the Underground station, where she becomes aware of the houses and streets of the city minutely fitted together like a honeycomb, of the overpowering weight of buildings pressing down on the network of underground railways, and of the men in the past who had first burrowed out the tunnels through the mud beneath the city – beneath houses and streets and even beneath the ships on the river.

Although none of the three novels by Penelope Farmer concerned with marvellous perception is entirely successful, they are interesting as illustrating a concern with 'experience liberated' for its own sake. In almost every other novel considered in this study, including the other works discussed in this chapter, the element of the marvellous is in some way fairly closely related to other elements in the work – to the structural technique or the symbolism, to the illumination of character or to an underlying religious or social theme. Penelope Farmer is here primarily interested in the imaginative experience itself. Even where she makes some attempt to relate it to character or theme, her treatment of these lacks the conviction of her imaginatively intense evocation of marvellous perception of the primary world. Possibly the fact that the experiences are not fully integrated helps to account for the comparative failure of these three novels (a failure which does not occur in *Charlotte Sometimes* or *A Castle of Bone*).

As a marked contrast with these three novels by Penelope Farmer, Susan Cooper's *The Dark is Rising* sequence is concerned with many issues besides 'experience liberated'. Its main theme is the eternal conflict between ultimate evil (the Dark) and absolute good (the Light). The Dark is always 'rising', growing gradually in strength, partly through its own inherent force, partly through corrupt human nature, until it is powerful enough to confront the Light in the battle for control of the world. Unlike Madeleine L'Engle, Susan Cooper does not set her conflict on a cosmic stage; this struggle is a struggle for the world, but the implications throughout are that the reverberations of the struggle reach out beyond the earthly world and have a universal significance. The morality, moreover, is not specifically Christian; it is much more ancient, and the novels draw on much pre-Christian symbolism and lore, including the mandala symbol, Celtic tradition, ancient British folklore, classical magic and Caribbean voodoo. At times the ruthless absolute good of the Light may even seem opposed to the gentler Christian virtues, as John Rowlands points out in the fourth book, *The Grey King*:

> 'But those men who know anything at all about the Light also know that there is a fierceness to its power, like the bare sword of the law, or the white burning of the sun. . . . At the very heart, that is. Other things, like humanity, and mercy, and charity, that most good men hold more precious than all else, they do not come first for the light. . . . At the centre of the Light there is a cold white flame, just as at the centre of the Dark there is a great black pit bottomless as the Universe.' (p. 135)

In the conflicting claims of absolute good and humanity, John Rowlands himself becomes the decisive factor in the final crisis of the fifth book.

When the Dark periodically rises it is combated by the Old Ones, agents of the Light, in minor skirmishes or major battles, one of the greatest of which was King Arthur's great victory at Mons Badonicus, a campaign which runs parallel to the main action of the last book, *Silver on the Tree*, in which the culminating supernatural battle takes place. There is a sense, throughout all the last four books, of the coexistent nature of all time, and the characters slip back and forth through time by simple shifts in the visual perspective. This is one of the ways in which Susan Cooper liberates experience in the perception of the primary world. The past is very much about us in these books – old roads remain, old buildings, old ports, the ageless mountains and rivers and woods. When Will awakes on Midwinter morning, his eleventh birthday, in *The Dark is Rising*, he finds more trees and fewer buildings than he is used to, and a smithy where no smithy stands today. But the roads and lanes run the same ways, and the general shape of the land is much the same, even though he has gone back seven hundred years in time. In *Silver on the Tree*, Simon, Jane and Barney turn from watching a gull flying over the harbour of Aberdovey to see a quay built of wooden piles, not concrete, an active shipyard, and the clothes subtly changed: they are standing on the same spot a century earlier, but the same houses surround the harbour, the same faces meet them in the crowd – grandparents and great-grandparents of people they know.

This acute awareness of the historical perspective of the surrounding primary world is perhaps the most important aspect of heightened perception in this group of novels, and it is enhanced by the careful structuring which relates the stages in the various quests with movement back and forth through many-layered time to periods of similar struggle or endeavour, and with ancient festivals and rituals of the changing year. The series began unpromisingly with *Over Sea, Under Stone*, a light-weight novel with many flaws. Then, after a gap of eight years, Susan Cooper virtually restarted the sequence with *The Dark is Rising*, which showed a remarkable advance over the first book. Here the action takes place over the period from Midwinter's Eve to Twelfth Night – the period of the winter solstice which has very ancient religious associations. This is the period when the physical dark of the northern world is at its peak, and the terror and awe of man reaches a similar peak, until the season turns, light gains the ascendance, and hope returns to the world. It was no accident that the early Church calendar located Christmas at this time of year, but the roots are much deeper, and throughout *The Dark is Rising* Susan Cooper draws on all the ancient rituals of the pagan Midwinter festivals as well as those of Christmas, to heighten the reader's sensitivity to the seasons of the circling world and their ancient significance for man.

Midwinter is related, of course, not only to the cycle of darkness and light, but also to cold and warmth, and one of the most forceful qualities in this novel is the evocation of weather. As the Dark grows in power, so the cold weather intensifies. Will greets the first snow with delight; it is something he has always desired for his Midwinter birthday, but never had before. However as the days go on, and the snow falls and the cold intensifies, the snowbound world becomes more and more terrifying. Everyone is locked in a frozen and silent world, the village cut off, the elderly and the poor in real danger. Only when the Old Ones, of whom Will is the last to be born, defy the Dark and seize the fifth of the Signs of the Light, the Sign of fire, does the thaw begin. The last of the Signs, the Sign of water, is brought to Will by the ensuing floods.

The six Signs of the Light, which Will, born to be the Sign Seeker, must find and unite, are themselves of an elemental nature: iron, bronze, wood, stone, fire and water, and each search probes some aspect of the earth's physical nature. The finding of each sign is related to Will's growing confidence as he discovers his unsuspected powers, and the completion of the quest with the symbolic joining of the signs as a powerful weapon of the Light against the Dark gives the structure of a satisfying shape. At the same time there is a clear onward drive towards the rest of the sequence inherent in the story, unlike the clumsy plot device of the dropped manuscript at the end of the first book.

There is a sense in *The Dark is Rising* of great reaches of time, and there is also a sense of both vast spaces and specific places. The Old Ones are spread throughout the world – one even approaches Will's brother Stephen in Jamaica – and so the struggle, in one way, is not localized. Yet in another way it is, because it is primarily British folklore on which Susan Cooper draws, so that Herne's Oak in Windsor Great Park and the Wild Hunt become very important. In other books in the sequence significant parts of Wales, Cornwall and the Chilterns all provide a very specific locale for events. The awareness of the special qualities of certain places in the primary world is thus linked with the historical awareness as the principal liberation of experience in the whole sequence of novels.

Place, time, natural forces – all these are perceived by Will more acutely as he grows in knowledge. He also develops a special awareness of the animals he encounters. The rooks become sinister, first brooding and watchful, then attacking the old tramp who is the Walker. They have fallen under the influence of the Dark. As Will, unknown at first to himself, comes into his powers, normally friendly animals become uneasy, avoiding him. Even one of the family dogs, leaning against his knee, seems to sense an electric shock. The animals, with their sense perceptions so much more acute than those of humans, are part-way to the kind of extra sense powers possessed by the Old Ones. Even in *Over Sea, Under Stone* the dog Rufus has an uncanny awareness of evil, and in *The Grey King* the dog Cafall has silver eyes which can 'see the wind'. Here Susan Cooper is using a perfectly well documented phenomenon, animals' acute senses, and relating it to other kinds of heightened perception.

Will's own gifts, like the animals', are largely innate, although unrealized until his eleventh birthday. He is made convincing as an exceptional hero from the outset by his unawareness of his own abilities together with the fact that his family (an excellent series of character studies) regard him as unusually mature for his age. He is also, as is only gradually revealed, the seventh son of a seventh son, and so destined by all the canons of folklore to be exceptional. It is, moreover, appropriate that his father is a jeweller, and that his mother comes from old farming stock, while Will and two of his brothers have musical gifts – the blend of the creative and artistic talent with the ancient family link with the land seems fitting for the last in the line of exceptional people of whom Merriman/Merlin is the first. The beauty of music and art, and a closeness to the land, are important aspects of the special vision of the primary world which Susan Cooper is concerned to develop.

In addition to his inborn abilities, Will receives a training in 'Gramarye', something like the training of Ged in *The Earthsea Trilogy*, although not expounded in the same detail, and very condensed in time. During his reading of the *Book of Gramarye* Will experiences a series of physical liberations – he flies like a bird, swings through the stars, passes beneath the sea. Later in the sequence of novels he will use many of the powers he learns here, as in *Greenwitch*, when he and Merriman travel to the depths of the ocean and confront the Wild Magic of the elemental forces of nature, which is older than the magic of the Light, and beyond its control.

Despite all the magical liberations of experience which Will undergoes, Susan Cooper constantly reminds the reader that besides being an Old One he is also a young boy with normal interests and affections. The discovery that he is not normal is profoundly disturbing. Although there is an excitement, a challenge, in the discovery, there is also a deep sense of loss – Will loses not only his childhood, but his right to the simple pleasures of a normal human life. The human issues are significant throughout the sequence. The Walker is Hawkin, loyal liegeman of Merriman in the thirteenth century, who has been tried past breaking-point, made into an agent of the Dark, and doomed to wander down the centuries carrying an intolerable burden. Neither wholly of the Dark nor of the Light, he is finally cast aside by the Dark and given peace by Merriman. This same human frailty is part of Will's nature also, and the Dark tries to break him through his human qualities – his love for his family and his natural compassion.

Bran, who first appears in *The Grey King*, is all human, not an Old One, but he is an exceptional human. Son of King Arthur and Guinevere, he has been brought out of his own time in infancy, by the contrivance of Merlin, and reared in a twentieth-century Welsh farming valley, not knowing his parentage, as his father, the half-legendary Arthur, was secretly reared by Sir Ector, also through the contrivance of Merlin. After the final battle in which the Light achieves 'the silver on the tree' and routs the Dark, Bran is given the choice either to pass with his father to the Isles of the Blessed, or to remain in the twentieth century as a normal boy. This is virtually the same choice which is offered to Taran, at a different period of history, in Lloyd Alexander's *The High King*. Bran, like Taran, chooses to remain behind, because this is where his human affections and responsibilities bind him. The battle now, Merriman warns, will no longer be fought at the supernatural but at the human level:

'For remember . . . that it is altogether your world now. You and all the rest. We have delivered you from evil, but the evil that is inside men is at the last a matter for men to control. The responsibility and the hope and the promise are in your hands – your hands and the hands of the children of all men on this earth. The future cannot blame the present, just as the present cannot blame the past. The hope is always here, always alive, but only your fierce caring can fan it into a fire to warm the world. . . . For Drake is no longer in his hammock, children, nor is Arthur somewhere sleeping, and you may not lie idly expecting the second coming of anybody now, because the world is yours and it is up to you. Now especially since man has the strength to destroy this world, it is the responsibility of man to

keep it alive, in all its beauty and marvellous joy. . . . And the
world will still be imperfect, because men are imperfect. Good
men will still be killed by bad, or sometimes by other good men,
and there will still be pain and disease and famine, anger and
hate. But if you work and care and are watchful, as we have tried
to be for you, then in the long run the worse will never, ever
triumph over the better. And the gifts put into some men, that
shine as bright as Eirias the sword, shall light the dark corners of
life for all the rest, in so brave a world.' (*Silver on the Tree*, pp.
282–3)

This, after all, is the theme of the whole sequence, and the reader
who has entered imaginatively into the liberated experience of Will
and the other characters is better able to perceive the world's 'beauty
and marvellous joy', and perhaps may learn to work and care and be
watchful.

In his lecture 'On Fairy-Stories', J. R. R. Tolkien stresses the point
that the appeal of fantasy is closely connected with man's desire to
transcend his own limitations: 'At least part of the magic that [the
folk of Faërie] wield for the good or evil of man is power to play on
the desires of his body and his heart' (*TL*, p. 15). The 'primordial
desires' enumerated by Tolkien have been discussed above, but it is
worth recalling them in conclusion, for they are closely related to the
imaginative desire for 'experience liberated':

> there are ancient limitations from which fairy-stories offer a sort
> of escape, and old ambitions and desires (touching the very
> roots of fantasy) to which they offer a kind of satisfaction and
> consolation. Some are pardonable weaknesses or curiosities:
> such as the desire to visit, free as a fish, the deep sea; or the
> longing for the noiseless, gracious, economical flight of a bird.
> . . . There are profounder wishes: such as the desire to converse
> with other living things. On this desire, as ancient as the Fall,
> is largely founded the talking of beasts and creatures in fairy-
> tales, and especially the magical understanding of their proper
> speech. . . .
>   And lastly there is the oldest and deepest desire, the Great
> Escape: the Escape from Death. (*TL*, pp. 58–9)

It is with one form of the Escape from Death, belief in the immortality of the soul, that the next chapter will largely deal.

Idealisms: Religious and Philosophic

An issue which has arisen repeatedly in earlier chapters is the concern of many modern writers of fantasy to use the form in order to present moral, religious or philosophical ideas. This conscious moral basis of much serious fantasy may be revealed in a number of ways. It may be implicit in the numinous quality of the marvellous experience. It may be present in the structural patterns of the work, in the use of mythic elements or in the quest tale form. Similarly, the creation of a secondary world may provide a utopia or dystopia, or, simply by its very quality of 'otherness', cast a sharp light on the primary world. The moral basis may occur obliquely in symbolic language or in an allegorical narrative. Or it may arise in the overt discussion of moral principles.

Some brief discussion of moral issues has been included in earlier chapters, but, where many works have had to be considered as characterizing a particular type of fantasy, there has been no place for detailed examination of individual writers. In this chapter, by contrast, a closer look will be taken at three writers only: C. S. Lewis, Leon Garfield, and Ursula Le Guin. C. S. Lewis wrote within the tradition of Christian apologetics. Whether his theology and ethics were purely traditional and conventional requires further discussion. In *The Ghost Downstairs* Leon Garfield takes as his starting-point one of the greatest post-Classical legends of Western Christendom, the story of Faustus – in which sin leads to eternal damnation – and by inverting the story considers how repentance can remould the past and lead to redemption. Ursula Le Guin is both more iconoclastic and more original than either Lewis or Garfield. In *The Earthsea Trilogy* she re-evaluates the whole basis of religion, science and belief. By creating a secondary world where even the natural law differs from that holding in our own, in which magic operates both mystically and as an accepted part of daily life, she is able to create a new philosophic basis for considering man in relation to eternal verities. What these verities are, she does not assume, but seeks to define.

The didactic element in the fiction of C. S. Lewis is more overt than in the work of any other recent English author, with the possible exception of the political and social satirists Orwell and Huxley. This is evident not only in his concern to employ the medium of fiction as a vehicle for Christian teaching, but also in the whole cast of his mind as a critic. As he wrote in *A Preface to Paradise Lost* in 1942, 'giants, dragons, paradises, gods and the like are themselves the expression of certain basic elements in man's spiritual experience' (p. 56). All of Lewis's fictional works are cast in the form of 'theological romance', a genre employed extensively by his predecessors George MacDonald and G. K. Chesterton.[1] The theological romance is a fantasy structured upon elements of myth, legend, folk-tale or romance, which embodies symbolic theology[2] and a clear ethical code. *The Chronicles of Narnia* are thus fantasies in which all the themes have a religious basis and culminate in a significant 'eucatastrophe'. The climax of each book and the final climax of the *Chronicles* parallel the great eucatastrophes of the Christian faith, and form a *praeceptio evangelica*.

The central theme which provides the entire framework of the *Chronicles* is the archetypal Christian battle between good and evil, the Holy War. Led by Aslan, the virtuous forces of Narnia constantly repel the invading forces of evil until the final Armageddon. The lines of battle, however, are not always clearly drawn. The human children and the more complex of the Narnian characters are flawed – some slightly, some more seriously – and the course of their salvation is determined by the vital choices which they must make, each choice involving either a rejection of self and a movement towards God, or an assertion of self and denial of God. Thus Lucy chooses to follow Aslan across the ravine, despite the scepticism of her companions; Jill, Eustace and Puddleglum struggle to follow Aslan's signs and choose to free Rilian in the face of almost certain disaster; Edmund chooses to follow the White Witch, ignoring a nagging suspicion about her good faith; Digory yields to the temptation to strike the bell in Charn, but resists the temptation to eat the apple of life. In spite of this emphasis on individual choice, Lewis is not primarily interested in character. In this, his fiction is diametrically opposed to the mainstream of English fiction during the last two hundred years or so. His interest in metaphor and analogy, in the symbolic presentation of the central experiences of the Christian faith, focuses attention on narrative structure, incident and image, while the protagonists become less central – not mere mouthpieces, it is true, but actors with given roles to play in the drama. This shifting of focus from what is more customary in the modern novel was clearly intentional, and is borne out by Lewis's evaluation of J. R. R. Tolkien's *The Lord of the Rings,* which he praised for being 'so disinfected from the *taint* of an author's merely individual psychology' (my italics).[3] Such a condemnation of the individual personality, while it does not in fact reflect either J. R. R. Tolkien's or C. S. Lewis's works, which bear the clear impress of their authors' personalities, certainly indicates Lewis's priorities. The world of Narnia embodies Lewis's belief in the ordered, hierarchical world of medieval Christianity, which is so at variance with the modern interest in the development of the individual, the unfolding of personality. Characters in Narnia achieve virtue and eventual salvation in so far as they conform to an external hierarchical order, and repress or deny the promptings of individual personality.

The repression of self in order to conform to an external pattern is an idea generally distasteful to post-Reformation man, but Lewis makes this theme more palatable by the stress which he places in his fiction – as he felt it had occurred in his life – on the theme of 'joy'. Joy as a concept in Lewis's work has two main stages: in the first place a kind of 'divine discontent', a longing for God, and in the second a sense of inner communion with God. The nature of joy may vary from brief moments of simple pleasure to the elevated and extended religious ecstasy which permeates the final chapters of *The Voyage of the 'Dawn Treader'*, in which the whole ship's company is sustained by the sweet waters of the eastern sea and the almost tangible light until, at the Utter East, there is a vision of the celestial mountains, and Reepicheep is translated to Aslan's country.

This sense of joy arises partly from an inner compulsion towards good, but it is repeatedly fostered by the presence or remembrance of Aslan, the Christ-Lion. No character in Narnia ever remains indifferent to the presence of Aslan. The sinful are struck with guilt or terror, the virtuous feel a lift of the heart, a renewal of courage, a surge of joy. Aslan embodies the 'inexorable love' of God, a central concept in the theology of George MacDonald, the writer who was probably the greatest individual influence on Lewis's fiction. The love of God is seen to be irresistible, all-consuming and relentless. It demands from man a bitter, painful rejection of self, a surrender portrayed in the incidents of Aravis and of Eustace. In *The Horse and*

His Boy Aravis is lacerated by the lion's claws in punishment for the beating given to her maid as a result of her own self-centred actions. When she meets Aslan again after her wounding she is subdued and repentant. The denial of self in Eustace is the subject of a much longer episode, in *The Voyage of the 'Dawn Treader'* – the conceited, egotistical boy is humbled into an abasement of self. On an enchanted island Eustace, in his greed for gold and importance, dons a gold armband, sleeps in a dragon's cave, and is changed into a dragon, the physical manifestation of his personality. Deprived of human company and speech, suffering acute pain from his swollen foreleg imprisoned in the symbolic armband, Eustace repents, seeks out his human companions, and tries to convey to them his predicament. His sense of his own unworthiness eats into his mind, just as the armband does into his foreleg. At last Aslan comes to him in the night and leads him to a well in which he is not allowed to bathe until he has been 'undressed' from his dragon skin. In a very masochistic scene, Eustace scratches and tears until he has peeled off three layers of skin, but without the help of Aslan he cannot be restored. Finally the Lion rips off the dragon skin, causing Eustace agonizing physical pain, and then throws him into the well in the centre of a paradise garden high in the mountains, from which he is reborn, and the cure of his character begins. In recounting the events afterwards Eustace says that in spite of the irrefutable fact that he is no longer a dragon, the episode by the well seemed like a dream. In the narrative and imagery there are indeed close parallels with medieval dream visions, and the garden on the mountain is the twin of the one in the far west, Narnia's Eden.

The inexorable love of Aslan can thus be a painful experience for the recipient, but the Lion himself also suffers and grieves. Aslan weeps when Caspian dies: 'great Lion-tears, each tear more precious than the Earth would be if it was a single solid diamond' (*The Silver Chair*, p. 202), and Caspian is resurrected through the shedding of Aslan's blood, as Edmund was redeemed through the passion and death of Aslan in *The Lion, the Witch and the Wardrobe*. The crucial issue of personal redemption, brought about through the driving love of Aslan and the inner prompting of joy, is constantly reiterated. Lucy, pure and humble, follows Aslan with only one brief moment of deviation while glancing into Coriakin's book of spells. Edmund, the traitorous Everyman, is saved from Hell – the power of the White Witch – by the self-sacrifice of Aslan. The quest for Rilian underground and the sea voyage to the east are both personal quests of faith.

The alternative to the redemption of the faithful in the Narnia books is sometimes seen as the active malevolence of the evil forces which gather about the White Witch, and of those characters who deny the existence of Aslan, confounding all deities in the name of Tashlan, in *The Last Battle*. The image of Hell, however, is more often one of blind stupidity, as in the self-deceiving dwarfs of *The Last Battle* who deny Aslan even after death, or in Ginger's loss of reason and articulate speech. The earthmen of Underworld, beneath the spell of the Green Enchantress, live in darkness, cold and gloom. The innocents of Narnia, trapped by the White Witch, are frozen into white statues. They become, in fact, an image of the innocents in Hell, before the advent of Christ. When Aslan is resurrected, his first action is a 'Harrowing of Hell' scene, in which he redeems these innocents by breathing upon them.

The alternative to the frozen despair of Hell is the warmth, movement, colour and joy of Heaven. The stone Narnians are restored to life and a hope of reunion with the Lion in Aslan's country. The earthmen are freed from the Green Enchantress and restored to their land of Bism deep in the hot heart of the earth, where living gems grow by the side of the rivers of fire. In the garden in the far west of Narnia, on Aslan's mountains, and on the waters of the silver sea of the Utter East, all the senses are delighted. Paradise is not ethereal, intangible, but a rich banquet which feasts all the earthly senses as well as satisfying spiritual needs. In the vivid imagery of these scenes the medieval influence on Lewis is seen most clearly.

Not all men can be redeemed. There are two contrasted images of death in *The Voyage of the 'Dawn Treader'* and in *The Silver Chair*. In the first, Caspian and the children discover, on one of the islands they visit, a lake whose water turns everything to gold, and lying on the bottom of it the golden figure of a man. One of the lost lords of Narnia lies forever frozen into an image of worldly greed, in the lake at the sight of whose waters even Caspian and Edmund are momentarily struck with the dragon-sickness, the lust for gold and power. This scene is echoed later, in *The Silver Chair*, when Eustace, who had stood beside Caspian looking down at this golden figure of a man in the water, finds himself in Aslan's country, looking down at the body of the aged Caspian lying in a stream. At the Lion's bidding, Eustace drives a thorn into his paw. Then comes the eucatastrophe:

And there came out a great drop of blood. . . . And it splashed into the stream over the dead body of the King. At the same moment the doleful music stopped. And the dead King began to be changed. His white beard turned to grey, and from grey to yellow, and got shorter and vanished altogether; and his sunken cheeks grew round and fresh, and the wrinkles were smoothed, and his eyes opened, and his eyes and his lips both laughed, and suddenly he leaped up and stood before them – a very young man, or a boy. (p. 202)

The central symbolic figure in the theology of the *Chronicles* is Aslan. Around the figure of the Christ-Lion cluster the outstanding incidents of Narnian history which are analogous to the major events in Christian theology: the Creation, the Fall, the Incarnation, the Passion, the Resurrection, the Day of Judgment. Most of the biblical events are very closely paralleled in the Narnian episodes, with the exception of the Fall. Digory, in *The Magician's Nephew,* does *not* yield to temptation, and does *not* eat the apple. Instead it is planted to grow into a tree of protection for Narnia, to fend off the evil which Digory's folly has introduced. At some time between these events and those of *The Lion, the Witch and the Wardrobe,* evil – in the form of the White Witch/Jadis – does succeed in entering Narnia, but this is never accounted for. On the other hand, the scenes of the Passion in Narnia are closely modelled on the Gospels, and the eschatology of *The Last Battle* on Matthew 25, Mark 13, II Timothy 3 and the Revelation of St John the Divine.

Although these major events in Narnian history have their source in the Old and New Testaments, they are realized through settings and characters which are primarily medieval, with strong classical and folklore influence. The blending of the serpent in the garden of Eden with the enchantress Jadis has been mentioned earlier. The Green Enchantress also manifests herself sometimes as a serpent, and the whole world of *The Silver Chair* is part medieval and part folk-tale. The initial and final Narnian scenes are formal and courtly, and enclose the wild fearful quest with its folklore elements, its incomprehensible tests and its temptress, precisely in the same pattern as *Sir Gawain and the Green Knight.* It is worth noting that while the sins of the flesh in Narnia are usually represented by gluttony and sloth, as those most appropriate to the younger reader, the sin of lust is implicit in the relationship between Rilian and the Green Enchantress.

The battles in the Holy War are sometimes waged against evil forces which take the form of folklore monsters and sometimes against Calormenes, worshippers of Tash, the 'Saracens' of the Narnia world. In the final Armageddon the opposition is composed of Calormenes and, more poignantly, fallen Narnians. The dwarfs, who refuse to be 'taken in', sit in the middle and shoot with their arrows whoever seems to be gaining the upper hand.

Lewis thus uses the common European cultural heritage of classical myth, folklore and medieval romance to provide the settings, the narrative structure and the characters of the *Chronicles*. The monsters and demons of folklore 'are themselves the expression of certain basic elements in man's spiritual experience', while the humans or humanized animals provide examples of sin – for example, Edmund (in *The Lion, the Witch and the Wardrobe*) of greed and treachery, Rabadash of worldly vanity, Jadis of spiritual corruption. Edmund is saved, Rabadash punished, Jadis damned. In keeping with Lewis's vision of Hell, Jadis becomes bitter and frozen in her self-imposed torment. In this conception of Jadis as she is transformed into the White Witch, freezing both countryside and hearts by her presence, Lewis is considerably indebted to Hans Andersen's Snow Queen, another symbol of spiritual death.

In their overall structure, the *Chronicles* form an extended psychomachia, comprehending the creation, fall, moral struggle and last judgment of an entire spiritual world. There are many battle scenes, and an analogy to the Crusader–Saracen wars, with their clash of cultures and religions. This is entirely in keeping with the ethical code which is presented throughout. It is the 'martial virtues'[4] which are constantly stressed – courage, obedience, fellowship. The followers of Aslan are 'soldiers of Christ', and they must exhibit personal courage in the face of danger and despair, whilst remaining unquestioningly obedient to Aslan. Explanations are not necessary for the faithful. All of this is in accord with Lewis's stress on the attainment of virtue through the imitation of a revealed pattern of faith and godliness. Unselfishness, kindness, compassion, pity – the various qualities of 'charity' – are rarely urged, and it is certainly never required of the children to forgive their enemies. Edmund, the repentant traitor, is forgiven, but he is one of the 'fellowship' of children. All other enemies are ruthlessly hunted down and destroyed. It is a code not only militant but vengeful. There are two possible ways of interpreting this attitude towards the 'enemy'. If the whole of the *Chronicles* is intended to be taken as an extended allegory, so that the monsters, the enchantresses, the giants of Harfang, the evil Calormenes and the lapsed Narnians are Vices, then this code of vengeance is perfectly acceptable in conventional Christian terms as an allegory of the suppression of evil within one's own heart. However, Lewis does not seem to intend the characters to be seen in this way – the very fact that some are 'lapsed' Narnians belies their interpretation as Vice figures. This more complex attitude is clearest in *The Last Battle*. One of the traitorous dwarfs is admitted to Aslan's doorway at the Last Judgment. Moreover Emeth, a devout follower of Tash, has fought against the Narnian fellowship in the last battle, but finds himself in Aslan's country:

> 'I said, Alas, Lord, I am no son of thine but the servant of Tash. He answered, 'Child, all the service thou hast done to Tash, I account as service done to me. . . . Not because he and I are one, but because we are opposites, I take to me the services which thou hast done to him. For I and he are of such different kinds that no service which is vile can be done to me, and none which is not vile can be done to him.' (p. 166)

Certainly, whatever his view of the evil characters in the earlier books, by the time of writing *The Last Battle* Lewis regarded them as capable of salvation. This ambiguous attitude makes the scenes of vengeance and destruction more difficult to accept. The treatment of the non-talking animals of Narnia is another questionable area of Lewis's ethics. Ginger's loss of speech and rational thought is an image of the self-imposed Hell of sin and apostasy. Similarly, in the judgment scene, the creatures who deny Aslan look into his face, and the expression on their faces changes to fear and hatred – except in the case of the Talking Beasts. They cease to be Talking Beasts and become dumb animals. All these, the sinful and the dumb animals, disappear into the black shadow on the left hand of Aslan.

The disturbing aspect of this symbolism is that the non-talking beasts are not simply those damned through sin. Many beasts in the world of Narnia are born without speech, are hunted and eaten by their more fortunate cousins, and have no opportunity for faith and redemption. Except in the Creation scene, no animal in Narnia is seen to earn speech and the chance of salvation.[5] Their position in Lewis's symbolic theology is never made clear, and the ethics of their treatment by the other Narnians are highly questionable. When

Tirian sees the horses being brutally maltreated by the Calormenes in *The Last Battle* he is not really concerned until one of the horses speaks, and he realizes that it is a Talking Beast. This is regarded as 'the really dreadful thing'.

Just as ambiguous as Lewis's treatment of the Vice characters and the non-talking beasts, is the position of Susan in the *Chronicles*. One of the original four children to visit Narnia, Susan becomes a High Queen, and is given the magical horn for summoning help, which plays a notable part in subsequent books. She returns in *Prince Caspian* and is told, like Peter, that she will not visit Narnia again. Similarly Edmund and Lucy, at the end of *The Voyage of the 'Dawn Treader'*, learn that they must seek for Aslan now in their own world. The visits to Narnia thus serve as an education for the soul, a preparation for the devout Christian life in the primary world. There is no indication at this stage that Susan has in any way failed in her spiritual training. She never appears again in any of the later episodes (*The Horse and His Boy* being out of chronological sequence). There is perhaps a slight hint that all is not well at the beginning of *The Voyage of the 'Dawn Treader'*: 'Grown-ups thought her the pretty one of the family and she was no good at school work (though otherwise very old for her age)' (pp. 10–11). There is no real evidence in this, which sounds more like sibling jealousy than anything else – an interpretation borne out by Lucy's desire, when looking in Coriakin's book, to become more beautiful than Susan. However, in the final scene of redemption in *The Last Battle*, when all the previous visitors from the primary world return to the 'real Narnia', and even the Pevensey parents are gathered in, Susan is absent, denied entry to the final paradisal scene: 'she's interested in nothing now-a-days except nylons and lipstick and invitations. . . . She wasted all her school time wanting to be the age she is now, and she'll waste all the rest of her life trying to stay that age' (p. 138). 'All her school time' includes, of course, the period of her visits to Narnia.

In her appearances in Narnia Susan has not been given over to worldly vanity, so that this condemnation comes as a great surprise. Moreover, these small vanities seem hardly comparable with the acts of treachery for which Edmund was forgiven. Did Lewis jettison Susan because he wanted to make a final attack on worldliness, however inconsistent with the earlier portrayal of the character? Or was there no more vital reason than a desire to achieve the mystic number (with its multiple significance in both pagan and Christian belief) of the 'seven friends of Narnia' – to maintain the pattern of the seven books published in seven years, one of which involved a quest for seven lost lords? Such an idea sounds ludicrous, but there seems no more convincing reason. It is in any case further evidence of Lewis's tendency to make his characters into lay-figures, vehicles of his ideas rather than fully realized people in their own right, and an indication of his submerged, but very clear, dislike of women.

The emphasis on the martial virtues, on a stern and unrelenting code of morality, involving much vengeance and little mercy, inevitably has its disturbing aspects. Lewis, like MacDonald, felt that fear had a natural place in religious training. The chain of development should be from fear to awe to joy. However, the stress on punishment, denial, discipline, can lead to definite suggestions of sadism and masochism – the very flaws which Lewis found in Kipling.[6] At times the imagery of violence, as it is associated with the *consuming* love of Aslan, becomes too extreme. The Lion has 'swallowed up' girls and boys, cities and realms. The gentle mare Hwin says, 'I'd sooner be eaten by you than fed by anyone else.' The distasteful episode of the stripping away of the dragon skin from Eustace has already been cited.

Lewis's underlying religious themes are most persuasive when closely related to the structural patterns of the books. The theme of divine love, as embodied in Aslan, is most fully and convincingly presented in the Passion scenes of *The Lion, the Witch and the Wardrobe* and the resurrection of Caspian in *The Silver Chair*, but it recurs constantly whenever Aslan appears as guide or adviser: in the crossing of the ravine in *Prince Caspian*; in his brief appearances at moments of crucial choice or danger in *The Voyage of the 'Dawn Treader'*; in the opening and closing episodes of *The Silver Chair* and in the series of 'signs'; in his appearances as both cat and lion in *The Horse and His Boy*, especially when he guides Shasta over the mountain pass.

The concept of the soul in search of God naturally dictates the quest structure, and forms the central pattern of *The Voyage of the 'Dawn Treader'*. There are two layers to the quest story here: Caspian's quest for the seven lost lords of Narnia, and Reepicheep's quest for the fulfilment of the prophecy made at his birth, that he would find his heart's desire in the Utter East. Caspian's journey is a voyage to maturity through self-discovery, a training in kingship; Reepicheep's is purely a spiritual quest, its hero the valiant and chivalrous mouse, its culmination the mouse's translation – alive – to Aslan's country.

The Silver Chair is also cast in the form of a quest, and involves following the signs given by Aslan until the two final tests in Underland: the faithful adherence to the commands of Aslan in freeing Rilian, however dangerous the outcome appears, and the assertion of faith in the face of the numbing enchantments of worldliness and rationality. (Puddleglum's deliberate self-mutilation here is another example of the masochistic element in the ethics of Lewis's fiction.) The same theme of the soul's quest for God emerges briefly in *Prince Caspian*, when Lucy, the pure in heart, is alone able to see Aslan. Gradually, one by one, the other children see the Lion, enacting the slow turning of soul after soul to God.

The quests end in moments of joy: the termination of the voyage in the eastern sea; the emergence of Rilian, Puddleglum and the children from Underland into the sun and fresh air of Narnia; the reunion with Aslan before the battle of Beruna. This is a constantly repeated pattern in Narnia, when the dark moments precede a eucatastrophe. Such are the Resurrection scene and the reanimation of the statues in *The Lion, the Witch and the Wardrobe*, after the humiliation and murder of Aslan. In *Prince Caspian*, interwoven with the harrowing scenes of the Hag and the Wer-Wolf in Aslan's How are the Bacchanalian scenes of feasting when those in misery or drudgery are released and water is turned to wine – Bacchus and Aslan unite in a ceremony of life-enrichment. Here more than anywhere else in the *Chronicles* the classical and Christian symbolisms are united. Perhaps the clearest example of the internal eucatastrophe before the final culmination of a book is to be found in Chapter XII of *The Voyage of the 'Dawn Treader'* in which the ship sails into a darkness – never physically perceived as an island – 'the Island where Dreams come true'. Dreams, not daydreams. In the horror which comes upon the ship's company at the thought of what dreams they have all suffered, the darkness seems to close in upon them inescapably. Then, in answer to Lucy's prayer to Aslan, a beam of light appears, 'like a cross', which resolves itself into an albatross, who speaks to Lucy in Aslan's voice and guides the ship out of the darkness.

Every individual eucatastrophe of this type leads up to a final one in each book, and each book leads on to the culminating *Last Battle*. Whether or not Lewis conceived the whole series when he started to write,[7] the pattern is certainly present by the end. In contrast with the general mood of excitement and gaiety of the earlier books, *The Last Battle* is an almost uniformly sombre and tragic story, in which the Holy War takes on its final and explicit form. Many of the characters are archetypal – the apostate, the rational agnostic, the tyrant who manipulates the credulous, the doomed champion of the faith, the Abdiel. The allegorical action is of central importance. The dark and tragic tone remains unrelieved until the violent reversal of the final eucatastrophe, when the Holy War ends in triumph for the righteous, the virtuous souls are united with Aslan-Christ, and the consuming love of the Son of God culminates in the release of Joy for all the redeemed characters.

The central themes in *The Chronicles of Narnia* are quite explicit. C. S. Lewis is not interested in character or individuals, in social relationships or the growth and development of societies,[8] but in Man, and in the soul's constantly threatened struggle towards good. It is therefore the narrative patterns and theological substructure which are most important in an appreciation of his work, the recurrent Christian symbolism and the allegorical action. The effectiveness of these qualities in Lewis's work is enhanced when his imaginative gifts are given free rein, and not restrained by the need to satisfy some didactic purpose. His imaginative power is most evident in many of the descriptive passages which set the Narnian scene, and which make the otherworld of the *Chronicles* so immediately attractive: the wintery landscapes of *The Lion, the Witch and the Wardrobe*, the Oriental glitter and filth of Tashbaan, the rich banquet on Ramandu's island. It is also evident in the creation of the particular 'flavour' of the individual books.[9] Each book in the *Chronicles* has its own web of sensations: the Spenserian and slightly 'pseudo-medieval' quality of *The Silver Chair* combined with elements from very primitive folk-tale and from George MacDonald's *Princess* books; the Arabian Nights and Crusader–Moor atmosphere of *The Horse and His Boy*; Edwardian London in *The Magician's Nephew*, with its gas-lights, steaming cab-horses, and raffish dandy, Uncle Andrew.

These strengths in Lewis's work can be contrasted with the curiously unsubstantiated and bitter attacks on 'modern' education[10] and with the awkward, superficial portrayal of the primary world children. A good index of Lewis's own ease with the imaginative situation in his books is the dialogue. At its best – in the smooth-tongued viciousness of the Calormenes, or the courtly speech in *The Silver Chair* – it is superbly evocative and witty. At its worst, primarily in the unreal slang of the children, it is clumsy and embarrassing. The insincerity of Rilian's exaggeratedly courtly speech is used by Lewis to indicate the falsity of his character under enchantment. Lewis's own failures in dialogue reveal the moments when he too rings imaginatively untrue.

The outstanding qualities of C. S. Lewis, as they appear in *The Chronicles of Narnia*, are thus two: his ability as a picture-maker and the creator of an imaginatively tangible otherworld with its own distinct 'sensations', and his quite definite and avowed moral purpose. Sometimes the two work against each other, as when his moral purpose distorts his artistic integrity, leading to the superficial portrayal of many characters, and perhaps above all in the inexplicable fall and damnation of Susan. However, when the two work in harmony, the finest Narnian scenes emerge: Aslan resurrected to vital power and energy, saving the frozen innocents from the Witch's Hell; the 'Dawn Treader' drifting through silver water-lilies over the sweet waters to the Utter East, where Aslan waits as Lamb and Lion; the Creation of Narnia, with the singing stars and the creatures drawn forth from the rich earth; the final cataclysm, the calling home of the stars, and the crushing of the Narnian sun, followed by the dawn of new hope. The undoubted flaws – the imaginative failures, the occasionally dubious ethics – should not blind us to the outstanding achievement of the Narnian books, and although the most immediately memorable qualities are the nature of the otherworld itself, its vivid life and profuse images, yet the backbone of the whole, providing both themes and structure, is Lewis's religious belief.

Like Lewis's *Chronicles of Narnia*, Leon Garfield's *The Ghost Downstairs* also has a clear moral framework. Based primarily on the Faustus legend, it also draws on the tradition of the nineteenth-century ghost story, particularly those ghost stories where the spirit which appears initially to be malevolent is shown in the end to be benevolent (as in a number of stories by Dickens). Dickens's frequent use of the trappings of the legal profession to symbolize human bondage, most notable in *Bleak House,* probably influenced Garfield's choice of which of Faustus's many professions[11] Mr Fast should pursue. Indeed, Garfield takes the symbolism much further than Dickens, realizing in concrete terms Blake's view that 'the fetters of Law are the fetters of Hell' ('The Marriage of Heaven and

Hell'). The central theme of the book is embodied in the reversal of the Faustus legend, in which the damnation of Faustus becomes the salvation of Dennis Fast. The buyer of souls, it emerges, is not always the Devil. Moreover, through repentance and clear-eyed self-sacrifice, redemption is possible even for the formerly twisted and damned soul. A related theme is the inescapable unity of the child-hood and adult selves – injury to the child injures the adult. Garfield externalizes this concept through his use of the marvellous: *physical* injury to the child has a physical effect on the man. In Mr Fast and the child phantom he shows the destruction of childhood purity, inno-cence and dreams by the hardening adult self, even to the selling of the child soul into (apparent) damnation. But the torments suffered by Mr Fast are those of self-created damnation,[12] followed by the struggle of his half soul in its striving towards redemption.

In order to explore Garfield's dominant religious and moral con-cerns, it is useful to examine the way in which the entire book – themes, structure, images – is built up from a mosaic of these concerns. The plot is an inversion of the Faustus story, and the mirror image effect of this structure gives it great impact by con-stantly drawing on the reader's partly unconscious awareness of the legend. By presenting it as the obverse of the damnation legend, Garfield makes the redemption much more dramatically effective. The atmosphere is tense throughout, and the irony of it is that Mr Fast, fully aware of the Faustus story, believes himself, or his child-hood soul, to be doomed to damnation through his act of signing the contract. The real nature of Mr Fishbane is only revealed symbolic-ally and through hints, as the reader grows aware, first, that Mr Fishbane is a devil only in Mr Fast's imaginings, and secondly, that the evil and suffering in the book all arise from the actions or in the thoughts of Mr Fast. They are not inflicted upon him from without.

There are two main types of symbol in the book: traditional Christian symbols, and parallels with elements from the Faustus legend. Often the two are combined, as in the beetroot soup/wine/ biscuits incident, when Mr Fast sells his childhood soul, signing the contract with the wine-laced soup. Minutes before he has uncon-sciously been celebrating the Eucharist with it. Scenes and objects in the book constantly operate on this double level: 'Down the endless streets, avenues, roads, lanes and crescents whose names were epitaphs to a green life long buried under the grey – Mountgrove, Woodberry, Seven Sisters, Brownswood – trudged the clerk who'd sold his childhood to the old man in the basement' (p. 51). Both the deadened, stifled life of the city and that of Mr Fast are captured here. Moreover, it is largely the life of the city which has made the clerk the kind of man he has become. Even the word 'basement' is significant, as is the reference to 'downstairs' in the title. The reader is intended to be confused, as Mr Fast is, in identifying 'down' with Hell. Such identifications are never what they seem. When Mr Fast begins to think he may be able to obtain money from Mr Fishbane by some means, he spends his evenings daydreaming of the possibilities: 'The clerk's imagination, liberated nightly from the twisting and turning and screwing down of his daily labours, spread its wings and soared in the direction he'd always supposed to be up' (p. 14).

The double meanings of words and images are also reflected in the way the adult and the child react to the same scene. When the clerk and the child visit the street market, both are caught by a vision of 'the riches of the world'. For Mr Fast, as before, these are the material objects, silver salt-cellar or pearl-handled knife; for the child they are the dreams which lie behind them: 'The child's lips parted at the bright piece of silver cracked and scored by the legendary rages of a mad king ... its weird eyes gleamed wistfully for Nelson's miraculous knife' (pp. 57–8).

The mirror image technique means that Garfield often reverses elements from the Faustus legend: Faustus moves from friendship to greater and greater egoism and isolation, Fast moves from egoism and isolation to compassion, friendship and love. The reversal of pattern occurs in the whole shape of the plot, together with certain parallels. Faustus passes from the sin of pride to the selling of his adult soul to the Devil in return for worldly power, and after a period of power and pleasure suffers a horrible death and damnation. Garfield reverses this for Mr Fast. The clerk is guilty of the sin of envy, and he sells his child soul to Mr Fishbane for 'all the riches of the world'; after a period of agonizing repentance and inner struggle he undergoes a heroic death followed by salvation. An additional irony is that Faustus gets precisely the worldly reward he bargained for, but Mr Fast, estimating 'all the riches of the world' at one million pounds (which he does receive), does not realize that Mr Fishbane is also attempting to fulfil his part of the bargain in spiritual terms. These reversed patterns are constantly present. Faustus signs the contract in his *own* blood, Fast signs it in *Mr Fishbane's* wine-laced soup. 'I ain't got so much [blood] to spare as I had in the old days,' says Mr Fishbane (p. 28) – a comment whose significance is lost on Mr Fast, who is locked in his obsession that the old man is the Devil. For the reader it helps to build up the true significance of Mr Fishbane. Faustus is tempted to suicide as a sin, and as a quicker path to his own damnation (VI, 21–5, XVIII, 57–9); Fast's self-sacrificing suicide, intended to save others, is in fact his own direct route to salvation (pp. 92–5). Occasionally elements from the Faustus legend are paralleled, not reversed. Both men sell their souls, as they believe, to the Devil, in return for worldly power. Both, initially, hold the soul cheap: 'these vain trifles of men's souls' (*Doctor Faustus*, III, 64); ' "For my soul, you said." "Ain't that nothing, Dennis?". . . . "After all, what is it?" ' (pp. 24–5). One could continue multiplying examples: the skill in the law, the temptation scenes, the heart's blood dried with grief, the visions of Hell.

However, Garfield's method of revealing his meaning through images reflected back and forth is not confined merely to the direct relationship with *Doctor Faustus* and the more slightly suggested relationship with the nineteenth-century ghost stories. It also operates within the book itself. In the first place, Mr Fast himself is mirrored in a number of images, some of which he perceives. When he brings home a decanter, 'picked up' at a sale of effects of a client who had committed suicide, Mr Fast begins 'to see himself twinkling away in the decanter's myriad facets – a whole world of peering, prying clerks, each in his own little sepulchre of glass' (p. 15). Mr Fast carries these imprisoned images of himself down to Mr Fishbane's basement, and the decanter of port, together with the beetroot soup, form the centrepiece of the scene. Just before he sells his soul 'stains and trickles of the wind adhered to the sides so that the gallery of entombed clerks seemed daubed and smeared with blood' (p. 23). In his excitement at the signing of the contract, Fast knocks the decanter off the table and cracks it: 'The crack was echoed in every facet; and the little clerks in their glittering cells stared out in sudden dismay. Slowly from the decanter's bowl, the dark wine dripped and leaked away . . .' (p. 29). It seems an ominous sign at first, associated with the drying up of the heart's blood and the death of Dr Herz, and also with the draining away of Mr Fast's youthful dreams and aspirations; but the prisons which contained the mirrored clerks are cracked – there is a way of escape from his self-imposed fetters, his 'mind-forg'd manacles', if only he can find it. Fast also recognizes himself as one of the tormented figures in Mr Fishbane's painting of

Hell in Threadneedle Street. He perceives this immediately before drawing up the contract, and his own period of torment begins when he sells his childhood soul. Too late he realizes that 'the ghost of his childhood, with all his longings, hopes and dreams, had gone with the terrible old man' (p. 62). One final time Fast sees himself, in the Guy burnt on the bonfire. At this point the last traces of the old self are destroyed. The child's hand is touched by a red-hot stick, but it is Mr Fast's hand which is burnt, as the Guy, the cast-off self, is consumed in the fire. From this moment Dennis Fast begins the climb up out of the trough of despair. His first spontaneously generous action for many years takes place a few minutes later.

There are also, however, images of Mr Fast which he does not perceive. He knows that the child is a manifestation of his seven-year-old self, but he never fully comprehends that the child *is* himself, still. Although this is repeatedly brought to his attention, in their mirrored relationship of physical and mental contact, Fast persists in thinking that the child has a separate will, malevolent because influenced by the Devil. When he clasps the child's slim hand he feels 'cold damp fingers engulf his whole hand' (p. 54); when he attempts to strangle the child, fingers close around his own neck, leaving it bruised; when the child begs to be blessed in St Paul's, Fast's horror at a demon child seeking blessing shoots like an unbearable pain through his head and twists the child's face with fury; when the child is seen joyfully driving the train through the night, his face reflects Mr Fast's own spirit, which is at last in a state of grace. Moreover, the young man in the train, with his innocent face and outstretched hands, trusting his soul to Fast's keeping as he sleeps, is in turn an image of Fast himself, purged of sin and at peace with the world.

It is not only Fast's own person which is reflected back and forth through the book. Other images, and situations realized through images, also operate at this level. At the time of signing the contract, Fast decides that his soul is easier to part with than £1: 'you can't be detailed about a soul. After all, what is it? How much does it weigh? Do you keep it on the public highway? Do you license it – or pay any tax on it?' (p. 25). The only problem is a legal one – how should the soul be pinned down in a legal document, so that it will not be laughed out of court? When at last Mr Fast has realized just what it means to part with even half his soul, he is nevertheless willing to sacrifice the rest (as he believes) to save the sleeping passengers on the train. Mr Fishbane turns his words back on him. It is too late for bargains: 'Souls, souls, souls! How much do they weigh apiece? Do you pay tax on 'em? Do you keep 'em on the public highway?' (p. 87) Fast is alone. All he has left to give is his life.

Another recurring image is the hoop. Mr Fast glimpses a street urchin, whom he takes to be the phantom child, playing with a twisted iron hoop. Immediately afterwards he sees and buys a 'magnificent hoop, painted silver and with coloured glass buttons glued round the rim. An eternity ring for a lady giant. . . . The clerk knew that no child, living or dead, could have resisted this hoop' (p. 61). Mr Fast is genuinely delighted with the hoop he buys for the phantom child, but his delight is marred by his miserly pleasure in having bought a bargain. In the night he finds the child rolling a battered iron hoop in the street – the child who has the same dreams and desires as the adult, without the stain of worldliness. The child refuses to part with his dreams in exchange for the glittering hoop, but for a brief moment the two are in accord, rolling their hoops together down the street. This temporary union is shattered, however, as Fast tries to embrace the child, feeling its cheek (his own cheek) like a stone against his lips, and then in a sudden rage encircling its throat with his hands. The image of the hoop recalls the constantly circling relationship between the adult and the child, and occurs finally when Fast sees the wheels of the train 'like stupendous iron hoops' (p. 85) – the same wheels which carry off the joyful child, and which crush Mr Fast to death.

One predominant cluster of images through which Garfield brings out his religious themes, and their realization for Dennis Fast in the objects of an industrial age, is the group including churches, cathedrals, railway stations and trains. As the clerk and the child wander the streets of London together, they see an exquisite model of St Paul's in the window of a retired cabinet-maker. As a joke, the cabinet-maker has placed his spectacles on Ludgate Hill, surrounded by a crowd of tiny spectators. The child is distressed by this mockery: 'Its eyes were huge and lost-looking, as if the cabinet-maker's little joke had destroyed a world of dreams. But to the clerk, the very destruction of the tiny dream had been its joy. It had seemed like an ingenious Writ or Injunction served on the lawless soul' (pp. 58–60). The cold, destructive touch of the adult, 'rational' world kills the living and vibrant imagination which the child embodies. Moreover, Mr Fast is unaware that his own thought has a double meaning. The 'fetters of the law' may indeed entrap the 'lawless soul' of winged imagination, which soars free of the narrow restrictions of the law and worldly vanity. There is, in fact, yet another meaning implicit in the word 'lawless'. The clerk has himself been instrumental in serving a Writ or Injunction on his own lawless soul, lawless because lost to God.

Later the child climbs the steps of St Paul's in search of blessing and salvation. Mr Fast attempts to frustrate him, his own fury becoming imprinted on the child's face, but the child remains, begging to be blessed, as Mr Fast stumbles out of the cathedral. Groping his way up Ludgate Hill in the fog, as dimensions and perspectives become confused, Mr Fast treads on another pair of spectacles, Mr Fishbane's. It is with the aid of these that the old man has been able at last to read the Contract drawn up by Dennis Fast himself – 'an ingenious Writ or Injunction served on the lawless soul'.

After Mr Fast's hand has been burnt like the Guy in the purging fire, he turns aside selflessly in the fog to guide an old woman to Charing Cross station, 'a huge iron cathedral of wrought arches that soared and lost themselves in a high nothingness' (p. 80). Ironically, Mr Fast will find salvation through entering the church-like station and later falling beneath the wheels of the train. Ironically, because earlier a train has seemed, like Mr Fishbane, an image from Hell. After buying the hoop to tempt the child to part with their shared dreams, Fast had hurried home:

> Already he felt quite redeemed . . .
>
> Suddenly there was a violent commotion in the air and a sound of iron thunder. A black shadow engulfed him and down streamed a shower of fire. He all but shrieked aloud in terror – when he saw he'd walked under the railway bridge that crossed Seven Sisters' Road, and a train had passed overhead, scattering tiny cinders as it went. He mopped his brow and dusted his ash-dappled hat.
>
> Calm yourself, Mr Fast. Did you fancy you'd been snatched into hell – right out of the middle of Seven Sisters' Road? No one goes to hell any more, Mr Fast. Take Counsel's opinion on it. Besides, it would hardly be *you* who'd go, sir. (pp. 61–2)

Having boarded the train to Chatham with the old woman he assisted in the fog, Mr Fast is happy and at peace amongst the other passengers until, at a sharp bend in the track, he glimpses the cabin of the engine as a 'fiery scarlet chapel' containing the phantom child (p. 84). Again in his confusion, misled by his preconceptions about the child and Mr Fishbane, he concentrates on the significance of the flames, and not on the significance of the chapel.

Fleeting glimpses of a church which he longs now to enter, a policeman 'about some ferocious business of the law', and 'a ruined abbey, all gnawed and ragged to the night' (p. 89) pass by Mr Fast in his violent cab drive through the night, caught up amongst other images, like a drowning man's vision of his past life. Looking down upon the railway line when the cab stops, Fast imagines what the wreckage of the train will be like: 'rearing up like an iron cathedral, filled with tangled tombs' (p. 91). The train is not wrecked, but it does become Mr Fast's doorway to death and salvation.

The whole work is structured about such recurring images. The child wants people to make a space for him in their hearts; the crowds at the bonfire and the passengers on the train make a welcoming space for Mr Fast, for the first time in his adult life. Mr Fast's furniture is coffin-like and imprisoning, Dr Herz is pictured enclosed in coffin and tomb, the mirrored clerks are imprisoned in the facets of the decanter, the city cabs enclose the clerk like leather coffins – all this imagery culminates in the final wild ride in the enclosed hansom cab driven by Mr Fishbane, out into the open country with its panorama of visions, to the railway line where Dennis Fast must make his final choice, to turn aside and ignore the train and its passengers, or to break out of his imprisoning coffin of self and make a solitary act of renunciation and sacrifice, all unaware that this will win his own redemption.

The tightly knit form of this book, uniting theme, structure and imagery, extends even to apparently casual phrases and ejaculations which are revealed, on closer scrutiny, to have tremendous significance. In the second paragraph of the book we learn that 'Wills were child's play to Mr Fast – though God help the child who played thus' (p. 9). It is only as the story unfolds that we realize this does not merely reveal Mr Fast's character. God does indeed help the child who played thus.

In the Contract scene, Mr Fishbane asks: ' "Wouldn't you like to have done with loneliness and envy, Dennis?" Damnation!' thinks Mr Fast, seeing his chance of the money slipping away. But 'damnation' is more than an ejaculation. Mr Fishbane has just analysed the state of damnation in Dennis Fast's soul, and echoed the opening sentence of the book: 'Two devils lived in Mr Fast – envy and loneliness' (p. 9). When Mr Fishbane suggests that, as his part of the bargain, Dennis should give up his soul: ' "Bless me!" said Mr Fast' and then continues, with an irony which is totally unconscious, 'I do begin to suppose you must be the devil himself, sir!' (p. 24). Mr Fast's own blindness to the true significance of his unthinking exclamations leads him into the purgatory of confusion and doubt. After Mr Fast's death under the wheels of the train, the child appears and cradles the man's head in his hands – the first time he has voluntarily touched his adult self: 'the fireman could have sworn he heard the words, "My son . . . oh my son . . ." ' (p. 94). The child and the adult are reunited at last in that brief exclamation which recalls both Wordsworth's 'The Child is father of the Man' (from 'My Heart Leaps Up') and David grieving over Absalom: 'Would God I had died for thee, O Absalom, my son, my son!' (II Samuel 18:33).

The adult Dennis Fast never really grasps who Mr Fishbane is, although he is aware of some mysterious power in the old man. He comes nearest to perceiving the true nature of the shabby old man in black during the final scene in the cab:

> There was a moment's silence. The old man's face, peering down through the hatch, seemed curiously softened. His rheumy eyes blinked like vague stars – and the clerk was caught in them as might be a child under the roof of heaven. His dread began to tilt towards awe . . . (p. 87)

The hints have been there from the beginning: the concern for Dr Herz, the sacrifice of blood, the celebration of the Eucharist – all these characterize the buyer of souls who is not the Devil. The final identification is left to the sensitivity of the reader:

> Then this weird pair – the shabby old man and the little boy in the sailor's suit – drifted away from the glowing scene and seemed to mount the embankment and so dissolve in the upper reaches of the night.
>
> 'Where shall we go now?' whispered the little phantom, its pale face smiling up into the old man's.
>
> 'God knows,' answered Mr Fishbane; and his beard streamed out to catch the stars. (pp. 94–5)

The Ghost Downstairs is marvellously close-worked, as finely wrought as a poem in prose. Not a word is wasted, for what appears at a first, casual reading as a somewhat flamboyant style is revealed on closer study to be a tightly structured web of interrelated images which convey the two themes with precision. First, the child and adult selves are one, only to be severed at the risk of permanent damage. The adult, worldly, rational self has, moreover, a duty to retain and protect the ideals and dreams of childhood. Secondly, the buyer of souls need not be the Devil, even to one sunk in bitterness and sin. Repentance is possible. Salvation is possible. Even, and especially, for sinners like Dennis Fast.

> See, see where Christ's blood streams in the firmament!
> One drop would save my soul.[13]

Ursula Le Guin's philosophy as displayed in *The Earthsea Trilogy* is not in any direct way based on Christian belief. At first glance it may seem almost anti-religious. The only regular religious practices depicted are the empty rituals of the Kargs in *The Tombs of Atuan*, with their manipulation of the superstitious terrors of the people by means of a sanctified brutality exercised by largely cynical priestesses, and including the politically opportune use of a 'Godking'.

However, certain cultural practices with religious implications do unite the scattered people of Earthsea. The Long Dance is danced all night on the shortest night of the year when Ged is an apprentice wizard at Roke. Years later, the Raft People dance the same dance on their sea-borne homes: 'so it was done on every island of the Archipelago that night: one dance, one music binding together the sea-divided lands' (I, p. 68).[14] On each occasion the turn of the year heralds a turn of events. In the first case the Long Dance takes place the night before Ged makes his fatal mistake of attempting to summon the spirit of Elfarran, and actually loosing the shadow which pursues him nearly to his death. In the second, the sudden faltering silence of the chanter before the breaking of dawn signals the arrival of the mental paralysis brought on Earthsea by the actions of the fallen wizard Cob – it has reached even to the remote sea-dwellers. As the chanter ceases, Arren sees 'high up, yellow Gobardon, and below it the eight companions, even to the last: the rune of Ending clear and fiery above the sea' (III, p. 141). The ominous constellation has appeared, star by star, foretelling doom, and is revealed at last at that moment in the year when the darkness begins to encroach on the light, as the days grow shorter. The Long

Dance is thus not simply an example of Earthsea culture, it is closely related to the themes of the trilogy. The constellation can be seen only at the end of the world in the far south-west, and further north in these seas lies the gateway to the land of the dead. The Long Dance is an attempt by the people of Earthsea annually to assert the strength of light and life in the face of the encroaching dark.

The Kargish rituals are the trappings of a largely dead religion, carried on in dusty and collapsing temples. Yet they still demand human sacrifices in the form of girls delivered over to a lifetime of priesthood, boys castrated to become eunuchs – the only men allowed into the temple precincts. Once in each generation an infant girl is chosen to replace the chief priestess when she dies. She is deprived of family, companionship, love, and – most significant in Earthsea – name. She becomes the Eaten One, vowed for life to the service of the dark powers inhabiting the subterranean labyrinth. Such is Tenar, in *The Tombs of Atuan*, rescued from this living death by Ged, whom she spares from the horrific death usually meted out to men who trespass on holy ground.

A novice priestess, Penthe, has earlier shaken Tenar's faith by her assertion that the gods are shams because the Godking is only a man. Kossil, Tenar's chief instructress, a cruel and embittered woman, uses the rituals of faith for political purposes. Tenar's lowest point of demoralization comes when she finds Kossil digging in the sacred tombs, and burning a forbidden lamp. The gods of darkness seek no revenge for this impiety – surely there can be no gods, and all her life, all that she has suffered, has been a mockery. Ged, however, asserts the existence of the Nameless Ones. They are not gods, but they are real powers of darkness. They are as real as tragedy and loss, pain and death, but they only grow in strength by feeding on the rituals of conciliation carried out by a fearful and superstitious people. Their existence must be acknowledged, but their dark power over mind and spirit must be resisted. Through her examination of the Kargish practices, Ursula Le Guin rejects any form of religion which is either empty ritualism or superstitious placation of unknown sources of terror.

In the final book of the trilogy, *The Farthest Shore*, there is a brief, disturbing image. Ged and his young companion, Prince Arren, are searching for the corrupt sorcerer Cob, who is gradually destroying all faith in magic throughout Earthsea. In a dark, fume-filled room, half hypnotized, Arren sees a vision:

> There, in the vast, dry darkness, there one stood beckoning.
> *Come,* he said, the tall lord of shadows. In his hand he held a
> tiny flame no larger than a pearl, held it out to Arren, offering
> life. (III, p. 65)

This seems a blasphemous parody of the figure of Christ, one who
has passed from death to life, bringing life. However, it is only what
the Master Hand would call a 'mere seeming' (I, p. 56). It is simply an
outward appearance, an illusion cast by Cob to conceal his present
form and to tempt people to come under his sway. When struck by
Orm Embar on Selidor, Cob is revealed in his true earthly form:

> But where [the dragon] had struck his enemy to earth, there lay
> something ugly and shrivelled, like the body of a big spider dried
> up in its web. It had been burned by the dragon's breath, and
> crushed by his taloned feet. Yet, as Arren watched, it moved. It
> crawled away a little from the dragon.
>   The face lifted up towards them. There was no comeliness left
> in it, only ruin, old age that had outlived old age. The mouth was
> withered. The sockets of the eyes were empty, and had long been
> empty. So Ged and Arren saw at last the living face of their
> enemy. (III, p. 186)

Cob, like a perverse version of Tithonous, has contrived a kind of
immortality for himself, but at a terrible price, and the Christ-like,
lordly, light-bearing figure he assumes is nothing but empty illusion.

The references to established religion thus tend to be negative in
the trilogy, and the secondary world of Earthsea is primarily significant in so far as it illuminates the primary world in its present state of
rationalized materialism, an arid desert of lost faith. Thus where C.
S. Lewis and Leon Garfield draw on a long tradition of Christian
culture, Ursula Le Guin takes no such basis of generally accepted
belief. Setting to one side the barren, late twentieth-century primary
world, she creates a secondary world where nothing can be deduced
automatically from our primary experience. The act of sub-creation
is even more necessary for Ursula Le Guin than for C. S. Lewis, for
she re-examines, from first principles, the most fundamental and
profound issues of human life: the essence of an individual's being,
the relationship between life and death, the possibility of immortality, the relevance of belief to daily life. Her philosophic position is
never simplistic, and rarely consoling, but it has the great virtue of

unflinching honesty.

Faith in Earthsea is faith in magic, during the settled times before the universal tragedy of *The Farthest Shore*. Magic replaces the religion, science and art of the primary world, in all of which it partakes. Magic resembles religion in that it demands faith and a belief in transcendent powers. Like science it acknowledges certain natural laws, although it can overstep the natural laws of our primary world, and like science it requires a laborious training in technique. Unlike science, however, magic cannot be practised by anyone who simply possesses the required knowledge of the skills. A wizard is born with innate gifts, which can be developed, but never created *ex nihilo*, gifts which may vary in quality and degree. In this the wizard resembles the artist, and much of his skill is closer to that of the artist than of the scientist. Mages with these gifts and this training are regarded with some awe by the common people of Earthsea, as priests in the primary world have often been regarded by the faithful, but they may also be mocked by the sceptic – usually to his cost. There are many levels of magic, from the rustic spells of a village witch or the clever but superficial illusions taught by the Master Hand, to the art of mental communion with those who are far away, the art of changing the true nature of things, or the art of summoning the spirits of the dead. Such power carries an inevitable burden of responsibility. The Master Hand makes this distinction between the skill he teaches and that of the Master Changer:

> Illusion fools the beholder's senses; it makes him see and hear and feel that the thing is changed. But it does not change the thing. To change this rock into a jewel, you must change its true name. And to do that, my son, even to so small a scrap of the world, is to change the world. It can be done. . . . But you must not change one thing, one pebble, one grain of sand, until you know what good and evil will follow on the act. The world is in balance, in Equilibrium. A wizard's power of Changing and of Summoning can shake the balance of the world. It is dangerous, that power. It is most perilous. It must follow knowledge, and serve need. To light a candle is to cast a shadow. (I, p. 56)

The lessons of this for a primary world caught in an age of nuclear power and biological engineering are immediately obvious.

Ged ignores the warning of the Master Hand, dismissing it with dissatisfaction: 'surely a wizard, one who had gone past these childish tricks of illusion to the true arts of Summoning and Change, was powerful enough to do what he pleased, and balance the world as seemed best to him, and drive back the darkness with his own light' (I, p. 57). The key word in this is 'powerful'. The young Ged's combination of supreme natural gifts with quick temper, pride and impatience with his masters leads to the near-fatal summoning of the shadow in *A Wizard of Earthsea*. He learns only gradually the bitter but essential lesson that more important than power is the wisdom to exercise it with restraint. In *The Farthest Shore,* to Arren's surprise, he hardly uses magic at all, husbanding his resources for the final encounter with Cob in the land of the dead. Ged has learned also that a man, a wizard, is not a mere manipulator and destroyer of the natural world. He is himself a part of it. In his youth he learns from the 'dumb instinctive wisdom' of the wild otak, and 'in later years he strove long to learn what can be learned, in silence, from the eyes of animals, the flight of birds, the great slow gestures of trees' (I, p. 97). This is very different from the attitude expressed by C. S. Lewis in the Narnia books towards the natural world and 'dumb beasts'.

Magic, in Earthsea, thus implies something much more profound than science in the primary world. It involves not only the study and knowledge of the appearance of objects and other phenomena, but a probing into the spiritual realities which lie behind them, a grasping not only of their physical but also of their metaphysical relation-ships. Ursula Le Guin's definition of magic is closely related to the importance she attaches to names.[15] The source of all magic power is the knowledge of names. Animals and even objects in Earthsea 'know' their true names and must answer them when summoned, or obey the commands of the wizard who addresses them. The essence of any creature or object is contained in its 'true name' (as opposed to its 'use name') and not in its physical appearance. True names are expressed only in the Old Speech, not in the common Hardic tongue. All of this is violently opposed to the modern primary world obses-sion with tangible objects, physical details, scientifically measurable data. As the Master Hand points out, the mage can easily manipulate the physical appearance of objects, on which we of the primary world have so much reliance. To alter their true essence is both more difficult and more dangerous. Knowledge of true names gives the mage power over the inanimate objects of the world of Earthsea, and over the animals and people. However, power brings its concomi-tant, responsibility, and power abused becomes corrupt. Any man who knows another's name has power over him, but this has its obverse – the greatest act of trust is for one man to tell another his true name. When Ged is at his lowest moment of despair, after his maiming by the shadow he has loosed, his friend Vetch comes and tells him his own true name:

> Ged stood still a while, like one who has received great news, and must enlarge his spirit to receive it. It was a great gift that Vetch had given him, the knowledge of his true name. . . . If plain men hide their true name from all but a few they love and trust utterly, so much more must wizardly men, being more dangerous, and more endangered. Who knows a man's name, holds that man's life in his keeping. Thus to Ged who had lost faith in himself, Vetch had given that gift only a friend can give, the proof of unshaken, unshakeable trust. (I, pp. 82–3)

The same qualities of love and trust hold in Ged's relationships with animals. He summons the otak first by speaking its true name, but it stays with him subsequently, even enduring death, through the power of love. He summons a rabbit for Tenar when they are fleeing from Atuan, and very hungry, but he will not kill it: 'would you catch and skin and cook a rabbit that you'd called to you thus? Perhaps if you were starving. But it would be a breaking of trust, I think' (II, p. 136).

The knowledge of names and of the art of summoning give the wizard also the power to summon up the dead. If it is dangerous to manipulate objects, animals and men from the land of the living, how much greater is it, Ursula Le Guin implies, to disturb the balance between life and death. To summon the dead to return to the land of life is always wrong. The young Ged calls up the spirit of Elfarran for no better reason than to display his cleverness to a rival. It is only by progressing from cleverness to wisdom that he is able to undo the damage he has done. In the past the Grey Mage of Paln 'summoned up the spirits of the heroes and mages, even Erreth-Akbe, to give counsel to the Lords of Paln in their wars and government. . . . [but] the counsel of the dead is not profitable to the living. Paln came on evil times. The Grey Mage was driven forth. He died nameless' (III, p. 85).

The dead may be summoned simply for money, by those whose wizardry has been turned to corrupt ends. Ged tells how Cob in the past misused his knowledge: 'I saw him summon from the Dry Land my own old master who was Archmage in my youth, Nemmerle, for a trick to entertain the idle. And the great soul came at his call, like a dog to heel' (III, p. 86). Nemmerle had died in protecting young Ged from the shadow and in exerting the last of his strength to close the crack Ged had inadvertently opened between the lands of the living and of the dead. In revenge for this outrage, Ged forced Cob to accompany him to the dead land and back. Yet in his desire to punish Cob, Ged acted wrongly, for this terrifying journey started Cob in his search for immortality, and so the chain of events is linked together across the years, and across the trilogy.

In the philosophy of Earthsea, when a man is alive, the most important single fact about him is his name. It expresses the essence of his being. When he is dead, he must answer to his name, but living body and name have now been separated. When the dead are summoned, they have the same outward appearance as they had in life. Does this then imply a belief in the resurrection of the body in Earthsea? It would seem not, for the dead are constantly referred to as 'shadows'. The dead who dwell in the Dry Land, the dead as they are summoned back to the land of the living are 'but a shadow and a name' (III, p. 197). 'But . . . a name' – this is a curious shift in the importance attached to names, as compared with their vital significance for the living. Ursula Le Guin does not spell out her meaning, so that one may only make conjectures. When the name is separated from the living man it ceases to contain his essence. It becomes a label for the shadowy form which represents the shape of his former body, an identity without living consciousness or emotions, a dry husk of the man who once was.

Names are the most important part of language, but all language is important in Earthsea. 'In the beginning was the Word' becomes in Earthsea 'Segoy . . . spoke the First Word, raising up the isles from the deep sea' (III, pp. 10–11). The greatest power and freedom, as well as the heaviest responsibility, lies in the word, in language, which distinguishes men and dragons from the inarticulate beasts. The greatest harm which can be done to an articulate creature is to rob him of speech. The dragons are ancient, often destructive to men, whom they rarely heed more than a man heeds the ants at his feet, but they are the guardians of traditional wisdom and of the Old Speech. They honour Ged as a dragon-lord and seek his help, while he in turn kneels to Orm Embar, dragon Lord of Selidor, as a liegeman to his king. When Cob, whom they call the Unmaker, begins to deprive the dragons of speech, it is a terrible fate:

> '[The dragons] fear him as a creature outside nature; and their fear gives his wizardry hold over them, and he takes the Speech of the Making from them, leaving them prey to their own wild nature. So they devour one another, or take their own lives, plunging into the sea – a loathly death for the fire-serpent, the beast of wind and fire.' (III, pp. 168–9)

The loss of speech implies a profound spiritual loss, a sinking into the state of a beast and far worse – into unnatural perversion and corruption. Ged translates for Arren the account given by the dragon Orm Embar of the horrors he has witnessed:

> 'On Kaltuel I saw villagers killing a baby on an altar stone, and on Ingat I saw a sorcerer killed by his townsfolk throwing stones at him. Will they eat the baby, think you, Ged?. Will the sorcerer come back from death and throw stones at his townsfolk?' I thought he mocked me, and was about to speak in anger, but he was not mocking. He said, 'The sense has gone out of things. There is a hole in the world and the sea is running out of it. The light is running out. We will be left in the dry land. There will be no more speaking, and no more dying.' (III, p. 169)

Both speech and dying are, as Orm Embar points out, essential elements of living. Those who fall first into Cob's power lose their facility in speech. Certain words, words of moral or spiritual significance, they cannot bring to their lips: 'magic', 'wizard', 'trust'. They stammer and grope for speech, their words float, unconnected, in the air: ' "I cannot speak," Hare said . . . and crouched down on the empty floor, weeping' (III, p. 56). They surrender their true names, and with them their lives, in return for a shadow life, a living death, meaningless and disintegrating as their speech. Cob himself has lost his true name and must be addressed simply as 'my enemy' when Ged summons him, although Ged holds the secret of his true name. The unmaking of the barrier between life and death has unmade Cob as a full man. Having lost his name he can neither truly live nor truly die.

The significance of words extends beyond the power of names. There are many languages and dialects in Earthsea and the Kargish lands, but the common tongue is Hardic. The mystic language, the

language of dragons and power, is the Old Speech. There are also
two forms of writing, the writing of everyday, and the mystic runes
which decorate the staffs of wizards or ancient swords, and which
are used in ritual inscription. Two words of the Old Speech have
particular significance – the first word, spoken at the beginning, at
the Creation, and the last word, which will not be spoken until the
end of time. The first book of the trilogy, which deals with the
childhood and youth of Ged, constantly refers to the song *The
Creation of Éa*. The last book is haunted by reference to the last
word, and to Agnen, the rune of ending, 'which closes roads and is
drawn on coffin lids' (III, p. 202). Agnen appears as the constellation
Gobardon over the southwestern seas, and with its sign Ged closes
the rent in the rocks which Cob opened between life and death. The
writing of Agnen on the rocks of the Dry Land marks also the ending
of Ged's power. 'I am no mage now' (III, p. 210).

In the lines from *The Creation of Éa* which open the trilogy, Ursula
Le Guin sets out the central themes of her philosophy:

> Only in silence the word,
> only in dark the light,
> only in dying life:
> bright the hawk's flight
> on the empty sky.   (I, p. 7)

The word, for all its significance, can only be spoken against a
background of silence, and it is the silence which gives the word its
power and meaning. *The Earthsea Trilogy* is based throughout on
this duality of imagery and meaning, particularly on the dualities
from the creation song, that of dark and light, and that of death and
life. Until nearly the end of *A Wizard of Earthsea*, the reader is led to
believe, with Ged, that the dark shadow which he has loosed is some
manifestation of evil, a power which Ged must struggle with and
overcome. As long as Ged believes this, the shadow takes on shape
after shape of his own fear – an insubstantial darkness, a nightmare
beast, a *gebbeth* consuming the soul and inhabiting the body of a
man hostile to Ged. Constantly fleeing before it, a hunted prey, Ged
seeks brief sanctuary with his first master, Ogion, who advises him to
turn around, to become the hunter.

When Ged in turn pursues the shadow and calls to it, it begins to
take on a form like a man's, 'only deformed and changing' (I, p. 153).
Later it appears on Vemish and on Iffish in Ged's own likeness. He

realizes, after seeking to touch and hold it, that 'he had forged between them a bond, a link that had no breaking point. . . . Neither could escape. When they had come to the time and place for their last meeting, they would meet' (I, p. 165). Accompanied by Vetch from his homeland of Iffish, Ged overtakes the shadow at last on the eastern seas, where the boat *Lookfar* runs aground on invisible shoals over the abyss of ocean, and there, on the 'coasts of death's kingdom' (I, p. 200), Ged meets the shadow and names it with his own name:

> Light and darkness met, and joined, and were one. . . . And [Vetch] began to see the truth, that Ged had neither lost nor won but, naming the shadow of his death with his own name, had made himself whole: a man: who, knowing his whole true self, cannot be used or possessed by any power other than himself, and whose life therefore is lived for life's sake and never in the service of ruin, or pain, or hatred, or the dark. (I, pp. 198–9)

Light has meaning only when it shines in a surrounding darkness, Ursula Le Guin maintains. So the beauty of life has a true savour only against the background of un-life, of death. Tenar learns a similar lesson to Ged's, passing her girlhood 'in bondage to a useless evil', and suddenly realizing after her release from the temple what life can mean by contrast, in joy and light, and also in human responsibility. Life has great rewards, but it demands choice, action, *living*. It can never be cold and passive, as Tenar's life as a priestess is intended to be, for then it is indistinguishable from death. Yet in order to understand and value life the wise man in Earthsea, as in the primary world, must face the reality of death. In *The Farthest Shore* Ged says to Arren, before they enter the land of the dead, 'You enter your manhood at the gate of death' (III, p. 180). The full man must know death, in order to live life. He must not bow down in service to the powers of darkness and death, but take up the burden of life and liberty: ' "death is terrible, and must be feared. . . . And life also is a terrible thing," Ged said, "and must be feared, and praised" ' (III, p. 180). But one who has learnt this lesson has achieved true life and full humanity. After the crossing of the land of the dead, when Ged lies unconscious and possibly dying, Arren comes to understand what the older man has been trying to teach him:

> [Arren] held it in his hand, the unchanging thing, the stone of

pain. He closed his hand on it, and held it. And he smiled then, a smile both sombre and joyous, knowing, for the first time in his life, and alone, and unpraised, and at the end of the world, victory. (III, p. 208)

Death must be faced and, as the dual of death, life assumes its true meaning, but when death is inevitable it must be accepted. Ged can defeat the mighty dragon of Pendor, but not save a little child from dying – the one requires only intelligence, courage and skill; the other would involve the violating of a natural law: 'Heal the wound and cure the illness, but let the dying spirit go' (I, p. 94).

In the trilogy the land of the dead is the Dry Land, full of rocks, an arid desert: 'Here they drink dust' (III, p. 192). It is a more terrible land even than the underworld of the Greeks and Romans, more empty and more hopeless. Similarly, when Ged struggles with the shadow, on the 'coasts of death's kingdom', the seas of the world turn to sand. By contrast, the lands of the living flow with the waters of life, and at the heart of the House of the Wise there is a fountain. However, this is not a simple contrast. In the beginning, Segoy raised the islands from the sea – only *dry land* provides a suitable habitation for man. Even the Raft People, the most naturally pious and uncorrupt of Earthsea, must occasionally come to land. The inhabited regions themselves are called, collectively 'Earthsea', stressing this duality between water and dry land. The men of this secondary world spend much of their lives in boats and ships, many crucial incidents take place at sea, but all except the Raft People look forward to the return to harbour, and regard as home 'the lands where men were meant to live' (I, p. 193). But the dry land of the living is not the same as the Dry Land of the dead; crossing barren Selidor, Arren complains bitterly, 'The land is as dead as the land of death itself', and is rebuked by Ged:

> 'Look at this land; look about you. This is your kingdom, the kingdom of life. This is your immortality. Look at the hills, the mortal hills. They do not endure forever. The hills with the living grass on them, and the streams of water running. . . . In all the world, in all the worlds, in all the immensity of time, there is no other like each of those streams, rising cold out of the earth where no eye sees it, running through the sunlight and the darkness to the sea. Deep are the springs of being, deeper than life, than death. . . . I cannot say what I mean,' Ged said unhappily. . . .

[Arren] looked at his companion and said, 'I have given my love to what is worthy of love. Is that not the kingdom, and the unperishing spring?'

'Aye, lad,' said Ged, gently, and with pain.

They went on together in silence. But Arren saw the world now with his companion's eyes, and saw the living splendour that was revealed about them in the silent, desolate land, as if by a power of enchantment, surpassing any other, in every blade of the wind-bowed grass, every shadow, every stone. (III, pp. 181–2)

In contrast with this, the land of the dead is truly the Dry Land, a land itself dead: 'No tree or thorn or blade of grass grew in the stony earth under the unsetting stars' (III, p. 191).

If the dead are 'but a shadow and a name' dwelling in a barren land, does this constitute the only view of immortality in Earthsea? According to Kargish belief, only the devout Kargs will have life after death, constantly being reborn into new bodies, as Tenar is believed to be the One Priestess, the Eaten One, repeatedly reincarnated. Kossil voices the general view of the Kargs when she speaks contemptuously of the 'wizard-folk' of Earthsea:

'They have no gods. They work magic, and think they are gods themselves. But they are not. And when they die, they are not reborn. They become dust and bone, and their ghosts whine on the wind a little while till the wind blows them away. They do not have immortal souls.' (II, p. 57)

This is a terrible attitude towards fellow human beings – the attitude often adopted in other cultures towards slaves, reducing men to much the same level as Lewis's 'dumb beasts'. Yet in a sense Kossil is closer to Ged's own belief than one might expect. The Kargs themselves are losing their old faith, paying it mere lip-service. The current form of worship consists of cash-tribute and servile obedience to the 'Godkings', as the ruling dynasty of the Kargs style themselves. Religion has become a political and financial tool in Kargad, so that Kargish belief in the rebirth of the faithful rests now on a shaky foundation. Moreover, according to the old religion, the souls of the ungodly are not reborn. Tenar undergoes a crisis of faith: still half believing in the power of the dark gods she serves, but having been given back her true name by Ged, she has an opportunity to break away and live as a full person, with an identity of her own, and not as the Eaten One, the vessel of this dying religion. She dreams her spiritual crisis in images from Kargish iconography, in which the souls of the dead appear as 'great bedraggled birds with human hands and feet and faces, squatting in the dust of the dark places'. Amongst them one is different, and says to her 'tenderly, softly, "Tenar" ' (II, p. 103).

This memory of her mother has been lying in her subconscious mind until awakened by the discovery of her true name, Tenar. The mother's soul is like and yet unlike, the souls of those not reborn. They have the bodies of birds but human faces. A bird face replaces the forgotten face of her mother, although Tenar retains the remote memory of golden hair and her mother's voice. Yet the sinister bird image is transformed, even as Tenar is transformed. The despair which wakes her from this dream is 'like a bird of fire', and as she stands outside in the sunrise, rejoicing in her name and identity, she watches a hawk wheeling in the sky. The Kargish images of the devoured dead are a horrible mockery, while the distorted image of the dream unites the reawakened memory of her mother with the promise of a new freedom for herself symbolized by the bird's flight. Ged's use name is, of course, Sparrowhawk.

Kargish ideas of immortality are distasteful, yet the view of life after death which is held in the rest of Earthsea is far from comforting. The first glimpse of it is given when Ged, then a young wizard living in a poor fishing community, tries, against his better judgment, to save the life of the child Ioleth, son of the fisherman who has become his friend. He sees the boy running ahead of him, through some silent, unfamiliar landscape.

> The stars above the hill were no stars his eyes had ever seen. Yet he knew the constellations by name: the Sheaf, the Door, the One Who Turns, the Tree. They were those stars that do not set, that are not paled by the coming of any day. He had followed the dying child too far. (I, pp. 94–5)

Years later, when Ged and Arren cross the land of the dead, we are given a much more detailed description of this afterlife:

> There was no passing of time there, where no wind blew and the stars did not move. They came then into the streets of one of the cities that are there, and Arren saw the houses with windows that are never lit, and in certain doorways standing, with quiet faces and empty hands, the dead.

The market places were all empty. There was no buying and selling there, no gaining and no spending. Nothing was used; nothing was made. . . .

All those whom they saw – not many, for the dead are many, but that land is large – stood still, or moved slowly and with no purpose. None of them bore wounds, as had the semblance of Erreth-Akbe summoned into the daylight at the place of his death. No marks of illness were on them. They were whole, and healed. They were healed of pain, and of life. They were not loathsome as Arren had feared they would be, not frightening in the way he had thought they would be. Quiet were their faces, freed from anger and desire, and there was in their shadowed eyes no hope.

Instead of fear, then, great pity rose up in Arren, and if fear underlay it, it was not fear for himself, but for us all. For he saw the mother and child who had died together, and they were in the dark land together; but the child did not run, nor did it cry, and the mother did not hold it, nor even look at it. And those who had died for love passed each other in the streets. (III, pp. 189–90)

This is a horrifying picture, perhaps the more horrifying because it accords with an innate secret dread of what life after death may be – an empty, barren non-life, which is much more credible than the crude Kargish bird-men. In the trilogy this hollow life after death becomes no longer a fearful possibility, but a fact. Using the freedom of the marvellous inherent in her secondary world, Ursula Le Guin leads the reader through the land of the dead and presents the reality of this immortality of shadows and names in a land of dust. Throughout all the books, death has been presented as the engulfing dark within which the bright spark of life flickers for a time. It is a shadow, a denial, an ending of sentient and emotional life. Why, then, is Cob wrong in attempting to achieve unending life? The answer lies partly in the imagery which is constantly associated with him, of spiders and cobwebs. He is himself 'the spider' (cob, O.E.), and he spins a sticky web of illusions which traps the gullible. His everlasting 'life' is filled with dust, shadows and cobwebs, which gradually enmesh his victims and hold them suspended in a living death like the insects hung in a spider's 'larder'. His action in breaching the wall between life and death is not an assertion but a denial of what life really means.

The reader's perceptions about life, death and immortality are built up through Ged's experience and the views he expresses to Tenar and Arren. In his youth he flees from the shadow – the fear of death – until he has the wisdom to turn and face it, and by 'naming the shadow of his death with his own name, had made himself whole' (I, p. 199). The dark powers in *The Tombs of Atuan*, called appropriately the Nameless Ones, which Ged resists in the prime of his manhood, represent a kind of immortality, the immortality of evil: 'They are dark and undying, and they hate the light: the brief, bright light of our mortality. They are immortal, but they are not gods. They never were. They are not worth the worship of any human soul' (II, p. 113). The dark powers of the Kargish lands are primeval earth powers, active and malevolent manifestations of man's capacity for irrational, superstitious dread. They are 'the ancient and holy Powers of the Earth before the Light, the powers of the dark, of ruin, of madness' (II, p. 114).

Darkness and death are thus associated by Ursula Le Guin with destroying, with unmaking, with the loss of names. Cob loses his name. So also do his followers, as they lose speech. The old powers of Atuan are the Nameless Ones, who devour and destroy. And so we learn that immortality, life *after* death or life *without* death, because it is static, because it cannot involve decay and loss, likewise cannot produce growth and creation. This, essentially, is where Cob's pursuit of immortality is based on a false premise. 'Where are the servants of this – Anti-King?' asks Arren of Ged when, in middle age, he is about to face his final and greatest enemy.

> 'In our minds, lad. In our minds. The traitor, the self, the self that cries *I want to live, let the world rot so long as I can live*! The little traitor soul in us, in the dark, like the spider in a box. He talks to all of us. But only some understand him. The wizards, the singers, the makers. And the heroes, the ones who seek to be themselves. To be oneself is a rare thing, and a great one. To be oneself forever, is that not greater still?'

Arren knows that Ged is being ironic, but puts the question the reader himself will wish to ask: 'If I love life shall I not hate the end of it?' Indeed, as Ged points out, Arren is one who might achieve this desire, life without end:

> 'And then – this. This blight upon the lands. The arts of man

forgotten. The singer tongueless. The eye blind. And then? A false king ruling. Ruling forever. And over the same subjects forever. No births: no new lives. No children. Only what is mortal bears life, Arren. Only in death is there re-birth. The Balance is not a stillness. It is movement – an eternal becoming.'
(III, pp. 150–1)

Essentially, it is not an external force, but the traitor soul within us which may betray us into such evil. Arren is not exempt from such temptation, as Ged reminds him: 'Did you not hear a voice say *Come*? Did you not follow? . . . How could he speak to you, and to all those who know how to listen, but in your own voice?' (III, p. 152). Against this inner evil, and the temptations of such as Cob, there seems to be no defence outside a man's own will. There is no God in Earthsea to comfort or defend.

It is a bleak philosophy – a man has no source of spiritual help except from within himself, and at death he is not reborn, nor does he attain a joyous immortality. He becomes 'but a shadow and a name' in the arid shadow-lands of the dead. But this is not quite the final conclusion. In the last encounter between Ged and Cob in the Dry Land, Ged freely – heedlessly, it seems – reveals his true name to the lost wizard. But in the land of the dead, as we have seen, names no longer have the significance that they have amongst the living, and at last Ged asserts his belief in immortality, a very different kind of immortality from the Kargish cycle of rebirth, the shadow existence in the Dry Land, or Cob's illusory death-in-life.

'My name is no use to you,' Ged said. 'You have no power over me at all. I am a living man; my body lies on the beach of Selidor, under the sun, on the turning earth. And when that body dies, I will be here: but only in name, in name alone, in shadow. Do you not understand? Did you never understand, you who called up so many shadows from the dead, who summoned all the hosts of the perished, even my lord Erreth-Akbe, wisest of us all? Did you not understand that he, even he, is but a shadow and a name? His death did not diminish life. Nor did it diminish him. He is there – *there*, not here! Here is nothing, dust and shadows. There, he is the earth and sunlight, the leaves of trees, the eagle's flight. He is alive. And all who ever died, live; they are reborn, and have no end, nor will there ever be an end. All, save you. For you would not have death. You lost death, you lost life, in order to save yourself. Yourself! Your immortal self! What is it? Who are you? ... You exist, without name, without form. You cannot see the light of day; you cannot see the dark. You sold the green earth and the sun and stars to save yourself. But you have no self. All that which you sold, that is yourself. You have given everything for nothing. And so now you seek to draw the world to you, all that light and life you lost, to fill up your nothingness. But it cannot be filled. Not all the songs of earth, not all the stars of heaven, could fill your emptiness.' (III, pp. 196–8)

In life, then, Ged argues, life as we know it through the senses, we have a living body, and a name which embodies the essence of our being. The living body must age, wither, decay, suffer pain, and die. Immortality cannot mean the survival of the body. The land of the dead houses the shadows of the living bodies of the dead, each with its name, but without sentience or emotion, without change. It is these empty phantoms which a wizard may summon. The true essence of a mortal man, divided now from his name, lives on, caught up in the living world he savoured, dispersed when separated from the concrete form of the body, but forever present in the living and changing earth.

Thus, although Ursula Le Guin is a very long way from the Christian belief which underlies Lewis's and Garfield's books, she does offer a note of hope at the end. Moreover, belief is closely related to daily living, for joy in living is the predominant theme in Ged's philosophy. Earthsea, like the primary world, has undergone a spiritual decline before our eyes. From a period of faith in the first book, Earthsea deteriorates spiritually amidst growing atheism and political unease during the height of Kargish imperialism, which is reached in the second book. In the final volume, a degenerating Earthsea is depicted – with a commercial and materialist ethic, drug-taking escapism, a decline in craftsmanship, and a loss of history, tradition and culture. The parallels with modern society, and especially America in the Vietnam War period, are obvious. As so often, the secondary world is used to illuminate and comment obliquely on the state of the primary world.

This final decline in Earthsea is seen as the direct result of a loss of faith, and as such it could be taken to mirror primary world experience with the decline of Christianity. Faith in Earthsea is not, of course, faith in an established religion, but in magic, that amalgam of religion, art and science, and all its cultural associations. The sorceress whom Arren and Ged meet in Hort Town has lost her power and now sells cheap fabrics in the market place: 'maybe all the silks aren't silk nor all the fleeces Gontish, but all the same they'll wear – they'll wear!' Magic, she says, was mere lies and air, and now 'those who want lies and visions chew hazia' (III, p. 52). There is a prevailing mood of cynicism and lawlessness. Ged and Tenar have restored the King's Rune, the Rune of Peace, but Earthsea still needs a High King – it needs a man in the seat of temporal power who also possesses spiritual strength, and it is such a man that Prince Arren proves himself to be. Ursula Le Guin implies that it is only by uniting a spiritual awareness with a zest for life that a man can truly live, in Earthsea or in the primary world. Magic and the significance of names, the imponderable power of words, are vitally important in everyday living, and so also is an awareness of the dark side of existence. This awareness must be linked with the strength to resist either a shambling, superstitious ritualism, or the temptation to manipulate the faith of others who are more credulous.

The underlying spiritual and philosophical theme of the trilogy is the need to balance opposites, and to realize that although darkness is non-life, it is essential as a background to the illuminating light of life. The unmaking of this right relation results in the destruction of speech, the withering of body and mind, the loss of name and identity. Ged's ultimate triumph lies in his strength in accepting the inevitable shadow of his own death, his courage in withstanding the dark, blood-thirsty powers of primitive belief, and his compassion. It is perhaps his compassion as much as his wisdom and his strength which remain in the mind after reading *The Earthsea Trilogy* – compassion for the dying Ioleth and for his grieving parents, for Tenar in her ruined girlhood, for the speech-paralysed weather-worker Hare, for the dragons lost to their savage natures, and in the end even for Cob. Despite all the evil the fallen wizard has done, Ged restores his true name to him,[16] and so gives him the passionless death of the Dry Land:

> Cob stood up. He looked about him slowly, with seeing eyes. He looked at Arren, and then at Ged. He spoke no word, but gazed

at them with dark eyes. There was no anger in his face, no hate, no grief. (III, p. 202)

The Earthsea Trilogy is primarily concerned with the meaning of death and immortality – both have meaning only in relation to the beauty and vitality of a life fully lived, and a search for 'the springs of being, deeper than life, than death' (III, p. 181). Ged's experiences enforce the lesson that we cannot avoid the sorrow of deaths like Ioleth's, nor should we deny pity, compassion, and a sense of pathos a place in our lives, but we must learn to accept our own death without fear or conciliatory ritualism. When a man dies his mortal body exists no more, except as a shadow and a memory, attached to a name. The real essence of the man, separated now from his name, lives on in the rocks and winds, in the seas and changing seasons of the trees. In the philosophy of Earthsea, as it is expressed through Ged, failure to face these issues – death, life after death, and the elements in life which are mystic and non-rational – leads to a barren life of dreary materialism or the need to escape through artificial, drug-induced hallucinations. An obsessive fear of them leads to another kind of barrenness, the living death of Cob or of the spider's paralysed victim. The balanced life, the life of the good man, faces good and evil, life and death, dark and light, materialism and mysticism, and establishes an equilibrium between them.

It is clear from the foregoing discussion that the three writers considered in this chapter, C. S. Lewis, Leon Garfield and Ursula Le Guin, while they are all primarily concerned with personal morality, vary widely in their approach. C. S. Lewis, working within the conventions of the Christian faith and Christian theology, usually presents his ideas through acceptable analogies by the use of a secondary world. The creation and destruction of Narnia are patterned on the biblical Creation and Day of Judgment, while the fall of the corrupt world of Charn images the visitation of the wrath of God on the sinful. The miraculous movement between worlds, and the multiple images of Narnia in *The Last Battle*, provide the reader with a vision of Paradise, and of the relationship between temporal words and the eternal. The use of the structural pattern of the romantic quest tale serves as a framework for the quest of the soul in search of God, while the magical temptations *en route* become the temptations of worldliness and spiritual sin. Aslan as Christ incarnate, Lion of Judah, restores the innocents from Hell, provides his followers with magical feasts and water turned to wine, later resurrecting Caspian and all the other devout Narnians – the resurrection of the body to the life everlasting in the Paradisal Garden. Aslan takes other bodily forms, as the Son of God may come in many guises, as beggar or as king. The stable which, in the primary world, was the place where God became incarnate, is in Narnia the door to salvation. There are, however, some false notes. It is implied that some creatures are predestined never to have the opportunity for salvation. Moreover, one feels a little unease with some of the ethics, particularly the hints of sadism and masochism.

Leon Garfield starts, like Lewis, from a basis of accepted Christianity. Taking the famous Faustus legend and the Christian precept that repentance will lead to salvation, he places his story in the primary world, into which the marvellous irrupts. The phantom child, reborn from Mr Fast's act of heedlessly signing away his childhood soul, seems doomed to damnation, until the tormented and repentant adult ends his earthly life in an act of self-sacrifice. Again like Lewis, Garfield used established Christian imagery of bread and wine, flames and the imprisoning of the sinful soul by its own acts of sin. Like him, he uses a Christ-figure who comes in a strange disguise. Garfield's method, however, is to suggest, rather than to state. *The Last Battle* concludes *The Chronicles of Narnia* like the last line of a mathematical proof. Every end is woven in, nothing important is left unexplained. The reference to Plato is carefully inserted, Paradise is described. At the end of *The Ghost Downstairs*, however, Mr Fishbane and the child vanish into the upper reaches of the night, God knows where.

In sharp contrast to Garfield and Lewis, Ursula Le Guin overthrows any reassuring basic beliefs, and even the symbols of Christianity. So the Christ-like figure offering life is shown to be the illusory form of Cob, tempting the unwary to sacrifice life for an empty immortality. Ursula Le Guin systematically undermines the reader's preconceptions in order to start, in her secondary world, from a *tabula rasa*, not only with regard to setting and culture but also – unlike Lewis – with regard to spiritual beliefs. Something of the same process can be seen at work in J. R. R. Tolkien's *The Lord of the Rings*, although more Christian parallels may be found there. Tolkien, however, avoids the issue of life after death for the mortal creatures of Middle-earth, and does not examine as searchingly as Ursula Le Guin the relationship between death and life. The contrast between Lewis's Paradisal Garden at the end of *The Last Battle* and Ursula Le Guin's land of the dead in *The Farthest Shore* is horrifying. Lewis and Garfield offer hope of salvation and a life of everlasting happiness: Le Guin constantly frustrates and denies such a hope. The only hope of immortality in Ged's philosophy is the reunion of a man's being with nature, but only with the loss of personal identity.

The stress on moral values also differs between the three writers. Lewis combines Aslan's admonitions against conceit and selfishness with a blunt, sword-wielding and somewhat insensitive code of ethics. Almost the obverse of this occurs in *The Ghost Downstairs*, where Garfield depicts compassion and growing self-awareness which lead to repentance and self-sacrifice. Compassion is also a keynote of Earthsea ethics, while Ursula Le Guin makes the use and misuse of abilities and power a central theme – together with the courage to face death and to live the good life joyfully now, on earth, without any promise of a life hereafter. No man in Earthsea, by his acts of goodness and mercy, is laying up any store of credit for himself in Heaven.

The vividness and variety of Narnia are probably the most memorable qualities of the Chronicles, apart from the strong element of Christian didacticism. There is a certain unevenness, most noticeable perhaps in the dialogue, which can be both apt and witty, or embarrassingly puerile. Sometimes the 'message' is too overt, and so unacceptable. Although Lewis's best scenes arise from religious concerns united with imaginative intensity, the element of didacticism and Christian apologetics sometimes conflicts with the creative spontaneity of the novels. This dichotomy does not occur in *The Ghost Downstairs*. Garfield's imagination is fully engaged with the theme; the Christian symbolism and Faustian parallels in themselves constitute the concrete elements of the story. One never feels, as one sometimes does with Lewis, that the story is present simply as a vehicle for something else. Garfield's is a flamboyant, neo-Dickensian style, which does not have a universal appeal, but it catches the period flavour of fog-bound London admirably, and works upon the reader as much through its grim humour as through its stark symbolism. Just as the religious basis is the essential framework of the story, not an added element, so the marvellous in the fantasy is essential to its full meaning, for the marvellous symbolizes in concrete terms our burden of inner sin and betrayed innocence. This is a fable for all time, placed in a very precise primary world setting. Ursula Le Guin employs the secondary world of Earthsea in order to create a new scale of values, and to wipe out given assumptions about religious beliefs and the meanings and use of words. Something so radically new and creative could only be done in a secondary world.

Leon Garfield uses fantasy to introduce a mystic element into primary world reality, to make us consider the nature of sin, damnation and repentance, and so to force us to examine more carefully the mystic element in our own lives. C. S. Lewis creates a secondary world of medieval culture which reflects the elements of Christian theology and ethics – at least as he saw them. His avowed object is to persuade the reader to learn to know Aslan by another name in his own world. Ursula Le Guin creates an essentially new and different secondary world to embody her questioning, probing, restless attitude towards the fundamental issues in man's life. She constantly undermines the comfortable walls which we build around the dark and inexplicable areas of doubt and fear. The fantasy is used sometimes to illuminate them, sometimes simply to force us to face them in all their darkness. *The Earthsea Trilogy* is an uncomfortable work. It offers no final solutions, no easy reassurances, certainly no gardens of Paradise. Despite all their differences, however, there is one element which unites these three authors. In the work of each it is precisely the use of fantasy itself which embodies the vital religious or philosophic purpose.

· 8 ·
Idealisms: Social and Political

A further and interrelated group of idealisms occurs in the work of some modern fantasists, and is concerned with social and political issues. There is a difference in the mode of fantasy here as compared with those writers considered in the previous chapter. Philosophic and religious idealism tends primarily to be concerned with worlds beyond this world, with life in relation to death, with temporal existence in relation to eternity. Such idealism seems to find its natural expression in the fantasy of the secondary world, in a parallelism between worlds, or in a fantasy of the primary world with a strongly numinous quality. Social and political idealisms, on the other hand, are idealisms of this world. In order to remain relevant to the contemporary reader within the framework of his daily life, works in this genre may not stray too far from primary reality. The use of the marvellous tends to be strictly limited. Moreover, certain subdivisions of fantasy which have been found in the past to be useful tools for social criticism continue to lend themselves to variation and development. Thus, of the three writers to be considered centrally in this chapter, two use the beast tale and one the fantasy of the future. The former is a long-established vehicle for this type of writing, while the latter has gained considerable popularity since the late nineteenth century.

The two themes of this chapter are closely related and not usually easy to separate. Political idealisms have social implications, while social idealisms imply the development of certain desirable political institutions. While the two can never be fully disentangled, however, an individual writer may lay more stress on one or the other. Moreover, while it is convenient to use the term 'idealism', writers within this field more often lead towards 'proof by counter-example'. It is difficult to create a convincing and unflawed utopia.[1] One has only to think of Plato's *Republic* or More's *Utopia* to realize how often elements which seem distasteful creep into such creations. Writers usually find it easier to depict a dystopia, as a warning of the undesirable forms which our social and political institutions have taken or may take, and their ideals must be deduced as the converse of what they deplore. Often combined with grim satire, this admonitory vision of a dystopia has produced some of the most powerful and influential novels of the mid-twentieth century, such as *Brave New World, 1984,* and *Animal Farm.* None of the books to be considered in this chapter have the depths of despair and bitterness to be found in these novels. The darker moments are relieved by heroism and stubborn hope, and although *The Winchester Trilogy* is almost uniformly tragic, it is a personal rather than a social tragedy. The satire is often bitter in *The Mouse and His Child,* the condemnation of certain political systems violent in *Watership Down,* but in both there is a glimpse of a limited attempt at a utopia in the closing scenes.

Writers who are concerned with social and political issues are sharply aware of the relevance of contemporary history both for themselves and for their readers. Certain major twentieth-century disillusions are common to all: two world wars and the Vietnam War; the disintegration of urban life with the rise in crime and the decline in general moral values; the failure of Communism to achieve utopia; the tyranny of dictators and the reigns of terror in totalitarian states; the loss of religious faith and of inherited cultural values; encroaching industrialization and the growth of the 'expendable' society; the discovery of nuclear power with its proved and potential horrors of maiming and wholesale destruction. These known, and accepted, facts of the contemporary social scene colour the thinking of many writers of fantasy, not just those with a clear social or political message. For example, whether it is conscious or not, there would seem to be a clear parallelism with the persecution of the Jews by the Nazis in Mary Norton's *Borrowers* series. The long saga of pursuit and escape culminates in the Borrowers' capture by the Platters, who intend to imprison them in a glass-sided house and exploit them for commercial purposes. The Borrowers are not tortured or killed, but they are devalued, dehumanized – fed and handled like vermin. In one of the illustrations accompanying this episode, the Platters are made to resemble conventionalized Nazi prison guards (*BT*, IV, p. 74). Moreover, in the first book, *The Borrowers,* an attempt *is* made to kill the small, alien, fugitive people – by poison gas. Mary Norton's main purpose is to depict the miniature world-within-a-world inhabited by Pod, Homily and Arrietty, and her writing is both humorous and lyrical, but when this world comes into conflict with the almost entirely hostile human world, the political analogies are inescapable.

A natural outcome of the moral disillusionment which has followed on the disasters of twentieth-century history has been the questioning of traditional ideals, particularly those which have affected political thinking. Britain and America have both undergone a collective loss of national faith: Britain as a result of the crumbling of Empire and the loss of major world status, America in the aftermath of McCarthyism and involvement in Vietnam, when she could no longer deceive herself that she was an earthly utopia, pure and uncorrupted sanctuary of ideals in a corrupt world. The writers to be considered in this chapter can constantly be seen to be questioning inherited political and social systems, of all the many varieties which have existed in the Western world.

This questioning of existing systems leads to a consideration of the individual in relation to social and political themes. It might be supposed that a writer whose concerns were the larger political ones would lay less stress on individuals. How important is the individual seen to be, and are individual virtues necessarily public ones? It emerges that these writers weigh up the relative merits of courage, love, loyalty, and honour as against statesmanship, diplomacy, and political guile. They face the issue of whether the state should be flexible enough to accommodate individual capabilities and eccentricities. Richard Adams and John Christopher both probe the question of what makes a good leader. Thus, although the *exempla* are taken from contemporary experience, and although certain widely accepted social systems are rejected by these writers, the fundamental issues they raise are those which have exercised political thinkers since the beginning of organized societies.

Three writers will be discussed in detail in this chapter: Russell Hoban, John Christopher and Richard Adams. However, the criticisms they make and the ideals they posit are often so closely related to the thinking of other writers of fantasy considered elsewhere in this study that it will be revealing to trace some of the connections and outline the common grounds of belief. Russell Hoban's *The Mouse and His Child* is concerned primarily with social criticism, while John Christopher presents a wide variety of social and political institutions in his *Winchester Trilogy* and in *The Guardians*. The political idealisms which have been chosen for study in this chapter are not so central a part of *Watership Down*, by Richard Adams. It is a book notable for many different qualities, only a few of which it is possible to discuss in this study. However, while the political theme is only one among many, the whole form of the novel is the quest for a new home, the drive towards a more perfect community, so that the political and social issues, although less dominant than in Hoban or Christopher, are highly relevant to the whole.

'Society is a retarded child with a loaded gun in its hands; I don't completely accept society's terms,' writes Russell Hoban.[2] This refusal to accept society's terms comes across very strongly in *The Mouse and His Child*. As the mice pursue their quest for independence and personal fulfilment, a subworld of the primary world is unrolled before the reader's eyes. There are three main constituents of this subworld: the toyshop, the dump, and the surrounding countryside. The toyshop is glimpsed only briefly, but the child retains the image of its warmth and security, comfort and companionship, throughout all the dangers he endures. It is the passionate desire to create again for himself and his father such a haven of peace and love which drives him on, in spite of the manifest impossibility of his dream. When the dream is realized at last, the dolls' house is a battered wreck, crudely repaired, and the elephant and seal, like the mouse and his child, are permanently maimed, but this gives the ending a genuine fidelity to life. The mice, like their human counterparts, find far greater happiness in rebuilding their lives from the wreckage of cruel experience than they could ever have known had they remained cocooned within the warmth and shelter of the toyshop, where the child wept because he was afraid to venture out into the harsh, frost-bound world.

In fact, the first stage in the career of the mice is a safe but tedious existence as part of the Christmas paraphernalia of a careful family, their task in life to dance each year under the Christmas tree (where Hoban saw the originals of his characters). All is well for several years until the child, at the memory of the dolls' house and the elephant, 'cries on the job', and the family cat, startled at this occurrence, knocks over a vase which smashes the mice. It is from this moment on that the father and son join the great hidden mass of cast-offs from society, but another cast-off has already opened the novel. In the initial scene the tramp (shunned by the people of the town but adopted by a stray dog) stops in the crowded street to dance in a circle, imitating the toy mice and defying acceptable patterns of behaviour, while the disconcerted shoppers hurry past, all travelling in straight lines. It is the tramp who later finds the mice in a dustbin and, feeling an instinctive sympathy with them, repairs their motor and sets them on their way.

In the person of the tramp, who appears only at the beginning and end of the book, Hoban sets up the frame of reference for the whole tale. The tramp, like the mice, is a product of the expendable society, a society which uses objects – and people – until they have served some limited purpose, and then casts them out; a society which values only the tangible objects of this world, and values them only by some materialistic standard of usefulness. Like the mice, the tramp has no further usefulness in such a society, and so has been rejected. Like them, he does not 'completely accept society's terms'. Like them, he creates an alternative life for himself, outside and yet parallel to society's norms. He makes use of its products as it suits him, like the goods trains for travelling or the wrecked cars for sleeping in, but for the most part he lives aloof from it. Like the mice, he finds companionship in the animal world. After his initial appearance, the tramp departs for most of the book, and we are left to follow the other cast-offs as they struggle to survive. Overtly the story of two mechanical toys, the novel constantly operates at this human level also, reminding the reader of the people in our society who are battered, rejected, cast out: the homeless and unwanted of peacetime, and the refugees who have wandered Europe and Asia in recent wars.

Hoban's detestation of the expendable society, with all its filth and rubbish of the part-used, the broken and the damaged, is evinced most clearly in the scenes at the dump. In these mounds of human refuse, another society has grown up:

> Stumbling over snow-covered rubbish, they followed a path through a city of rats and other vermin, where little refuse fires tended by the inhabitants threw dancing shadows on the dirty snow. Tunnels and alleyways led through the rubbish to dark and filthy dwellings. Skulking figures watched them pass, and loud rat voices all around them quarrelled, cursed and sang. (pp. 28–9)

The rats of the dump are not refugees, they choose to live like this, and their society serves as a comment on modern city life, the second of Hoban's social targets. In the dump are portrayed all the horrors of the collapse of urban life into a primitive struggle for survival, set not in the jungle but amongst the dirty refuse of an industrial society. With a typical touch of his grim satire, Hoban has objectified 'the rat race': Manny Rat, boss of the dump, is more man than rat, a Chicago Mafia-boss figure, and the 'cream of rat society', invited to his party, could be either humans or rats. As with the pigs and men at the end of *Animal Farm*, the physical distinctions become blurred where the mental and moral resemblances are so close:

> Grizzled old fighters and their plump, respectable wives touched whiskers with gentleman rats grown sleek by cunning and lithe young beauties of vaguely theatrical connection. Debutante rats and dashing young rats-about-town, all the golden youth of the dump, arrived in little laughing groups that achieved an effect of brilliance even in the dark, while doddering dowager rats came escorted by gaunt artistic rats with matted fur, burning eyes, and enormous appetites. Last up the ladder were a scattering of selected social climbers, followed by various hired bravos, obscure ruffians, and cheap hustlers whose good will was worth cultivating. (p. 152)

As in a corrupt human urban society, the wealth of this 'cream of rat society' is based on 'an evil-smelling huddle of gambling dens, gaming booths, dancehalls and taverns' (p. 30). The rats live not by creating – not even at the mechanical level of manufacturing – but by scavenging and by exploiting the weakness and folly of others. There is only one moral principle in the dump – SURVIVE. Crime is rampant, and the mouse and his child are forced to take part in an abortive bank raid. By making the object of the raid so trivial – peanut brittle – Hoban underlines how much Manny Rat's greed resembles man's own worthless greed for material goods. And the death of the rat Ralphie, killed and eaten by the badger bank guard, is paralleled by the wasted lives and casual deaths of young criminals in human cities.

The materialism and decline in moral values in modern urban society has generally been accompanied by a similar loss of traditional culture. The itinerant theatrical company run by Crow and Mrs Crow ekes out a precarious existence in woods and meadows, where an enraged audience is likely to eat the cast alive – literally. Constantly changing their approach – the Caws of Art Classical Repertory Group, the Caws of Art Follies, the Caws of Art Experimental Theatre Group – the company only really achieves success with the follies, which included 'a line of red-hot chickadees . . . that everybody was crazy about' (p. 71). When they try to perform *The

Last Visible Dog, a modern drama of the theatre-of-the-absurd school, written by the morose nihilist C. Serpentina, a member of the audience shouts: 'We don't want none of your modern filth around here!' (p. 77). The irony of this is that the play is not even so coherent as to be 'filthy' in the sense the weasel means. Its filth is of a different order, symbolized by the rank mud in which Serpentina lives – a filth of rottenness and decay, but a mental decay rather than a physical one.

There is an uncrossable divide between 'the public', who only want mindless entertainment, and the writers and producers who see themselves as a cultural elite. But Hoban ruthlessly exposes the pretensions of this elite, who believe that obscurity and confusion are to be equated with profundity. The products of this modern theatre possess neither technical competence nor artistic merit. The author and 'philosopher' Serpentina is, in his way, as empty and mindless as the purveyors and consumers of the mass pop culture of crack-voiced carousel and jiggling celluloid doll, while the crows, who possess a certain shaggy generosity and charm, are too easily gulled by the playwright's own estimate of himself. Serpentina is just clever enough to deceive others with artistic pretensions into accepting him at his own valuation, just as in man's modern pseudo-culture the manipulation of clever publicity can create a spurious fame for an artist, a writer, a pop group or a film.

In a similar manner, Manny Rat, whose native wit considerably exceeds Serpentina's, establishes a petty tyranny over the other inhabitants of the dump by manipulation. He manipulates their fear rather than their pretensions, but both he and Serpentina depend on the credulity of their victims. Manny Rat's weapons are terror, protectionism, and a popular reputation for omniscience. When his teeth are knocked out in the battle with the mice and their friends, he can no longer sustain his façade as ruthless king of the dump. Once the façade crumbles, Manny Rat falls from his position of dictator.

Manny Rat's foundations of power are set in the urban jungle of the dump, and the reader might suppose that as the mouse and his child move outward into the countryside they will discover a purer, better world amongst the more natural animals of the woods and fields. Not at all. The first animal they encounter is the Frog, an itinerant pedlar, fortune-teller and mountebank, who travels between country and dump, managing to survive in a world full of predators by cunning and a smooth tongue. The mice, however, have an extraordinary effect on the Frog. In a long life of hypocrisy and guile, he has never encountered anyone like them. Their shining integrity and courage awake some dormant spark in this grotesque fraud of a fortune-teller, forcing him (against his will and his better judgment) to prophesy the truth. This alienates the dangerous Manny Rat, but the Frog throws in his lot with the mice, guiding and protecting them in their first initiation into the life of the countryside, where Hoban launches his next attack on the contemporary human scene.

The Frog and the mice are taken prisoner by a detachment of shrew soldiers who are involved in a campaign against a rival army. Like so many human soldiers, the shrews are confused as to which army invaded which territory. The only thing they are certain about is their hunger and their hatred of the other army. The sole motive of each army is to defend its own territory and seize that of its neighbours, at whatever cost in blood on both sides. The battle cries are 'Ours! Ours! Ours!' and 'Onward! Onward! Onward!' Up to this point Hoban might be castigating those responsible for any war fought for doubtful gains by violent but uncomprehending humans. The final scenes, however, as the blood-bath escalates and each destroyer is destroyed by another more powerful, immediately call to mind the whole doom-ridden history of the Vietnamese struggle:

> The weasels flowed like hungry shadows down into the hollow, and once among the shrews, struck right and left with lightning swiftness, smiling pleasantly with the blood of both armies dripping from their jaws. Not a single shrew escaped. When the weasels had satisfied their thirst for blood they bounded away, leaving behind them heaps of tiny corpses scattered on the snow.
>
> 'This is a *nice* territory,' said the female. 'It's the nicest we've had yet. I'd kind of like to settle down here for a while.'
>
> 'It's not bad,' said her mate. 'Not a bad little territory at all. I could see us making a home here.' They nuzzled each other affectionately as they ran, and their heads were so close together that when the horned owl swooped down out of the moonlight his talons pierced both brains at once.
>
> 'My land,' wheezed the owl as he rose heavily with the weasels' limp bodies dangling from his claws. 'Two at once! The missus won't believe me when I tell her. Yessiree!' he chuckled, 'as territories go, this is a might good one!' (pp. 63–4)

The animals of the wild are thus no more admirable than the rats of the dump, and they enact Hoban's vision of war, not as something noble and heroic (even in the defenders of their own territory) but as a horrible devaluation of life. There is a totally callous attitude on the part of all the participants in the battle towards wholesale massacre. The weasels kill from blood lust as much as from hunger, for while no shrew survives, only a few are eaten: 'heaps of tiny corpses' are left on the field.

It is in the country also that the mice meet other animals who embody human types which Hoban wishes to satirize. Serpentina, the pompous nihilist, they meet in the mud at the bottom of the pool into which they sink after the disastrous breaking of the beavers' dam. Prior to this they have spent an entire winter, wearing out their motor and their plush, labouring as slaves for Muskrat, in the hope that he will help them to independence through self-winding. Muskrat is the obsessed scientist (as Serpentina is the obsessed philosopher), totally absorbed in the problems of pure research and later of applied science. The living creatures he encounters have less meaning for him than the abstract symbols he manipulates, and he abandons pure research for applied science only in a bid for personal fame and public esteem. To him, the mice are simply another tool for the furtherance of his aims. He is less manifestly cruel and evil than Manny Rat, but his moral position is not very different. He typifies all those whose lives are absorbed by research into nuclear power, germ warfare, biological engineering and the like, but who justify such research by the argument that it is not their responsibility if politicians and others in power misuse the products of their research. 'Society is a retarded child with a loaded gun in its hands' – literally, in this case. Someone has to put the loaded gun there. Is the Muskrat admirable, Hoban questions, as a devotee of pure research and the furtherance of knowledge? Or is he culpable, because of all the destruction his actions trigger off?

The mouse child learns, however, from both Serpentina and Muskrat. After 'contemplating infinity' for months at the bottom of the pool, he realizes that 'there's nothing on the other side of nothing but us' (p. 126), and from Muskrat he learns that the mind, forced to find a solution to apparently insoluble problems, may be capable of a sudden leap into the unknown. It is the determination to find their own solution to their disastrous situation which leads to the turn in the fortunes of the small pair. From this point onwards, despite their

ruined motor and subsequent smashing, the book moves optimistic-
ally to its close. The mice are repaired by their animal friends, the rats
are defeated, the dolls' house restored as a haven for weary outcasts
and migrant birds. This optimistic note of the final chapters counter-
acts to some extent the sombre quality of much of the earlier part of
the book (sombre despite its satiric humour). The two poles of the
novel, dystopia and utopia, are not contradictory, however – as
Hoban himself indicates when discussing his own beliefs and the
literature which has influenced him: 'Myself, I can't use a mythology
in which there is nothing to win and consequently nothing to lose.'[3] It
is this dual attitude towards winning and losing which makes the
dystopia–utopia structure so suitable for Hoban's purposes. By
depicting those aspects of modern society which he considers
deplorable, Hoban implicitly constructs, in the abstract and always
out of sight, a utopia towards which it is desirable that we, like the
valiant mice, should strive.

The animal world thus appears in *The Mouse and His Child* as an
image of human society at its most ruthless. The values of the dump
are what Hoban sees as the values of modern urban society: an
obsession with the tawdry and gimcrack; an indifference to filth,
pain and terror, and to lives lived out in hopelessness; an admiration
of material wealth built on a foundation of refuse – broken objects
and broken lives. There is more than a hint here of the horror which
lies at the heart of Dickens's *Our Mutual Friend* and, as in that novel,
the horror is sometimes coldly explicit, as when the badger bank
guard eats the young criminal Ralphie, and then criticizes his technique while picking his teeth with a sliver of bone. This vein of
macabre humour runs through the book, and the suggestion that
society has a substructure of refuse, death and bones is continually
brought before the reader.

The society which surrounds the mouse and his child has as its
prime purpose in life the struggle for survival and supremacy,
unsoftened by any touch of compassion or charity. Against this
background of cruelty and persecution on the one hand, and destitu-
tion on the other, the defiant idealism of the mice shines out. Despite
their small stature, this quality in the mice makes them heroic, and
the strength of their characters constantly challenges the worthless-
ness of the social framework in which they are set.

One way in which the mice operate within the novel as a whole
becomes clear if we examine the species of the animal characters.

There are many different varieties of birds, animals and insects within the subworld of toyshop, dump and countryside, some hostile to the mice, some friendly. There is also another group, which can be seen to be interrelated in a way that the other animals are not: the two mechanical mice, Manny Rat and the rats of the dump, the shrews and, less importantly perhaps, Muskrat. All these mouse/rat characters are more closely human types than the other animals, and they themselves recognize a strange affinity with those who, on the surface at least, appear to be enemies. Hoban does not stress this relationship, except in Manny Rat's attitude to the mice, but it is present in a number of hints.

The shrews are an army of vicious fighters, but the gentle mouse child feels a curious attraction towards the little shrew drummer boy, who teaches him the meaning of 'territory': 'What chance has anybody got without a territory? . . . A territory is your place. . . . It's where everything smells right. It's where you know the runways and hideouts, night or day. It's what you fought for, or what your father fought for' (p. 58). After the drummer boy is killed, the child carries his nutshell drum everywhere with him, and sounds it as he and his father fight for their own territory, the dolls' house occupied by Manny Rat. Despite their cruelty, and their attitude towards the mice as 'rations', the shrews share a common core of 'humanity' with them.

Again, after their encounter with Muskrat and his belief in the power of abstract thought, the mice realize that they too have a similar potential, and learn to use it. It is as though in each of these encounters with others belonging to the rat–mouse type, the mouse and his child enlarge their own personalities and capacities. As their imaginative and reasoning faculties develop, as they realize the need for independence and for a home – which is part of their search for an identity – the mice become less and less mechanical and more alive, more human.

The most complex of these relationships which lead to growth is that with Manny Rat. Manny Rat is, on the face of it, the villain of the story. When he feels that 'those wind-ups' (a devaluing and abusive term which he uses like 'nigger') have made a fool of him, he vows to catch them and smash them, and to this end he tracks them across miles of snowy countryside, risking death from the shrews, birds of prey, and the enraged audience at the Caws of Art. Despite his villainy, his courage gives him an odd kind of nobility, and in a way his quest mirrors that of the mice. As they suffer and learn in a cruel world, the mice gradually discover what it is that they are seeking: the opportunity to live full lives in security and peace. The rat believes, initially, that his one aim is to destroy the mice, and yet he finds them oddly attractive: 'Manny Rat felt himself by some strange magnetism drawn to the father and the son, felt that something was wanted of him, forgot almost that he was there to smash them' (p. 54). He repeatedly allows opportunities for killing them to slip away, somehow sensing that he too is in search of something which he cannot identify. In the end, it is through Manny Rat that the mouse and his child win through to their goals. The dolls' house has been found and repaired by Manny Rat, and mounted on the old birdhouse pole, before the mice and their friends win it back. Moreover, it is the humbled and toothless rat, with his passion for mechanical gadgets, who devises a self-winding mechanism for the mice. As he works on the problem, Manny Rat begins to understand his real relationship with the mice:

> They were not unlike him, he realized for the first time; almost they were tin caricatures of himself. In their long exposure to the weather, moss had rooted in the crevices of their tin, and now it covered them like soft green fur. Manny Rat laughed inwardly. Perhaps they were becoming animals, and he, once the most powerful animal in the dump, would turn into a toy. After all, why not? Had not their roles been totally reversed? Had not they risen to his high place as he fell from it? (p. 180)

As this relationship between Manny Rat and the mice develops, the rat ceases to function in the novel simply as a caricature of the criminal boss, and becomes instead part of the spiritual quest of the mice. As he is socially humbled, he becomes morally more ennobled, as much through the loving generosity of others as through his own actions. When his last act of villainy fails (the attempt to blow up the dolls' house and all its occupants), the anxious animals surround the stunned rat with concern. Despite the harsh and ruthless nature of society which Hoban has depicted for most of the novel, there is still a place for compassion and the forgiveness of enemies.

Throughout *The Mouse and His Child*, it is the worth of the individual which is stressed. Against the social background which Hoban portrays in dump and fields is set the heroism and idealism of the mice. Constantly persecuted by a hostile society, they manage to survive against all the odds. By displaying explicitly in the animal world the horrors of our own lives – poverty, hunger, oppression, spiritual deprivation, persecution and bloody wars – and by mirroring, in the harsh attitude which prevails in most of the animal world, our own callous indifference to such horrors, Hoban both castigates our own society and implies the qualities he thinks desirable in a utopia. The tension between the surrounding society and the individual quest is resolved only at the end, when all the main characters contribute to establishing their final haven. It is a fragile utopia, the patched dolls' house swaying on top of its pole near the railway tracks, but Hoban suggests that it is only the frail, temporary utopia we can never aspire to, surrounded as we are by a hostile, dystopic world.

Unlike Russell Hoban, John Christopher, in *The Winchester Trilogy* and *The Guardians*, depicts society not of the present, but of the future. Christopher's portrayal of the future is an individualistic one, and it is different in the two works. In contrast to a number of twentieth-century depictions of the future (especially those which occur in science fiction), it is not a pure technocracy. In both cases the imagined future is seen to arise naturally from our present, and at the same time the society of the future rejects certain aspects of our own society. Indeed it tends, for the most part, to turn back to our past and adopt many of its forms.[4] There are certain prime issues which concern Christopher: the conflict between technology and civilization; the relative desirability of different forms of government; the apparently irreconcilable issues of personal freedom and social tranquillity; and the morality of powerful, centralized rule, however benevolent in its intentions. Christopher does not separate social and political systems, but sees them as mutually interactive. Moreover, his use of the marvellous is minimal, a characteristic of fantasies of the utopia–dystopia type, and is limited primarily to the assumption that the writer can portray the future. Other occurrences of the marvellous are hardly more than incidental features of his future otherworlds.

One major aspect of the contemporary scene provides the starting-point for *The Winchester Trilogy* – the threat of a world cataclysm. The necessity this suggests for reassessing fundamental values gives Christopher his basis of an England reverted to feudalism, in which machines are feared and banned, and yet continue to exist in secret, in the possession of the Seers (or religious leaders), who make use of them to delude a credulous populace. Throughout the trilogy the world of science and technology is contrasted with the world of feudalism. Technology can offer improved comforts in living, can aid communication, but it also stands for guns, bombs and the mass media. Feudalism means honour, loyalty and personal bravery, but it also involves bigotry and superstition.

A similar conflict occurs in the future England of *The Guardians*. Here the two cultures coexist, but are sharply divided, geographically, by the Barrier, into the Conurbs and the County. The Barrier is only a wire mesh fence, not very high, and hardly guarded. Yet it has a reputation for being impassable, and has created its own no-man's-land of desolate country about it. As one of the characters, a young man becoming involved with the revolutionaries, points out: 'There are two worlds, with a barrier between them. The barrier may not be strong in the physical sense but in people's minds it's enormous' (p. 118). The barrier which separates the two cultures is essentially a mental one, for the people on one side fear and despise those on the other, whom in fact they never meet. It is, in exaggerated form, the kind of psychological barrier of hatred and misunderstanding which so often separates nations.

In *The Winchester Trilogy*, the condemnation of technology is a highly emotional issue. Machines are banned, not simply lost, after the cataclysm. It is a ban which arises largely from the superstitious fear that the disaster may have been caused by man's heedless use of machines, although Christopher is at pains to assure us repeatedly, through his first-person narrator Luke, that in fact the disaster was due to natural causes. This ban is a social pressure enforced by the community on the individual by ostracism and punishment, and the ban has been further reinforced by the teachings of the Seers, who decree that any dealing with machines is an impiety. As a result of this, any interest in machines, any inclination towards scientific experiment, is ruthlessly suppressed. It is the social attitude, rather than a personal abhorrence of machinery, which causes the young Luke to destroy the old mechanics magazine which his friend Martin has found. He argues that it is 'a forbidden thing', forbidden by the Spirits; but the force behind the argument comes not from personal horror but from the punishment society will inflict on Martin, as it did on 'old Palmer':

this man, neither farrier nor armourer nor metal-worker, was

brazing metal and building something from it. The soldiers rode
out on the Prince's command and took him. He was tried and
found guilty and hanged. For a week his body hung on the
gibbet outside the North Gate. (*WT*, I, p. 58)

Even at as young an age as this, Luke realizes the distinction
between the two types of motive behind his action: 'I wanted to tell
him why I had been angry. Not because of the blasphemy in itself but
because of the risks that it involved. . . . One took risks, in battle for
instance, but only for a worthwhile end. There was none here' (*WT*,
I, p. 59). Luke is unable to understand Martin's restless intellectual
and spiritual hunger, which is not satisfied by the conditions of the
society in which he lives. Luke's attitude changes subtly as he
matures. Taken, after his father's murder by an enemy and his
half-brother's seizure of power, to Sanctuary, the headquarters of
the High Seers beneath Stonehenge, he is astonished to discover that
the Seers themselves build and use machines. The Seers are in fact not
a spiritual brotherhood, as they pretend, but an intellectual elite,
who use both their own position as religious leaders and the superstitious fears of the people to manipulate society into the forms which
they feel it should take. They are entirely devoid of religious feeling
and their politics follow quite a different channel from those of the
small city-states which they exploit.

Do the small feudal communities represent a desirable society?
Such a society does have many attractive qualities – a kind of
cleanness and strength which is lacking in industrial societies. But it
is also violent, prejudiced and riddled with superstition, though
notably lacking in spiritual strength except amongst the small,
despised sect of Christians. Violent death is common, and from the
time his father becomes Prince, Luke knows himself to be surrounded by enemies as well as flatterers.

The Seers, then, with their machines, and their plans for a united
England with Luke as Prince of Princes – perhaps theirs is a vision of
utopia? Luke becomes more and more willing to accept machines, in
the land of the Wilsh where simple machines like lawnmowers are
retained, and to feel less superstitious horror of 'polymuf' humans
and animals. This personal growth in tolerance and enlightenment in
Luke promises well for the reformed political system which the Seers
project, and their intentions for a time appear both worthwhile and
desirable. Luke's doubts, and the reader's, begin to arise when it is

revealed that the Seer Ezzard has killed Luke's pregnant sister-in-law by sending an electric charge through her metal bathtub. This has been done in pursuit of the Seers' aims, to secure the succession for Luke, but he instantly and unhesitatingly condemns such a use of machines, and such callous disregard for human life.

Yet Luke himself does not remain guiltless. After he is deposed by a coup at Winchester and his betrothed bride is taken from him by his best friend, he persuades the Seers to design for him, and the Wilsh to manufacture, a Sten gun. With a Wilsh army and three hundred guns he returns to the south and slaughters the army of Amesbury which comes riding out to meet him, leaving an 'ugly rampart that marked the scene of carnage. It was made up of the broken bodies of horses in their hundreds, mingled with the bodies of men' (*WT*, III, p. 133). Luke, hardened and embittered, points out the battlefield to Prince Eric of Oxford:

> 'The old battles achieved nothing: you told me that in Winchester. They had horses and honour but they brought no resolution. Things will be different from now on. There will be no room for horses or honour in the battles we shall fight, but we shall have victories of a kind men have not known before.'
> (*WT*, III, p. 134)

The ruthless pursuit of his political objectives means the laying aside of his ingrained moral code, and when he reaches Winchester Luke's nerve fails him. He gives the signal to fire too late. The Winchester army is not annihilated, and the Wilsh suffer some casualties. By allowing the remnant of the army to retreat to Winchester, Luke involves the Wilsh in a long siege. By this time the reader has realized that Christopher is not holding up as ideal the imperialist aims either of the Seers or of Luke.

After the siege has continued for some months, the Seers offer Luke further technology, a mortar to destroy the walls of the city, and with it the beginnings of a breach are made. In this final confrontation between the world without technology and the murderous technology of warfare, the battle is won by a moral victory. At first the Christians, and after them all the people of Winchester, place themselves in the gap in the wall. Looking through fieldglasses, Luke recalls the words of the Christian Bishop: 'If killing there must be I would rather it were done by a warrior who kills with his own hand, and knows what bloody corpse he leaves behind' (*WT*, III, p. 149).

All the strength of his new-found technology and of his bitter sense of betrayal cannot rob Luke of his moral sense, or of his conviction of the worth of human life and dignity:

> They lined the parapets, in scores, in hundreds. There were not so many Christians in Winchester. These were the people of the city, human and dwarf and polymuf, offering their bodies as its bulwark.
>   I said to Martin: 'Go back to them. Tell them they can keep their freedom.' (*WT*, III, p. 149)

The final condemnation of technology, in Christopher's view, is that it dehumanizes people. It makes it possible to destroy other human lives at a distance, at the press of a button or a trigger. It shields us from the true horror of our own actions. Violence and cruelty are inherent in man's nature, and a society which kills by the sword in close combat or mounts a man's head on a pole is not essentially more violent and cruel than a society which, superficially, keeps its hands clean, but kills at a distance by electrocution or bullet. There is, as the Bishop points out, more chance of appealing to a man's conscience in the first case, for at least he knows 'what bloody corpse he leaves behind'.

At the end of the trilogy Luke looks ahead to the future which must come, for technology does not consist merely of weapons, and once the spirit of scientific inquisitiveness is released from its unnatural bondage, it cannot be contained:

> So we shall meet with the cities of the south again, and when we do we shall conquer them. It will not serve them to line their walls with the living bodies of their citizens. We shall have weapons more subtle and more powerful than Sten guns and mortars: weapons of ease and novelty and riches. We shall conquer them because we represent the strength of the future, and they the past which must always bow to it. It will happen because it must, but I am in no great hurry to see it. (*WT*, III, p. 152)

In *The Guardians*, John Christopher considers twin societies, with and without technology, at peace rather than at war. In the Conurbs, a materialist society taken to extremes, technology is the dominant force in life. The people of the Conurbs live crowded together in skyscrapers interpenetrated with narrow caverns of streets. The working week has been halved, and the populace are entertained in their prolonged hours of leisure by games held in huge stadiums. Favourite sports are terraplaning, in which the frequent accidents make it popular with the spectators, and high-wire gladiatorial combats in which the losers 'always got hurt, sometimes badly, occasionally fatally' (p. 24). With their taste for violence directed into these safe channels, and kept happy by inane holovision programmes, the people remain relatively peaceful, but the intense overcrowding occasionally explodes in riots.

In the Conurbs, John Christopher depicts a society in which technology is entirely devoted to man's comfort and surface tranquillity (the only war is a far-distant one in China). There is no poverty. Food is plentiful, although of a tasteless, prepackaged variety. Everyone has work, everyone has leisure. The people of the Conurbs actually prefer their crowded living conditions, fearing solitude. Their festive occasions, however, have the contrived atmosphere of a holiday camp. And there is virtually no personal freedom. This lack of freedom is only gradually borne in upon the hero, Rob, when his father dies as the result of an 'accident', and he is sent to a State Boarding School, which is more than half Borstal.

The County, to which Rob escapes after a lonely and perilous journey, seems at first to be free of technology. There is space and air, a small population living in scattered farms and manor houses or in a few fine cities like Oxford, where the car works have been razed to the ground, and the fields replanted. The roads, it is true, have a plastic surface, but it is a special plastic designed for horses' hooves – the only transport being on horse-back or by horse-drawn carriage. The only exceptions are the occasional copters of the Commuters, professional men who live in the County but work in the Conurbs until they can afford to retire entirely to the County. Gradually Rob learns that other forms of technology are used in the County, but generally kept out of sight because it is 'customary'.

Much store is set, in the County, by what is 'customary', by good taste and elegance. Care is taken to preserve the landscape, to fill interiors of houses with elegant traditional furniture, paintings, bowls of flowers. It may take longer to light one's way from room to room by oil lamp, or for the servants to maintain open fires, but a fine standard of living is worth the effort. Food is prepared to gourmet standards, clothing is elegant. The pastimes are garden parties, fêtes, riding events, cricket, archery, regattas, dinner parties.

There is, however, little reading, although Mike's family possesses a large library of inherited books. This is a hint, casually dropped, that all is perhaps not perfect in the County: 'The books were various but had one thing in common: none had been published within the last thirty or forty years' (p. 101).

Attending school with Mike, the County boy who has befriended him, Rob finds the discipline sometimes even more severe than at the State Boarding School, and yet the schools are not the same. 'The difference between the two places was not easy to grasp at first, but it was distinct. Gradually Rob worked it out as having to do with pride and self-respect. . . . Here there was a sense of being trained, and trained for eventual authority. . . . They belonged to a special, a privileged group, and this was never allowed to be forgotten' (p. 115). One of the distinctions lies in the fact that, despite the cold showers, early morning runs, hard benches and plain food, the boys are served their meals by servant girls. At the State Boarding School the boys queue for hours at mealtimes and are constantly bullied; the atmosphere is compounded of fear and factory-like dullness and rigidity. Christopher is working at two levels here. The contrast between the two schools brings out essential qualities in his two societies – the submissive, disciplined populace of the Conurbs and the healthy, tough gentry of the County preparing, as of right, for positions of power in the ruling class. At the same time he is also attacking the extremes towards which British education has swung from time to time: the elitism of the nineteenth-century public school, the training-ground for empire-builders, and the vast, homogeneous modern comprehensive, with its expectation that every child will conform. By showing both systems taken to extremes, Christopher illuminates the faults of both, although it is noteworthy that Rob is happy at the County school, which recognizes his value as an individual. This is, of course, a part of the subtle temptation to which he is subjected.

The validity of traditional culture in a society of the future is closely related to Christopher's exploration of societies with and without technology. It has been hinted that there is little reading in the County of *The Guardians*. Although life is gracious, and the forms of elegant social living are constantly adhered to, there is no true artistic culture. The fine furniture and paintings are a background to comfortable living. The craftsmen make copies of antique furniture – they do not create afresh. There is a stagnation here in the arts. The clock has deliberately been turned back to the social forms of the Edwardian period, and this has been accompanied by a drying up of artistic and literary inventiveness, and of any public interest in the creative arts.[5] What Rob must learn in order to be accepted in the County are the social graces of a gentleman: when to stand up and when to sit down, the correct mode of addressing people, the clothes suitable for each occasion, proper table manners. It is an essentially surface grace to a superficial style of life.

In the Conurbs, of course, there is no culture, only the mass-produced entertainment of the holovision. The prefix 'holo-' is significant. This mass medium dominates *all* the senses, fills the whole mind of the spectator. The intention is that no corner of the mind should be left free to wonder and speculate. Books have even less value in the Conurbs than in the County. The gentry of the County take some pride in their fine libraries, even if they do not read the books in them. In the Conurb where Rob lives, the public library is a decaying old building, with a staff of one morose old man past retiring age. Rob is the only person under fifty to use the library. Sent away suddenly to the State Boarding School, he still has two library books in his possession, which are found by a master at inspection:

> 'Library books,' the master said. He prodded one contemptuously. 'Objects which have been passed from hand to unwashed hand. Filthy insanitary things. Traps for germs. You disgust me, Randall.' The calmness had gone and his voice was hard and angry. 'You are a disgrace to the House and to the School. . . . See that these things are removed and burnt.' (p. 39)

The overt anger and hatred is symptomatic of the underlying fear of books in the Conurbs. Schoolchildren are taught by a carefully controlled use of audio-visual aids, and are never allowed the dangerous freedom of developing their own minds through contact with books. This scene is recalled, as a faintly disturbing memory, when the reader realizes that even the beautiful, calf-bound volumes in the County are rarely used.

In the world of *The Winchester Trilogy*, there is little artistic culture in the towns of the south. There is one not very skilled portrait painter, some jugglers and clowns who perform at traditional festivals, and no books except a few handwritten manuscripts. Only after the beginnings of social and political changes does a group of actors come to perform a play at Winchester. The story of Tristram and Iseult which they act is taken by Luke to reflect his own position, and causes him to precipitate an emotional situation which might have remained under control. The coming of this new cultural force to Winchester thus initiates a new phase in the tragedy, and in the further social changes which follow.

At first it appears that Christopher is presenting the Wilsh as a cultured people in contrast to the people of Winchester: they love music, both instrumental and vocal; they paint portraits and huge murals; they enjoy drama and dancing. Yet somehow it is all of a piece with their fine clothes, their perfumes and jewellery. They are, it is true, more genuinely artistic than the County gentry of *The Guardians*, but it has still a light-weight, superficial quality. Such culture, Christopher implies, without true depth of feeling behind it, never becomes more than a surface polish to life. The Wilsh are capable of strong feelings – firm friendship and implacable hatred – but these are essentially narrow and egotistical emotions. The Wilsh show no responsive sympathy to the feelings of others. The people of Winchester, for all their rough, uncultured ways, all have much more highly developed feelings and sensibilities – human, dwarf and poly-muf alike. Their emotional strength is evinced in their individuality, their pride in their city, their fierce love of freedom. It is these qualities, the qualities from which an artistic culture can grow, which overcome their mutual prejudices and unite them in their heroic resistance on the walls of the city. Culture is something both more complicated and more profound than paintings and musical instruments. It manifests itself on the surface of a society, but it arises initially in the hearts of the citizens. As we have come to expect with Christopher, neither Winchester nor Klan Gothlen represents a utopia. Both are incomplete and flawed, and in many ways they are complementary.

Although the cultural issues explored by John Christopher are partly spiritual, he does not consider religious matters in any depth. Any form of religion is totally absent from *The Guardians* – in itself an oblique criticism of the two societies depicted there. In *The Winchester Trilogy* only two forms of religion have any promin-ence, Spiritism and Christianity, although other, smaller religious sects are mentioned. Spiritism is gradually revealed as a sham religion, its seances and the public pronouncements of its Seers serving as convenient tools in manipulating the populace. The Seers are deeply involved in making use of the politics and power struggles of the small city-states. The Christians take a far less prominent part in the action. A poor, politically powerless group, they are outside the normal structure of society, even breaking ancient taboos by admitting dwarfs and polymufs to their brotherhood. Their moral position seems strange, sometimes even laughable, to the majority of the citizens. Advocates of peace and opponents of corporal punishment and the death penalty, they constantly set a moral standard by which others may be measured and found wanting. Nor are they totally negligible as a social force. Their influence within the city grows, almost imperceptibly. Luke is won round to a half-grudging admiration of them, while never fully comprehending their views. And at the city's greatest crisis the courage of the Christians, willingly going to their deaths in order to save their fellow citizens, provides the example which unites all the people of Winchester in their final act of heroism.

The actual forms of society and government which Christopher depicts in *The Winchester Trilogy* and *The Guardians* are considerably varied. In the trilogy, the two main forms are the separate city-states of the south, each with its own hereditary or elected Prince, and the strong centralized government of the Wilsh, with its capital and only large town at Klan Gothlen. Other attempts at social organization which have emerged since the Disaster are glanced at briefly. The cannibalistic, matriarchal Sky People are certainly not presented as a desirable social group, but as a warning of the degradation into which human beings can sink. The men are unmanned by their subservience to the women, which is all the more distasteful in that they have shown themselves skilful and cunning hunters. The women, never stirring from the platform village in the trees, fed prodigious amounts of food from babyhood so that they may become physically distorted – ponderous mountains of gross flesh – are equally degraded. Even their religious practices have become a meaningless cruelty. At one time young men of the tribe died willingly as part of the religious ceremonies. Now the hunters catch young men from distant villages to sacrifice and eat. This tribe indulges in monstrous practices and yet, as Christopher takes care to remind us, they are human like ourselves. To aid Luke's escape from the Sky People, Hans sets fire to the platform in the tree tops where the village huts stand:

Sickness and anger rose in me again. I looked up and rejoiced at the spreading fire. The cries were thinner but more anguished. I rejoiced at that, too.

Not until we were clear of the forest, whose whole heart seemed to be consumed in a conflagration that crimsoned the sky like the flaming mountains of the Burning Lands, did I remember the children trapped in it with the rest. Then I felt only sickness, and no more anger. (*WT*, II, p. 135)

By contrast with the Sky People, the society of the Bell People seems idyllically happy. They live a kind of commune life: there is no individual marriage and the children of the tribe call all the men 'Father' and all the women 'Mother'. There is no headman – decisions are reached when the common consent of all the people becomes clear. All the members of the tribe are healthy, smiling and clean, their farmlands are prosperous, their huts well built. Yet behind and beneath all this contentment, there is a distant background of cruelty. All polymufs and dwarfs are smothered at birth. 'This was not out of revulsion or in obedience to the behest of Spirits, but from kindness. It would be cruel, they felt, to let a crippled child live, different from his brothers and sisters and deprived of the fullness of activity which they enjoyed' (*WT*, III, pp. 113–14). Should an adult become crippled, everything would be done to help his recovery, but if it failed and 'he knew he would not regain his true strength, he would bid farewell to the Tribe and leave the village. There was a herb growing in the woods which brought a quiet death' (*WT*, III, p. 114). This recalls the euthanasia of More's *Utopia*. Luke is offered the chance to remain with this tribe, where he knows that his desire for vengeance will soon be lost in the atmosphere of love and happiness, but he clings to his vengeance and leaves.

This is the nearest Christopher approaches to depicting a utopia, yet, as we have seen, the general happiness is in part founded on a certain ruthlessness. In some ways it resembles the society of the Raft People in Ursula Le Guin's *Earthsea Trilogy*. Like them, the Bell People live in simple contentment, free from ambition and strife, but they do so only by cutting themselves off from all other people. There is an essential selfishness in such a society. It recognizes no claims but its own, it has no compassion or concern for the rest of humanity. In the end, it can never provide a utopia, only an escape from the commitments of a full human society.

While the more developed town societies are not as strongly

contrasted as these tribal ones, there are certainly major differences between the small city-states, of which Winchester is the main example, and the strong central government of the Wilsh. The differences in their attitudes to technology and culture have already been mentioned. The Wilsh are also more tolerant towards dwarfs and polymufs – a polymuf, Snake, is King Cymru's Chancellor and most valued advisor. In its tolerance, the Wilsh society is certainly superior to the south, although one begins to suspect, when Cymru with casual indifference mentions the Christians and the White Witches in close conjunction, that perhaps this tolerance arises in part from the very superficiality of the Wilsh, and their insensitivity to the deeper and more complex areas of human emotion and belief.

In both the city-states and Klan Gothlen, supreme power rests in one man. The dynasty of the Cymru amongst the Wilsh has endured for many generations, and appears throughout the trilogy to be absolutely secure from attack or rebellion. The courtiers plot and flatter, but only with a view to advancement within the existing power structure. In the south the position of a Prince is far less secure. It is relatively easy to dispose of Prince Stephen, Edmund's father, when the nobility of Captains and the religious leaders, the Seers, both determine upon it, even though the family have ruled for some time. The task is made even easier by Stephen's unpopularity with the people of the city. Luke's father is made Prince in his stead, although he is virtually an upstart – an ennobled commoner, who has risen through military abilities. This is a diplomatic move, designed to forestall rivalry between the two powerful families of the Blaines and the Hardings, perhaps no more than a stop-gap, until one faction or the other feels sure enough of its strength to attempt a coup. (One is constantly reminded of medieval and Renaissance Italy throughout all these power struggles.) Later, when through personal grief and suspicion Luke becomes too authoritarian, he is as easily deposed as Stephen had been. Times are changing, however. This time it is not a coalition of nobility and church which deposes one Prince and creates another. The Captains act without the Seers, and determine that in future there shall be no single Prince, but a Council of Captains. It is a step, a small step, towards democracy.

The Seers are planning for a far different political structure. From boyhood they select Luke as their future Prince of Princes, and this is one factor, at the time not known to Luke or his family, in the choice of his father as Prince of Winchester. Winchester itself is chosen, as a former capital of England and a geographical centre of the south, to be the focal point from which the Prince will unite all the civilized lands against the barbarians in the far west, who are becoming a serious threat.

The plans of the Seers go somewhat awry, for they have failed, in drawing up their political plans, to allow for human nature; but the trilogy ends with Luke, named heir to the Cymru, preparing for the day when he will conquer the whole of the south. Although Luke sees that a future of technology and science must defeat the past, whose values and social structures he really prefers, there is a note of irony at the close of *The Sword of the Spirits*, in that Luke seems unaware that he too may be part of that past which will be swept away – the rule of an absolute monarch may be as doomed as the heroic but indecisive battles on horseback. Even if he is not fully aware of all the political implications of his position, Luke is conscious of the finality of his own personal tragedy, which has come about mainly through his position at the political storm-centre of the times. The final words of the trilogy make this clear:

> The Sword of the Spirits lies in a golden casket in the throne-room. Swords have no use any longer, though there was a fashion last winter of wearing ornamental daggers, but this one is treasured for its history and will be as long as the towers of Klan Gothlen stand and Cymru rules there. It is a trophy, a legacy, that a man would be glad to leave to his son.
> But I shall have no son. (*WT*, III, p. 153)

Despite the fact that, in *The Guardians*, the people of Britain are divided into two apparently disparate societies, they are in reality – as Rob and the reader gradually learn – under one government. The most sinister aspect of this government is that it is always out of sight. In the Conurbs Rob meets hosts of minor officials – officials of the Stadium, the hospital, his schools, the Education Office, the police, the railway but no one ever sees who gives the orders, makes the decisions, establishes the laws. In the County, he is informed that the gentry are the ruling class, although he sees little evidence of it. Some serve as officers in the army, or have careers in the foreign service, but most appear to live at leisure on the income from their estates or from their investments in the factories in the Conurbs. Mr Gifford spends most of his time growing Bonsai, Mr Penfold tinkers with clocks. Rob's eyes are first opened to the true state of affairs by

Mike's restless discontent and the haranguing of Daniel Penfold, a clever but 'unreliable' boy at school, who has secretly joined a revolutionary group:

> 'The point we have to start from is the realization that we're all conditioned – that we live in the most conditioned society the world has ever known. We have our special position drilled into us from childhood. The servants here in the County are taught to despise the Conurbans and the Conurbans despise them in return. They never meet – they know scarcely anything about the way each other lives – but they despise them all the same. And we are the privileged ones at the top of the pyramid.' (p. 118)

Rob refuses to heed what Penfold says, and refuses Mike's invitation to join the revolutionary group. Having found a haven in the County, he is not anxious to be discovered and sent back to the Conurbs. Yet all the time he has been living in a fool's paradise. After the revolution in Oxford and Bristol has failed and Mike has fled into the Conurbs to join the scattered revolutionaries, Rob can no longer hide from the reality of the political situation.

Sir Percy Gregory, whom Rob has taken to be 'friendly and not particularly intelligent' (p. 161), reveals that Rob's true identity has always been known to 'the guardians', of whom Sir Percy is one, and who have been observing him as a potential recruit. The guardians are the true ruling class, not the gentry; they rule in secret and absolutely. Their intentions appear to be perfectly benevolent, as do those of the Seers in *The Winchester Trilogy*. As Rob knows, no one is hungry, the people are contented: 'For the first time in human history we have peace, plenty, the greatest happiness for the greatest number' (p. 166), and as Penfold, who has been killed in the revolution, predicted to the other boys, the Conurbans will not initiate any revolutions, for they are kept in controlled comfort, with their occasional riots as deliberate safety valves. The only hope for change in the structure of society and government must come from within 'the ruling class' – the gentry. The guardians are aware of this potential threat, and as Sir Percy explains, both halves of society must be controlled:

> 'It must *appear* natural because people cannot be contented unless they believe their lives to be natural. But to do this and to keep everything in balance requires intelligence and planning. It

requires a special group of dedicated men who will act as guardians over the rest. Thus guns are abolished but a reserve is kept to protect society against insurrection. Not only that – we have psychologists to help us mould people into proper courses of action. We are constantly on the alert for trouble. The Conurb is easier to control than the County in that respect. Anyone showing creative intelligence and initiative stands out conspicuously from the mob and can be dealt with. Here it is less easy. Aristocracies have always provided the seedbeds for revolt. However well we manipulate the gentry, sooner or later there must be an eruption. This is what we have just had. We have watched it gather like a boil and at the right moment have lanced it. It will be fifty years at least before it happens again.' (pp. 166–7)

By this point in the novel, the reader has already begun to wonder how close are the parallels between Christopher's utopic–dystopic otherworld, and the primary world which he himself has experienced. The otherworld experience is exaggerated, but it springs from a basis in reality. How much, we are forced to ask, are we manipulated and moulded here and now?

The ultimate test of a political and social system is the relationship between the individual and society as a whole. In *The Winchester Trilogy* Christopher explores the ways in which political tyranny and social prejudices can warp and stunt people even more decisively than the physical effects of the Disaster can deform their bodies. Some measure of personal freedom a human being must have, so long as he does no harm to others by his aspirations: the freedom to realize his potential in the kind of life appropriate to him, to develop his mental capacities and satisfy his spiritual yearnings. Hans as a warrior, Snake as Chancellor, Martin as a poor Christian, are all – dwarf, polymuf and man – fulfilled human beings, although they contravene social taboos of long standing. On the other hand, Christopher stresses, each man must live as part of a society, and Luke's final, tragic mistake is a failure in communication and mutual understanding: he is unable to tell Blodwen that he loves her, he cannot discuss the situation rationally with Edmund, he becomes overwhelmed by groundless suspicions implanted by a few jealous words. Consequently, he attempts to assert his personal rights at the expense of others and is justly, if tragically, punished for it.

In *The Winchester Trilogy*, Christopher highlights the individual tragedy which is set against a background of changing and conflicting social systems. In *The Guardians* the individual's story is dominated by the major problem presented by the social system – is revolution justifiable when the majority of the people are happy? At first Rob denies that it is, until he learns just how the contented acceptance of the guardians' rule is secured. Mike, he is told, will not be killed or imprisoned if he is recaptured:

> 'We guardians are not limited by the moralities we lay down for others but I hope we retain human feelings. He will be all right: you have my word for that. A very small operation on the brain, performed by expert surgeons. It won't hurt him. He'll remain active, intelligent, capable of a full life. But he won't want to rebel any more. It's a tried and tested technique. We keep it in reserve for cases like this.' (p. 169)

This claim to be beyond the restraints of accepted morality recalls the similar position maintained by the Seers, and has a ring of familiarity about it for twentieth-century readers from their own primary world experience. Moreover, the calm assumption of the right to destroy the mind and personality of another individual has uncomfortable parallels also in contemporary experience, in the use of lobotomy and of brain-washing.

Awake at last to the reality which surrounds him, Rob tells Mrs Gifford in horror of what will happen if Mike is recaptured. She accepts it with apparent indifference, strong and intelligent woman though she is. Her husband had had the same operation when he was a young man, she tells Rob.

> It was only now, listening to her quiet voice, that he realized the full horror. . . . Mr Gifford watering and pruning and pinching the buds off his tiny trees, had once been like Mike, thought as he did. And they had opened his skull and nipped out the core of his manhood as he himself might nip the growing heart of a plant. (p. 173)

Mike had not known about his father's operation, but the father's rebellious spirit had been inherited by the son:

> to spring into growth when he found a ragged boy, and helped him, and understood that someone from the Conurb could be a

human being like himself. And then he had looked around and
seen the stagnation and rottenness festering under the elegant
surface of the life he knew: the corruption that could manipulate people like puppets, and the acquiescence of the puppets in
their silken bonds.

Mike had seen things to which he, almost deliberately, had
blinded himself. The bait which he had been offered today and
had so nearly taken had been more subtle and powerful but no
less poisonous. The chance to be not a puppet, but a puppet-
master. (pp. 173–4)

Utopia has become dystopia, and at last everything falls into place
for Rob, and for the reader. Incidents in Rob's childhood take on a
new meaning, and he understands the reason for his father's 'accident', with which the novel began, and Mr Kennealy's remark that
Rob will be 'safer' not staying with him. Both Penfold and Sir Percy
have been wrong. It is not only among the gentry that the spirit of
rebellion can spring up. Remembering his father, Rob has 'a strange
feeling as though after all it had come right. He was going with his
father, long years behind but following' (p. 175). He leaves his
sanctuary in the County, and the invitation to become one of the
guardians, and goes to join Mike and the other revolutionaries.
Perhaps, as Christopher implicitly suggests in *The Guardians*, the
right relationship between the individual and state can never be
found. Uncontrolled individualism leads to anarchy, while totalitarianism reduces the individual to the level of an automaton. Perhaps
the only way for society to survive is in a perpetual state of tension
between the two conflicting demands. Certainly this promises no
utopia.

Like John Christopher, Richard Adams is acutely aware of the
dangers of a totalitarian state, and like both Hoban and Christopher
he detests the encroachment of man's industrialization on the
natural environment of the countryside. The world of *Watership
Down*, however, is much closer to our normal primary world reality
– despite the fact that the protagonists are rabbits – than either
Hoban's or Christopher's otherworlds. Hoban imputes rational
thoughts and feelings to mechanical toys as well as to animals, while
Christopher's worlds of the future are radically changed from our
own. *Watership Down* is set, with meticulous and abundant detail,
in the Berkshire Downs of today. If the reader will only accept that

rabbits have some mental and oral method of articulating their thoughts, everything else follows. Christopher distances his various political structures, enabling us to regard them objectively, and yet still be shocked. Hoban's animals and toys form a small-scale version of modern American society. So also, in the warrens of the Berkshire countryside, surrounded by the everyday human pursuits of a contemporary farming community, Adams depicts four main types of human political systems: a totalitarian state, a community of lotus-eaters, a once healthy social group sinking into stagnation and complacency, and an attempt to set up a utopia.

Watership Down is not a straightforward political allegory like *Animal Farm,* but like Orwell's animal society it shows the influence of particular aspects of twentieth-century history on the author. Adams himself served in World War II, and a parallelism with the political atmosphere of the 1930s and 1940s lies behind all the Efrafan sections of the book. One cannot draw up a precise table of equations, as one can between *Animal Farm* and revolutionary/post-revolutionary Russia, but General Woundwort has all the attributes of the ruthless head of a totalitarian state, whether he be Franco, Mussolini, Hitler, Stalin or Amin. In particular, the police states of Nazi Germany and Stalinist Russia provide the background for Efrafa. Woundwort has none of the sophisticated technology, but he has the mentality of the twentieth-century dictator, and the most illuminating characteristic of this is the determination to prevent his subjects from escaping from the state. In the past, rulers' energies were almost entirely directed towards preventing a political coup at home or an attack from outside. Exile was a common punishment for political dissidents. It is a modern tendency to fear and prevent the departure of 'citizens'. This is also one of the most notable features of Efrafa.

Like other totalitarian states also, Efrafa has a highly efficient army, the Owsla, kept in regular fighting order, and a secret police, the Owslafa, chosen for their strength and brutal nature. Obedience must be unquestioning and is enforced by punishment, torture, mutilation and even death. The expression of views possibly unacceptable to the state is suppressed by fear of retribution. The inhabitants of the warren are divided into 'Marks', and a bite in ear or flank scars them for life with the appropriate mark. The different Marks live in separate burrows with no intercommunicating passages, in order to prevent the spread of disease or rebellion. They are allowed outside for exercise and feeding only at certain set times, to prevent rabbits of different Marks from meeting. The Owsla officers have considerable powers within their Marks, although they too are always subject to Woundwort and his Council. The attitude of the Owsla towards the other rabbits is summed up in Chervil's remark to Bigwig about the does: 'If you want a doe you have one – any doe in the Mark, that is. We're not officers for nothing, are we? The does are under orders and none of the bucks can stop you!' (p. 324). In Efrafa individual rights and individual liberty count for nothing.

When Woundwort originally established Efrafa, his intention was to create a warren which was safe from the attacks of predators, men or disease, but his insatiable longing for power has developed into the determination to conquer and enslave all surrounding warrens, and to reduce his subjects to mere cyphers in his power game. Woundwort thus sets out, like John Christopher's Seers and guardians, to establish a utopia, and finishes by creating a dystopia. The dignity of the individual has become meaningless in this totalitarian state. Only the strength of the warren and the size of the geographical area which he controls through the Wide Patrols of his Owsla matter to Woundwort. As a result of these policies, the ordinary inhabitants of Efrafa are either cowed or rebellious. The unhappiness of the does has resulted in fewer and fewer litters being born, and here Adams uses one of his excellent touches of realism. It has been observed that in overcrowded warrens pregnant does reabsorb their unborn kittens instead of giving birth to young who will starve.[6] Adams uses this biological fact in two ways: first, as an illustration of the rabbits' religious belief in the divine dispensation of the Lord Frith (p. 202), and secondly, to make a moral point about the deterioration of life under a political regime like that in Efrafa (pp. 243, 327).

Efrafa is not entirely ruled by terror, although this is the main instrument of discipline. General Woundwort is more than a mere bully. He is clever, courageous and shrewd, with a genius for organization. Young bucks compete to gain entry into the Owsla, not only for the privileges, but in a spirit of emulation of the general. Once there, they are eager to volunteer for the Wide Patrols, on which many lose their lives, and their admiration for Woundwort is warm-hearted and sincere. (The Owslafa, or Council Police, are a different matter. They are ruthless and inhumane almost without exception.) The attitude of the Owsla illuminates Woundwort's good qualities, and even after the final battle with the dog some of the Efrafans refuse to accept that Woundwort has been killed (his body is never found). However, the General's attitude towards the courageous exploits of the members of his Owsla is not altogether attractive:

> the casualties ... suited Woundwort's purpose, for numbers needed keeping down and there were always fresh vacancies in the Owsla, which the younger bucks did their best to be good enough to fill. To feel that rabbits were competing to risk their lives at his orders gratified Woundwort, although he believed – and so did his Council and his Owsla – that he was giving the warren peace and security at a price which was modest enough. (p. 313)

At the opposite extreme from Efrafa is Strawberry's warren, which the band of wandering rabbits finds after a nightmare journey across heather and bog. As Efrafa is Adams's depiction of a totalitarian state, so this warren is his presentation, in rabbit terms, of a community of self-deluding lotus-eaters. (Significantly, this is the only warren in the book which has no name. Sandleford, Efrafa, Watership Down, even the briefly mentioned Nutley Copse, all have an identity, in which the inhabitants can take a pride.) To all outward appearances this warren seems to the weary travellers, with the exception of Fiver, to be a veritable utopia. All the rabbits are large, sleek and healthy. There is plenty of room for newcomers, for the warren is by no means overcrowded. It seems that the wandering rabbits have reached their goal.

The lives of the rabbits in this community are totally unnatural: they neither have to avoid *elil* (enemies) nor to defend themselves against them – the warren is open and conspicuous, and they rush out of the runs heedless of danger. (In Efrafa there is a headcount at the mouth of each run, supervised by the Owsla officers.) They do not even need to seek for food: *flayrah* (royal food) is provided for them, and they have developed the curious habit of storing and eating food underground, so that they need not go outside in inclement weather. (Efrafan rabbits tend to be somewhat undernourished. Feeding sessions are policed, and may be cancelled because of rain or a security scare for as long as twenty-four hours.) Unlike all the other rabbit communities in the book, they have lost their traditional rabbit culture, having forgotten the folk-tales and ceased to believe in the traditional religion of Frith and Inlé. Instead they have developed a curious, inward-looking culture of their own: they perform a ceremonial greeting dance, the does make a kind of singing noise to their young, and they devise pictures by pressing pebbles into an earth bank – but all of this is very superficial, only the outward forms and gestures of culture. It has no inner meaning for these rabbits, who are obsessed with the illusory surface of their lives, and will not confront reality. All their tales are introspective, shutting out any speculation about the world outside, while their decadent poetry expresses in veiled language what they dare not speak of openly – a longing for escape, even to some dream-shrouded, peaceful death kingdom. The fear and horror which permeate this warren are the fear of violent death, the horror of sudden strangulation by the wire snare. Fiver senses at once that this warren is a place of deceptive luxury and hidden terror, roofed with bones.[7]

The wandering band of rabbits, led by Hazel and incited by Fiver, comes originally from the Sandleford warren, a third type of society which Adams implicitly criticizes. Midway, in terms of social organization, between the extremes of Efrafa and Strawberry's warren, this is an old-established community (a parallel to modern Britain?) whose Chief Rabbit is the Threarah, and where many of the migrating band were 'outskirters', young rabbits with no social status within the warren. The Threarah possesses courage, resourcefulness, tact and strength of character, and his behaviour during the myxomatosis crisis has saved the warren. However, he is settled now, growing older, secure in the complacent estimate of his own wisdom and foresight, and he ignores Fiver's warning of impending disaster.

This warren is comfortable, secure against wild *elil*, happy and well organized. Nothing, of course, can protect it against the vicious destructiveness of man. Moreover, it is becoming overcrowded, and the young bucks feel that they have little future there. They decide to go in quest of a new home partly in response to Fiver's prophecy, and partly in order to make a better life for themselves. This tendency to colonize in order to absorb overpopulation is a natural phenomenon amongst rabbits, as it is amongst primitive peoples. After the departure of the small band, almost the entire population of the warren is deliberately exterminated by poison gas. In a community where there is no room for mental growth or the appreciation of fresh ideas, Adams suggests, social stagnation sets in, political development atrophies, and the community becomes a natural victim to outside forces. This happens at Sandleford. Complacency culminates in disaster.

All of these communities are rejected by Hazel and his companions, and so, by implication, by Adams: Sandleford is deteriorating from what was once a desirable society; Efrafa and the 'warren of bones' are both dystopias. The two dystopias are powerfully admonitory. The community of lotus-eaters appears to be a utopia, but the utopian superstructure is built on a foundation of horror and sudden death. On the other hand Efrafa, which is patently a dys-· topia, has evolved – and become distorted – from the utopian projections of its founder, whose obsession with ultimate ends has led to a corruption in the means, in this case in the lives of the members of the community. This is a reflection of much human experience, in which utopian ideals too narrowly conceived can, perversely, destroy human happiness. Warned by these examples, Hazel has only simple, but wide-reaching, objectives for Watership Down: that all the rabbits should be free and happy, and that the weaker members of the community should not be tyrannized by the stronger. The community established on Watership Down has no rules, only commonly accepted patterns of behaviour, and Hazel is accepted and respected as leader not because of superior physical strength (which is the attribute of Bigwig) or the gift of prophecy (Fiver) or ingeniousness (Blackberry), but for the breadth of his humane vision, and his compassionate understanding of his fellows.

Adams uses dystopias to illustrate what is necessary in a utopia. Inherited culture and religious faith give a strength and cohesion to the community. Both have virtually been stamped out in Efrafa (only the rebellious doe Hyzenthlay recites a poem, an elegy for the vanished freedom of the spirit), and have died a natural death in Strawberry's warren, where the fear of facing even the reality of their situation stunts any spiritual or imaginative growth in the rabbits. Hazel's group, by contrast, have a rich store of inherited tales, and a robust and unshakeable belief in the Lord Frith and the hero El-ahrairah. In addition, the overprotected life of the lotus-eaters has stultified all political energy and vigour. Their passive acceptance of their fate is as degrading as the submissive obedience of the majority of the Efrafans. They combine physical well-being with mental

torpor, demoralization and depression. This has led to such disintegration of personality under the strain of their unspoken knowledge
of the snares which wait to end their lives, that it can only find
expression through the decadent poetry of Silverweed, which is filled
with the death-wish. On the other hand, the tyranny of Efrafa has
resulted in a total loss of personal freedom and the victimization of
dissidents. In both of these communities, the inhabitants are protected from the outside world, from disease and from predatory
animals, but become instead the victims of the politically powerful
within the community: in Efrafa of Woundwort and the Council, in
the other warren of 'the man', the farmer who is effectively the ruler
of the community, protecting it, providing its food, and killing its
inhabitants.

By contrast with these two dystopias, and with the warren of their
childhood, the rabbits on Watership Down establish a small and
modest utopia. It is a loose democracy with a popularly acclaimed
leader or prince, which looks back to the traditional culture and faith
which the inhabitants, like human colonists, have brought with them
to their new home, and forward to the good life which is to be lived in
their new and freer community. It is a society without bigotry, in
which there is adequate accommodation for individual talents and
eccentricities, and each member can be valued for his own qualities.
Above all there is complete freedom of action, of thought and of
speech, within the limitations imposed by consideration for other
members of the community.

This respect for the individual within the political system is the
most notable feature of Adams's portrayal of Watership Down.
Hazel is the prince, Hazel-rah, but only by the consent of the community. The relationship between the individual and the political
system is fundamentally different in the two dystopias. Strawberry's
warren has no political head, because of the danger that the leader
might be the next victim of the snares, but it also has no sense of
direction or purpose. The lives of the individual members are not
restricted by political controls, but they are essentially futile; all have
equal rights, and all run an equal risk of death. At the other extreme,
Woundwort is a ruthless dictator, a psychopath with a lust for
bloodshed and tyranny. The rules of the warren have a logical basis
in the safety of the community as a whole, but they have been pushed
beyond the limits of reason. Individuals are cruelly suppressed.
Dissidents, even if their only desire is to leave the community, are

tortured and killed. The inhabitants of Efrafa are healthy enough, although not as sleek and well-fed as the lotus-eaters, but the sense of oppression and mental deprivation leads to discontent, psychological troubles, the death of unborn young, and a spirit of rebellion. Bigwig senses when he first meets them that the discontented does have become so desperate under oppression, so much in need of escape from the imprisoning atmosphere of Efrafa, that he is almost too late to rouse them to action. They are sinking into suicidal despair. Yet so strong is the will for freedom that even Blackavar, cruelly mutilated and condemned to death, brain-washed, bullied and half-starved, summons up the last of his strength to join in the escape, and reaches the utopia of Watership Down.

Watership Down is never described by Adams or any of the characters as utopian, but it functions, like most imagined utopias or visions of the Golden Age, by negatives. In presenting the two dystopias, Adams has prepared the reader for the utopian quality of Watership Down. It is utopian by what it is *not*. There are no snares in the grass, no sudden death, no tyranny, no sense of hopelessness, no secret police, no informers, no military law, no repression of individual freedom. The positive qualities, as in Hoban's utopia, are modest: a sense of personal and communal self-respect, faith and culture, security, and personal liberty. Modest riches to those who have always possessed them, but infinitely precious to those who have not.

It is interesting that two of the three writers considered in this chapter find animal fantasy the easiest way of presenting their ideas. The use of this particular type of the marvellous gives the writing a certain objective quality which makes it possible to view the political or social system from without. Similarly, John Christopher creates a secondary world of the future in order to produce the same distancing effect. There are certain other similarities to be observed in both their ideas and their methods of presenting them. One of the principal similarities lies in their uses of anger as a tool for directing the reader's responses. Hoban works largely through satire, with its twin implements of anger and mockery, in order to persuade us to condemn many of the values of contemporary America. Christopher arouses our anger by the calm acceptance, in the Winchester world, of the inferior social position of polymufs and dwarfs, and in so doing causes us to question some of the social injustices which we accept unquestioningly in the primary world. In depicting the cruelty and oppression of Efrafa, Adams directs our anger against other totalitarian states.

The uses of anger in the work of these three writers are closely allied to the echoes from contemporary history which sound through the novels. Their vision of the present state of the primary world is, on the whole, not a happy one, and they thus tend to stress the particular horrors of twentieth-century political and social systems which disturb them. The horror of mass tyranny, tyranny on a scale hitherto never conceived, is present both in Adams's Efrafa and in Christopher's *The Guardians*: whether the origins of totalitarianism lie in alleged benevolent social planning or in the pursuit of personal glory and power on the part of a dictator, the ultimate effects on the people living under totalitarianism are largely the same. All three writers detect a devaluation of life to the level of dump culture or through subjugation to ruthless and meaningless laws or harsh social pressures.

While the writers considered in the last chapter were centrally concerned with religious or philosophic belief, it is notable that Hoban, Christopher and Adams are also occupied by the loss of sincere, deeply felt and inherited faith and culture. Indeed, in *Watership Down* this constitutes a much more prominent part of the book than might appear in the present analysis, one of the most outstanding sections in the book being chapter 31, 'The Story of El-ahrairah and the Black Rabbit of Inlé', in which the strongly religious tone is linked to the questions of social responsibility, social morality, and the willing self-sacrifice of the leader for his people. All these writers deplore the vanishing of the numinous from modern society with its shallow materialism, leaving nothing in its place but barren and joyless pleasures – the surface comforts of life in the warren of the lotus-eaters, the mindless entertainment of the jiggling headless celluloid doll, the empty pretensions of cult art, or the decadent poetry of despair. There is a slight note of optimism in *The Winchester Trilogy*: although the empty and superstitious faith of the masses in Spiritism is purely a convenient tool for controlling them, yet true faith can still inspire humanity, compassion and selfless heroism, as it does in the acts of the Christians. As profound a horror, although one less often present in daily life than the devaluation of our status as human beings, is the horror of war. This is to be found in each of these novels – the bloodlust of Woundwort, the violence of the shrew war, the carnage of battles in which swordsmen face Sten guns, the cold efficiency with which the rebellion is suppressed in *The Guardians*.

It is clear from all this that these writers are remarkably united in what they condemn, although their approaches are different. Thus, Hoban sets the squalor of the dump against the countryside in which the fight for survival is equally ruthless; Adams, however, paints a varied and minutely detailed picture of the beauty of the countryside as a corrective to an urban-centred view of life. What do these writers offer as a goal? Certainly nothing so clear-cut as a simple utopia: The Last Visible Dog and the Watership Down warren are only tentative attempts at a utopia. The first is seen as fragile, probably transient, but the mouse and his child and their friends have found personal fulfilment. At the end of *Watership Down* Hazel dies, and leaves the warren in the company of the legendary rabbit hero El-ahrairah. Yet the sense here is not one of ending but of promise for the future: Hazel 'stopped for a moment to watch his rabbits and to try to get used to the extraordinary feeling that strength and speed were flowing inexhaustibly out of him into their sleek young bodies and healthy senses' (p. 478).

Utopia, to have any meaning, must not stand still, it must always look to the future. John Christopher is not so specific either about the shape of utopia or about the future direction of his future otherworlds. Luke knows that the age of technology must come, but he is in no hurry to promote it, even though it seems certain to bring his absolute rule. His heart is with the old culture, with the life of his childhood. Indeed, it is more complex than this, for he recognizes the inhumanity of some of the old beliefs, particularly in the treatment of dwarfs and polymufs, but he values the old sense of honour, the freedom of individual states, the general respect for human dignity. He survives as a man permanently damaged by the clash between political expediency and the social and moral values which he treasures. At the end of *The Guardians* the future is even more uncertain. The dystopias of Conurb and County have established the need for fundamental social and political change, and the novel ends with Rob leaving to join the revolutionaries, but there is no clear indication of what their aims are, or even of whether Christopher believes that any form of utopia can be achieved to replace the generally dystopic forms of political and social institutions which man allows to imprison him. Even if some improved form of society can be created, it is unlikely to leave men with the surface happiness they possess in the County: 'Being discontented is a part of being free. And we aren't free – that's what I'm trying to say' (p. 121).

Although no recognizably consistent view of utopia appears in purely positive terms from the works considered so far in this chapter, a great deal emerges by implication, both from what is deplored and from what is indicated as being desirable. Moreover, these hints find echoes in the work of virtually all the major writers considered in this study: Tolkien, Lewis, Le Guin, Kendall, T. H. White, Alexander, O'Brien, Selden, Whistler, Pearce, Garfield – all those who address themselves in some way to the question of what makes a desirable society. A general longing for the pre-industrial period is very dominant. If we must have machines, these writers imply, let us keep them simple, let us not become subservient to them. Moreover, all genuine work of mind or hand is seen to have value – the work of the craftsman, farmer, merchant, poet, musician, scholar. In the general lines of utopia as it emerges from the work of these writers, no one is fettered to the mindless labour of the factory – although perhaps the hard physical labour of the agricultural worker is sometimes a little idealized.

Arising from this view of a desirable society, desirable political structures are outlined by some, though by no means all, of these writers. Here Hoban tends to differ from the majority – although he deplores many of the same aspects of modern life as the other writers, his characters form a small community taking refuge from a hostile world, against which they remain at the end in a somewhat embattled position. A similar isolated community is deplored by Christopher (the Bell People), and another treated with some reserve by Ursula Le Guin (the Raft People). Speaking in very general terms, there seems to be a consensus in favour of loose federations of communities in which all the citizens take part in decision-making and local affairs. This is characteristic of the communities depicted in *The Chronicles of Narnia*, *The Lord of the Rings*, *The Earthsea Trilogy*, and *The Chronicles of Prydain*, amongst others. And – perhaps a curious and unexpected feature in twentieth-century writing – most writers visualize a High King or Prince, who provides leadership in both temporal and spiritual matters, and who is the font of pure justice. The loneliness, responsibility, integrity and heroic stature of such a leader are stressed, and by implication are strongly contrasted with the characteristics of contemporary political leaders. The training of such a leader is a central theme with T. H.

White, Alexander, Tolkien and Le Guin, while Christopher depicts the tragic demands which may be made upon him, and the near-impossibility of living up to them. Adams provides a double image of the leader – Hazel is the temporal and mortal leader of his community, but behind him is always the vision of El-ahrairah, the ideal to which he must aspire. In such a utopian political system, the remainder of the community would live with the greatest possible individual freedom within the constraints of mutual tolerance and consideration.

Harvey Cox, in his study *The Feast of Fools: A Theological Essay on Festivity and Fantasy*, has analysed two 'temptations' or 'malaises' in contemporary society: the temptation towards violence and the temptation towards withdrawal (p. 116). In the term 'violence' he includes both the direct violence of war and urban riots, and the indirect violence committed against personal freedom by organized bureaucracy. 'Withdrawal' includes both the more obvious forms taken by the communes, the hippies, the drug-takers, and the more indirect forms, in which people refuse to face their responsibilities towards their fellow-men. It is noteworthy that fantasy, which some might expect to be a literature of 'withdrawal', since it is so often carelessly dismissed as 'escapist', is in reality employed to condemn precisely those malaises towards which Cox directs our attention. The depiction of a pre-industrial society as desirable is not a withdrawal in the sense of a shirking of responsibility. Rather it is a revolt against precisely that indirect form of violence which has created a widespread need for release from a sense of imprisonment by regulations and data-banks, constant official prying into private life and a devaluation of personal dignity. The cheapening of humanity by a society which rates people as 'wind-ups' which may be cast aside when worn out lies behind Russell Hoban's dystopia of the dump and John Christopher's dystopia of Conurb and County. Those views of society which are expressed with such remarkable consistency by so many of the writers of serious modern fantasy arise from a desperate dissatisfaction with contemporary life, a need to break free and realize full human potential. These writers of fantasy are thus amongst the latest voices in the long tradition of liberal humanism in English literature.

· 9 ·
The Perilous Realm

If this study has demonstrated nothing else, it should have shown that the period under consideration has witnessed a substantial outpouring of creative fantasy. Possibly at no other period in the history of English literature has the writing of fantasy achieved such popularity amongst writers and readers alike. Inevitably, this flow has contained a proportion of mediocre and ephemeral works, but at the same time it has included a notable element of innovative literature of considerable merit – so much so that it has been necessary to omit a number of interesting books from the discussion. Some explanation of the large and still growing interest in this genre has been attempted. For some authors, the writing of fantasy has provided the most satisfactory mode of expressing their ideas about the contemporary world and contemporary values. They have used it to explore new methods of expression and to expound a deep-felt sense of moral purpose. What they have not done, in most cases, is to use fantasy as a means of escape from contemporary reality. Fantasy, it has been argued, is not escapism but a method of approaching and evaluating the real world.

It follows that the period has witnessed not simply an increase in the sheer volume of work in this genre, but also a development, both in relation to what has gone before and also within the period itself. Thus we have seen the emergence of what might be described as a new sub-genre of fantasy – time fantasy – in which complex ideas about movement through time, time-displacement, and the whole concept of the inter-relationship between time and eternity have received a more penetrating and sophisticated treatment than ever before. There has been development, further, in terms of technique and in particular in the evocation and portrayal of secondary worlds. Writers have had to learn the lesson that in the creation of a secondary world it is no less necessary than in the description of the everyday primary world to keep closely to the intrinsic reality of the created world, to observe a scrupulous inner consistency – in other words, to maintain the utmost 'realism'. Fantasies which fail to do this immediately lose credibility and cease to convince. Writers of fantasy are, like all other writers, engaged in literary expression of their ideas, and are thus part of the great and continuing tradition of English literature. Their modes of expression and construction should not fall below the most exacting standards of literary creation. The modes employed by our writers, including the modes of allegory, symbolism and satire, are those which have been and continue to be used by writers in other genres. Again, ample examples of the perceptive use of such modes in fantasy have been discussed in this study. In short, the literary skill employed by the best of our writers can withstand comparison with that of the best writers in other genres.

But what is fantasy, and what is its *raison d'être*? To what extent has this study borne out Tolkien's dictum that fantasy, like fairy-tales, is not really about marvellous beings, but about 'man in the Perilous Realm'? The point has already been made that fantasy, just as much as the 'realist' novel, is about reality – about the human condition. All serious fantasy is deeply rooted in human experience and is relevant to human living. Its major difference from the realist novel is that it takes account of areas of experience – imaginative, subconscious, visionary – which free the human spirit to range beyond the limits of empirical primary world reality. In a sense, then, fantasy provides the writer with greater scope to construct his own scheme of morality, his own time structure, his own political and social order. But at no time does this apparent freedom permit the author to escape from contemporary reality. Indeed the fundamental purpose of serious fantasy is to comment upon the real world and to explore moral, philosophical and other dilemmas posed by it. This process may be described less as didacticism, although this is sometimes present, than as a form of creative questioning; and, it may be argued, without such questioning in any intellectual field, there can be no advance.

Of the writers primarily concerned with moral and philosophical ideas, C. S. Lewis, in *The Chronicles of Narnia,* is the most didactic and, in terms of religious belief, the most traditional. The Narnian books are based on and provide an allegory of the major Christian precepts. If taken in logical but not chronological order of writing, they provide an embodiment of the Christian myth from the Creation to the Day of Judgment. In the process they examine not only the larger questions of Christian morality but the ethics of social behaviour, confronting the sins of treachery, deceit, conceit and petty egoism. Tolkien's novels, less obviously based on traditional Christianity, are nevertheless built around a psychomachia, as well as commenting on the lesser manifestations of human frailty. His characters may take the form of elves, orcs, hobbits, ents or dwarfs, but they all share in some degree the characteristics and foibles of human nature.[1] *The Earthsea Trilogy* of Ursula Le Guin perhaps goes further than any other of the fantasies considered, not so much in divorcing itself from the Christian tradition as in providing us with a new philosophical structure which, if it is derivative at all, is based upon a much wider philosophical and religious foundation, including the Hermetic and Neo-Platonic traditions and some elements of Zen. But these elements are not overt, and Ursula Le Guin demonstrates considerable skill in creating a world whose philosophy is, or at least appears to be, *sui generis*. Yet even here the problems are, above all, human problems. The central concept of balance, a balance which man disturbs only at terrible risk, has some connection with Zen, but is obviously directly relevant to contemporary concerns with ecology, the balance of nature and the risks of nuclear energy. The trilogy also considers the whole question of the control of scientific and technological advance – the extension of knowledge must involve an extension of responsibility, and an increasing dominance over the material world engenders an increasing dominance of materialism over human life. The same theme is taken up by John Christopher in his fantasies of the future in a transformed primary world, where he develops the political implications of technology and its control.

Political systems *per se* are one of the concerns of Richard Adams in *Watership Down*, where the secondary world of the rabbit community is used to explore a variety of possible political systems. Adams, like many of our writers, is deeply suspicious of totalitarianism whether of the Left or of the Right, and opts for a kind of liberal democracy, although interestingly he, like many of the other writers, depicts an ideal leader who emerges by informal common consent rather than through the formal workings of a representational system. In *The Mouse and His Child* there is no leader, and no overall system. The only character with any claim to authority is the boss figure, Manny Rat. Hoban's attitude to political systems and modern materialism is highly critical. The point is, however, that whatever form a writer's characters may take, whether human, animal, mechanical or marvellous, their fundamental characteristics and concerns are those of modern man.

The freedom which fantasy imparts from the need to depict the primary world in all its empirical reality does not, therefore, imply that the writer of fantasy is not concerned with the inner and transcendent reality of this world. Moreover, such freedom from the constraints of primary realism introduces its own, perhaps even more rigorous constraints. The marvellous, in order to be both satisfying and convincing, must maintain its own inner consistency. The writer of fantasy, therefore, cannot begin, as the realist writer can, with a given setting, a given heritage of ideas and beliefs, a given world order. These he must construct for himself, but having made his own rules, he must then abide by them. He must induce secondary belief or lose both the interest and credence of his reader.

The best works discussed in this study succeed in rising to this challenge. The work of Tolkien is notable for the extreme lengths to which the author is prepared to go, to establish credibility. His creation of a secondary world is accompanied not only by physical description but by an underlying philosophical purpose and the compilation of a massive substructure of history, myth, language and literature. Amongst more recent writers, the work of Ursula Le Guin is also distinguished by its secondary realism. While Ursula Le Guin is less concerned than Tolkien with the minutiae of her secondary world, it is arguable that her success in constructing a philosophical foundation for it exceeds that of Tolkien in its innovative quality. Few, if any, of the leading exponents of fantasy are not informed by a serious attempt to analyse the workings and inner meaning of their own primary world through the medium of the marvellous or the secondary world. Even when traditional material is used in modern fantasy, it may be transformed in the process. Alan Garner's *The Owl Service* draws upon *The Mabinogion* tale of Blodeuedd, Lleu Llaw Gyffes and Gronw Bebyr in both its general structure and its fine detail of language, and yet the ancient myth is blended with the modern primary world characters and setting in such a way as to create not only a fresh artistic work but also a fresh insight into the nature of the myth itself, and the nature of the human relationships which it reflects. Many other writers, like Philippa Pearce, Penelope Farmer, Norton Juster, Susan Cooper, William Mayne, Helen Cresswell and Catherine Storr, use the medium of fantasy in fresh and subtle ways to explore the inner workings of the personality and the fluctuating relationships between the individual and those around him.

Despite the many difficulties which may stand in the way of success in this genre, the principal advantage for the writer of fantasy is that it engenders an extraordinarily enhanced perception of the nature of the primary world, which is so often only imperfectly grasped until a shock is given to the senses by the introduction of the marvellous. Such enhanced perception of the primary world in turn develops the imaginative faculty for creating or entering secondary worlds. What emerges above all from this study, then, is that modern fantasy, far from being the escapist literature which it is sometimes labelled, is a serious form of the modern novel, often characterized by notable literary merit, and concerned both with heightened awareness of the complex nature of primary reality and with the exploration beyond empirical experience into the transcendent reality, embodied in imaginative and spiritual otherworlds. Through fantasy, man does indeed enter the Perilous Realm, and may find there both the familiar made strange, and the strange made familiar.

Notes

Chapter 1 Fantasy and the Marvellous

1 See, for example, Edmund Wilson, 'Oo, Those Awful Orcs'.
2 For example, C. N. Manlove, *Modern Fantasy*. This contains a short introductory chapter, followed by studies of five individual writers (Charles Kingsley, George MacDonald, C. S. Lewis, J. R. R. Tolkien and Mervyn Peake) and a conclusion.
3 Dante uses both *imaginativa* and *fantasia* to signify the faculty of perceiving mental pictures; such a picture he calls an *imagine*. In some contexts the imaginative faculty is seen as operating on images perceived through the senses (see *Convivio* III, iv; *Paradiso* X, 46–8). The significance of the passage quoted in the epigraph (p. vi) is that in moments of high creative power (*alta fantasia*, *Purgatorio*, XVII, 25, immediately following this passage), the process seems to originate outside the conscious human will, inspired by some celestial or divine power. (For *fantasia* as vision, see also *La Vita Nuova* XXIII.) Cf. St Thomas Aquinas, *Summa Theologiae*, Prima, Qu. lxxxiv, Art. 6.
4 Tolkien, 'On Fairy-stories', *Tree and Leaf*, p. 50. (Further references to *Tree and Leaf* will be abbreviated *TL*. For other abbreviations, see the Table of Abbreviations, p. ix.)
5 See, for example, the works by Harvey Cox, W. R. Irwin and C. N. Manlove listed in the Bibliography.
6 *BL* XIII.
7 This is Coleridge's view in his philosophical works. See, however, his 'Destiny of Nations' (1796), ll. 18–23:

For all that meets the bodily sense I deem
Symbolical, one mighty alphabet
To infant minds; and we in this low world
Placed with our backs to bright reality,
That we may learn with young unwounded ken
The substance from the shadow.
(The Complete Poetical Works of Samuel Taylor Coleridge, vol. I, p. 132.)

8 *BL* XIII.
9 *BL* Conclusion.
10 Shelley, of course, here interprets the word 'poet' very widely. A poet is seen primarily as a *creator* (cf. Tolkien's definitions, and the root meaning of the Greek word) who works through the medium of language (verse or prose). The quotations from Shelley in this paragraph are all taken from *A Defence of Poetry*.

Chapter 2 Talking Beasts

1 Edward Lee Thorndike, *Animal Intelligence*, quoted in Walter de la Mare, *Animal Stories*, pp. xlvii–xlviii.
2 Stith Thompson, *Motif-Index of Folk Literature.*
3 See Ned Samuel Hedges, 'The Fable and the Fabulous: The Use of Traditional Forms in Children's Literature'.
4 Lofting was originally inspired to write the first of these stories for his own children while serving in the trenches in World War I. His anger that the horses who served alongside the men received no medical care for their illnesses and war wounds gave him the idea of an animal doctor who could understand the language of his patients. See John Rowe Townsend, *Written for Children*, p. 167.
5 T. H. White, *The Sword in the Stone*, p. 28. Cf. Sir Thomas Malory, *Le Morte d'Arthur*, vol. I, book 1, ch. 19. (Throughout, the 1957 second edition of *The Sword in the Stone* will be used, and not the heavily revised, and considerably inferior, version in which it appears as part of *The Once and Future King*. The final version has one interesting addition, the portrayal of the ant colony, a satirical dystopia.)
6 This is not T. H. White's invention. See Sir Thomas Malory, *op. cit.*, pp. 16–17.
7 For further discussion of the political themes in *The Mouse and His Child*, see below, Ch. 8.
8 Robert C. O'Brien, *Mrs Frisby and the Rats of NIMH*, p. 198.
9 Cf. William Blake, *The Four Zoas.*
10 R.M. Lockley, *The Private Life of the Rabbit*, p. 164.

Chapter 3 Worlds in Parallel

1 A collection of papers dealing with some of the conceptual problems of time is to be found in R. M. Gale (ed.), *The Philosophy of Time*. Certain classical writers were concerned with the complexities of narrative time in their works (e.g. Lucian, *Verae Historiae*; Ovid, *Metamorphoses*; Apuleius, *The Golden Ass*; and Homer, *The Odyssey*), but the modern exploration of the time dimension begins with twentieth-century writers like H. G. Wells, T. S. Eliot, Virginia Woolf and J. B. Priestley.
2 E. A. Abbott, *Flatland*, pp. 65–73.
3 C. S. Lewis, *Prince Caspian, The Voyage of the 'Dawn Treader'*, and *The Magician's Nephew*, respectively.
4 Pages in this text are unnumbered.
5 See below, Ch. 5.
6 See Robert Graves, *The White Goddess*, chs 10–11.

Chapter 4 Secondary Worlds

1 However, genealogies are used to provide historical depth in such works as Spenser's *The Faerie Queene*, *The Mabinogion* and the stories

of the Arthurian cycle. See, for example, the chronicles of Britain given in *The Faerie Queene* II, x and III, iii. Note also the use of maps in *Gulliver's Travels* (1726). The later seventeenth and early eighteenth century saw the rise of this desire for realism in fiction, particularly in the genre of alleged travellers' tales.

2   C. S. Lewis, *The Magician's Nephew*, chs 4 and 5. In *The Last Battle* the dying sun of Narnia also appears large, red and tired, p. 158.

3   There is an interesting parallelism between Gurgi, moving from beast nature to human nature, and Gollum in *The Hobbit* and *The Lord of the Rings,* who is 'moving beastwards' (a phrase of George MacDonald's). Gurgi initially attempts to strangle Taran (*CP,* I, p. 28) and follows Taran and Gwydion by stealing through the trees, closely similar behaviour to that of Gollum. Gwydion understands Gurgi's nature and tolerates him, as Bilbo pities and spares Gollum. Gollum determines the final destruction of the Ring. Gurgi, through his inner growth and pathetic heroism, is fully redeemed.

4   Tolkien himself said that 'the book is about the world that God created – the actual world of this planet'. See Charlotte and Denis Plimmer, 'The Man Who Understands Hobbits', p. 35.

5   There have been some semi-serious attempts by critics to place the period of *The Lord of the Rings* in the Pleistocene era of Western Europe. See Paul H. Kocher, *Master of Middle-Earth: The Achievement of J.R.R. Tolkien,* pp. 3–7 and n. 5, and J.S. Ryan, *J.R.R. Tolkien: Cult or Culture?,* pp. 160–1.

6   Nemmerle's raven speaks (*A Wizard of Earthsea,* p. 49), but ravens are always a somewhat special case. Animals and birds understand and answer to their true names, and some of the mages are able to communicate with them (*The Farthest Shore,* p. 18).

7   The constellation Gobardon, which has the form of Agnen, the rune of ending, assumes symbolic significance in *The Farthest Shore.* See below, Ch. 7.

8   In *The Magician's Nephew* an apple from this tree is planted to grow into the Tree of Protection for Narnia (ch. 14). Compare the planting of the sapling in *The Lord of the Rings,* III, pp. 249–50.

9   Both Tolkien and his characters have a strong sense of history, 'a vision as it were of a great expanse of years behind them, like a vast shadowy plain' (*LOTR,* I, p. 157). In reviewing the first volume of *The Lord of the Rings,* C.S. Lewis wrote, 'in the Tolkinian world you can hardly put your foot down . . . without stirring the dust of history' ('The Gods Return to Earth', p. 1083).

10 E.g. *A Wizard of Earthsea,* p. 30; *The Tombs of Atuan,* p. 22; *The Farthest Shore,* pp. 82, 141.

11 *The Lion, the Witch and the Wardrobe,* pp. 70, 96, 101.

12 See, e.g., Alwyn Rees and Brinley Rees, *Celtic Heritage,* pp. 15–17; and Robert Graves, *The White Goddess,* pp. 18, 22.

13 Tolkien: 'the stories were made rather to provide a world for the languages than the reverse.' Plimmer, *op. cit.,* p. 36.

14 J. R. R. Tolkien, *The Father Christmas Letters.*

15 See Douglass Parker, 'Hwaet We Holbytla', and John Tinkler, 'Old English in Rohan', for useful discussions of this point.

16 Clearly Le Guin, Alexander, Lewis and Tolkien are all influenced by the long predominance of Latin, the Old Speech of Europe, as the language of learning, religion, medicine and magic, as well as the international mode of communication between scholars. There is an interesting discussion of Ursula Le Guin's use of language in T. A. Shippey, 'The Magic Art and the Evolution of Words: Ursula Le Guin's Earthsea Trilogy'.

17 See *The Lion, the Witch and the Wardrobe*, p. 131; *The Voyage of the 'Dawn Treader'*, p. 146.

18 For further consideration of these aspects of *The Chronicles of Narnia*, see below, Ch. 7.

19 The curious world of the Maborians in Keith Claire's *The Tree Wakers* suffers from this flaw; it is too alien, too many natural laws are broken, for the reader to establish a coherent frame of reference. Alan Garner's early work also needed more restraint in the use of the marvellous, a lesson he subsequently learned.

20 C. S. Lewis, *Surprised by Joy*, p. 13.

21 C. S. Lewis, 'On Three Ways of Writing for Children'.

22 For a discussion of Christian parallels and spiritual values in *The Lord of the Rings*, see Dorothy L. Barber, 'The Structure of *The Lord of the Rings*'.

23 C. N. Manlove, *Modern Fantasy*, pp. 185–92.

Chapter 5   Layers of Meaning

1 Jonathan Raban, *The Technique of Modern Fiction*, p. 101.

2 Alan Garner, 'Coming to Terms', p. 16.

3 Lloyd Alexander, 'The Flat-Heeled Muse', p. 244.

4 Amabel Williams-Ellis, 'Traditional Tales', p. 52.

5 Dorothy L. Sayers, 'Chronicles of Narnia', p. 123.

6 Joan North, *The Light Maze*, pp. 129–30, 153–4, 169–72. Cf. Ursula Le Guin, *A Wizard of Earthsea*. In both books the shadow of inherent evil is let loose on the world, although less terrifyingly in *The Light Maze* than in *A Wizard of Earthsea*.

7 The casting of flowers on the bare earth and the reawakening of the barren soil may derive from Botticelli's *Primavera* (which in turn draws on Ovid's *Fasti* – see Edgar Wind, *Pagan Mysteries in the Renaissance*, ch. VII). However, Vir'Vachal's inexorable creative force is a far cry from Botticelli's poised and lovely Flora.

8 Swine regularly have sacred associations in Celtic mythology. See Alwyn Rees and Brinley Rees, *Celtic Heritage*.

9 See Marcus Crouch, *The Nesbit Tradition*, p. 124.

10 See C. S. Lewis, 'It All Began with a Picture', *Of Other Worlds: Essays and Stories*, p. 42.

11 Roger Lancelyn Green and W. Hooper, *C. S. Lewis: A Biography*, pp. 239–40.

12 Leon Garfield, *The Ghost Downstairs*, pp. 94–5. This will be considered in greater detail in Ch. 7.

Chapter 6   Experience Liberated

1   Henry James, Preface to the New York edition of *The American*, reprinted in *The Art of the Novel*, p. 33.
2   For a discussion of Branwell Brontë's wooden soldiers and their influence on the juvenilia of the Brontë children, see F. E. Ratchford, *The Brontës' Web of Childhood*.
3   Mary Norton's own myopia helps to account for her precise vision of minute objects. See Margery Fisher, *Intent Upon Reading*, p. 106. In this study we consider the original group of four Borrowers books. Two more were published later: *Poor Stainless* (1971) and *The Borrowers Avenged* (1982), Harcourt Brace.
4   See Ezekiel 1.
5   According to the pre-Copernican theory of a geocentric universe in which the earth is surrounded by nine concentric spheres, Proginoskes the cherubim is correctly characterized as being by nature contemplative rather than active, and in being associated with the second highest sphere, the *Stellatum*. See C. S. Lewis, *The Discarded Image*, pp. 70–5, 96, and E. M. W. Tillyard, *The Elizabethan World Picture*, ch. 5, § I. Note that Lewis gives the order of the angelic hierarchies incorrectly, placing the Virtues below the Powers. (The hierarchies were first given by Dionysius the Areopagite, or the 'pseudo-Dionysius', a Christian Neo-Platonist perhaps of the fifth century A.D.)
6   Metron Ariston – 'the best measure' (Greek). There is considerable use of Greek terminology throughout the novel.
7   This description of the birth of a star should be compared with C. S. Lewis, *The Magician's Nephew*, ch. 8.
8   For the importance of names and naming, compare Ursula Le Guin's *Earthsea Trilogy*.
9   Clarence DeWitt Thorpe, 'Empathy', *Dictionary of World Literature*, ed. Joseph T. Shipley, pp. 186–8 (p. 186), quoted in Richard H. Fogle, *The Imagery of Keats and Shelley: A Comparative Study*, pp. 147–8.
10 R.H. Fogle, *op. cit.*, pp. 139–51.

Chapter 7   Idealisms:Religious and Philosophic

1   For a useful discussion of the theological romance, see John D. Haigh, 'The Fiction of C. S. Lewis', ch. VIII.
2   See 'The Myth Makers', *Times Literary Supplement*, 1 July 1955, Children's Book Supplement, pp. i–ii; and Haigh, *op. cit.*, ch. XVI.
3   Quoted on the dustjackets of *The Lord of the Rings*, source not given.
4   As noticed also by the *TLS* reviewer. (See n. 2, above.)
5   In *Prince Caspian*, p. 178, Aslan states that the mice first became talking mice after gnawing away the cords which bound him to the Stone Table, but this is an aside, very much after the event.

6 For C. S. Lewis on Kipling, see 'Kipling's World'.
7 See Marcus Crouch, 'Chronicles of Narnia'.
8 This is evident especially from his treatment of Narnian history. See above, Ch. 4.
9 For C. S. Lewis's interest in the 'sensations' created by the environment of stories, see 'On Stories'.
10 *The Voyage of the 'Dawn Treader'* (1952) and *The Silver Chair* (1953), in which these occur, were written long before the current developments in educational practice, and thus are presumably attacking the educational environment of the 1940s, or earlier. Lewis seems to have been particularly opposed to 'progressive' schools, which he depicts in exaggerated form, yet he himself was acutely unhappy at conventional boarding schools.
11 Christopher Marlowe, *The Tragical History of the Life and Death of Doctor Faustus*, Prologue and Scene i. All references are to the Revels edition.
12 See Marlowe, *Doctor Faustus*, Sc. iii, l. 78. Compare Milton, *Paradise Lost*, iv, l. 75: 'my self am Hell'.
13 *Doctor Faustus*, Sc. xix, ll. 146–7.
14 Elsewhere in this study, references to *The Earthsea Trilogy* are abbreviated *ET*. For brevity, in the remainder of this chapter references to *The Earthsea Trilogy* are given thus: I = *A Wizard of Earthsea*; II = *The Tombs of Atuan*; III = *The Farthest Shore*.
15 See above, Ch. 4, and also T.A. Shippey, 'The Magic Art and the Evolution of Words: Ursula Le Guin's Earthsea Trilogy'.
16 Cf. Shippey, *op. cit.*, p. 161. Shippey is here mistaken in saying that Ged does not restore Cob's true name to him. It is the recovery of his name which restores Cob's sight, and brings peace to his tortured existence. He is at last truly dead.

Chapter 8   Idealisms: Social and Political

1 The term 'utopia' will be used throughout in its generally accepted meaning of 'a good place'. It should be borne in mind, however, that Sir Thomas More, in devising the term, deliberately played on the two meanings εὐ τοπος = good place and οὐ τοπος = no place. His own attitude towards 'utopia' was, of course, ambiguous.
2 Russell Hoban, 'Thoughts on a shirtless cyclist, Robin Hood, Johann Sebastian Bach, and one or two other things', p. 13.
3 Ibid., p. 8.
4 A similar treatment of society is undertaken by Peter Dickinson in his fantasies of the future.
5 Such a stultification of the arts, taken to comic extremes, occurs in Carol Kendall's *The Minnipins*; see above, Ch. 4.
6 See Lockley, *The Private Life of the Rabbit*, pp. 91, 95, 126.
7 See *Watership Down*, pp. 124–6.

Chapter 9   The Perilous Realm

1   Cf. K. M. Briggs's *Hobberdy Dick*. In this book, which has not been
    considered elsewhere in this study for reasons of space, the central
    characters are all hobgoblins and other sprites. It is noteworthy that
    even here, where on the surface level the fantasy is concerned with
    'fairies' and not men, the fundamental issues are human ones. More-
    over, in the final dénouement Hobberdy Dick chooses, not the carefree
    and feckless future of a freed sprite, but the twin burden and joy of a
    Christian human soul.

Select Bibliography

Details of first publication are given in brackets where a different edition has been used for reference. Anonymous works are listed under title.

Primary Sources

Abbott, Edwin A., *Flatland: A Romance of Many Dimensions* (London, Seeley, 1884), Oxford, Basil Blackwell, 1962.

Adams, Richard, *Watership Down* (London, Rex Collings, 1972), Harmondsworth, Penguin, 1973.

Alexander, Lloyd, *The Chronicles of Prydain*:
> *The Book of Three* (New York, Holt, Rinehart & Winston, 1964), London, Collins, 1973.
> *The Black Cauldron* (New York, Holt, Rinehart & Winston, 1965), London, Collins, 1973.
> *The Castle of Llyr* (New York, Holt, Rinehart & Winston, 1966), New York, Dell, 1975.
> *Taran Wanderer* (New York, Holt, Rinehart & Winston, 1967), New York, Dell, 1973.
> *The High King* (New York, Holt Rinehart & Winston, 1968), New York, Dell, 1974.

Arthur, Ruth M., *The Whistling Boy* (London, Gollancz, 1969), London, Collins, 1973.

Boston, L.M., *The Children of Green Knowe*, London, Faber, 1954.

Briggs, K.M., *Hobberdy Dick* (London, Eyre & Spottiswoode, 1955), Harmondsworth, Penguin, 1972.

Calder-Marshall, Arthur, *The Fair to Middling* (London, Hart-Davis, 1959), Harmondsworth, Penguin, 1962.

Chant, Joy, *Red Moon and Black Mountain* (London, Allen & Unwin, 1970), Harmondsworth, Penguin, 1973.

Christopher, John, *The Guardians* (London, Hamish Hamilton, 1970), Harmondsworth, Penguin, 1973.

Christopher, John, *The Winchester Trilogy*:
> *The Prince in Waiting* (London, Hamish Hamilton, 1970), Harmondsworth, Penguin, 1973.
> *Beyond the Burning Lands* (London, Hamish Hamilton, 1971), Harmondsworth, Penguin, 1973.
> *The Sword of the Spirits* (London, Hamish Hamilton, 1972), Harmondsworth, Penguin, 1973.

Claire, Keith, *The Tree Wakers* (London, Methuen, 1970), London, Transworld, 1972.

Clarke, Pauline, *The Twelve and the Genii,* London, Faber, 1962.

Cooper, Susan, *The Dark is Rising Sequence*:
Over Sea, Under Stone (London, Jonathan Cape, 1965), Harmondsworth, Penguin, 1968.
The Dark is Rising (London, Chatto & Windus, 1973), Harmondsworth, Penguin, 1976.
Greenwitch (London, Chatto & Windus, 1974), Harmondsworth, Penguin, 1977.
The Grey King (London, Chatto & Windus, 1975), Harmondsworth, Penguin, 1977.
Silver on the Tree (London, Chatto & Windus, 1977), Harmondsworth, Penguin, 1979.

Cresswell, Helen, *The Outlanders,* London, Faber, 1970.

de la Mare, Walter, *The Three Mulla-Mulgars* (London, Faber, 1910), London, Faber, 1969. (Retitled *The Three Royal Monkeys* from the 1935 edition onwards.)

Eager, Edward, *The Time Garden* (New York, Harcourt, 1958), Harmondsworth, Penguin, 1972.

Farmer, Penelope, *The Summer Birds,* London, Chatto & Windus, 1962.

Farmer, Penelope, *The Magic Stone,* London, Chatto & Windus, 1965.

Farmer, Penelope, *Charlotte Sometimes* (London, Chatto & Windus, 1969), Harmondsworth, Penguin, 1972.

Farmer, Penelope, *A Castle of Bone* (London, Chatto & Windus, 1972), Harmondsworth, Penguin, 1974.

Farmer, Penelope, *William and Mary* (London, Chatto & Windus, 1974), London, Pan, 1977.

Gallico, Paul, *Jennie,* London, Michael Joseph, 1950.

Garfield, Leon, *The Ghost Downstairs* (London, Longmans, 1972), Harmondsworth, Penguin, 1975.

Garner, Alan, *The Owl Service* (London, Collins, 1967), Harmondsworth, Penguin, 1969.

Grahame, Kenneth, *The Wind in the Willows* (London, Methuen, 1908), 101st edn, London, Methuen, 1951.

Harris, Rosemary, *The Moon in the Cloud,* London, Faber, 1968.

Harris, Rosemary, *The Shadow on the Sun,* London, Faber, 1970.

Harris, Rosemary, *The Bright and Morning Star,* London, Faber, 1972.

Hoban, Russell, *The Mouse and His Child* (New York, Harper, 1967), London, Faber, 1972.

Jones, Gwyn, and Jones, Thomas (trans.), *The Mabinogion* (London, Dent, 1949), revised edition, London, Dent, 1974.

Juster, Norton, *The Phantom Tollbooth* (New York, Random House, 1961), London, Collins, 1974.

Kendall, Carol, *The Minnipins* (first published as *The Gammage Cup,* New York, Harcourt, 1959), Harmondsworth, Penguin, 1971.

Langton, Jane, *The Diamond in the Window* (New York, Harper, 1962), London, Hamish Hamilton, 1969.

Le Guin, Ursula, *The Earthsea Trilogy*:
  A Wizard of Earthsea (Emeryville, Parnassus, 1968), Harmondsworth, Penguin, 1971.
  The Tombs of Atuan (New York, Atheneum, 1971), Harmondsworth, Penguin, 1974.
  The Farthest Shore (New York, Atheneum, 1972), Harmondsworth, Penguin, 1974.
L'Engle, Madeleine, *A Wrinkle in Time* (New York, Farrar, Strauss & Giroux, 1962), Harmondsworth, Penguin, 1967.
L'Engle, Madeleine, *A Wind in the Door* (New York, Crosswicks, 1973), New York, Dell, 1976.
Lewis, C. S., *The Chronicles of Narnia*:
  The Lion, the Witch and the Wardrobe, London, Bles, 1950.
  Prince Caspian (London, Bles, 1951), Harmondsworth, Penguin, 1962.
  The Voyage of the 'Dawn Treader', London, Bles, 1952.
  The Silver Chair (London, Bles, 1953), Harmondsworth, Penguin, 1965.
  The Horse and His Boy, London, Bles, 1954.
  The Magician's Nephew (London, Bodley Head, 1955), Harmondsworth, Penguin, 1963.
  The Last Battle, London, Bodley Head, 1956.
Lively, Penelope, *The Ghost of Thomas Kempe* (London, Heinemann, 1973), London, Pan, 1975.
Malory, Sir Thomas, *Le Morte d'Arthur* (London, Caxton, 1485), ed. J. Cowen, 2 vols, Harmondsworth, Penguin, 1969.
Marlowe, Christopher, *The Tragical History of the Life and Death of Doctor Faustus* (The A text published 1604, the B text 1616); ed. John D. Jump, Revels Plays, London, Methuen, 1968.
Mayne, William, *Earthfasts* (London, Hamish Hamilton, 1966), Harmondsworth, Penguin, 1969.
Mayne, William, *A Game of Dark* (London, Hamish Hamilton, 1971), Harmondsworth, Penguin, 1974.
North, Joan, *The Light Maze* (New York, Farrar, Strauss & Giroux, 1971), London, Macmillan, 1972.
Norton, Andre, *Breed to Come* (New York, Viking, 1972), London, Longmans, 1973.
Norton, Mary, *The Borrowers Tetralogy*:
  The Borrowers (London, Dent, 1952), London, Dent, 1964.
  The Borrowers Afield (London, Dent, 1955), Harmondsworth, Penguin, 1960.
  The Borrowers Afloat (London, Dent, 1959), Harmondsworth, Penguin, 1970.
  The Borrowers Aloft (London, Dent, 1961), Harmondsworth, Penguin, 1970.
O'Brien, Robert C., *Mrs Frisby and the Rats of NIMH* (New York, Atheneum, 1971), Harmondsworth, Penguin, 1975.
Pearce, Philippa, *Tom's Midnight Garden*, London, Oxford University Press, 1958.

Robinson, J.G., *When Marnie Was There* (London, Collins, 1967), London, Collins, 1971.

Selden, George, *The Cricket in Times Square* (New York, Farrar, Strauss & Giroux, 1960), Harmondsworth, Penguin, 1963.

Sendak, Maurice, *Where the Wild Things Are* (London, Bodley Head, 1967), Harmondsworth, Penguin, 1970.

Smith, Dodie, *The Starlight Barking* (London, Heinemann, 1967), Harmondsworth, Penguin, 1970.

Spenser, Edmund, *The Faerie Queene* (originally published in two parts, 1590 and 1596). In *Spenser: Poetical Works*, ed. J. C. Smith and E. de Selincourt (London, Oxford University Press, 1912), London, Oxford University Press, 1970.

Storr, Catherine, *Marianne Dreams* (London, Faber, 1958), revised edition, Harmondsworth, Penguin, 1964.

Swift, Jonathan, *Gulliver's Travels* (London, Benjamin Motte, 1726), Harmondsworth, Penguin, 1967.

Thurber, James, *The Thirteen Clocks* (New York, Simon & Schuster, 1950), London, Hamish Hamilton, 1951.

Tolkien, J. R. R., *The Hobbit,* London, Allen & Unwin, 1937.

Tolkien, J. R. R., *The Lord of the Rings*:
The Fellowship of the Ring, London, Allen & Unwin, 1954.
The Two Towers, London, Allen & Unwin, 1954.
The Return of the King, London, Allen & Unwin, 1955.

Tolkien, J. R. R., *The Father Christmas Letters*, London, Allen & Unwin, 1976.

Uttley, Alison, *A Traveller in Time* (London, Faber, 1939), London, Faber, 1963.

Whistler, Theresa, *The River Boy* (London, Hart-Davis, 1955), 2nd edition, London, Oxford University Press, 1976.

White, E. B., *Stuart Little,* New York, Harper, 1945.

White, E. B., *Charlotte's Web* (New York, Harper, 1952), Harmondsworth, Penguin, 1963.

White, T. H., *Mistress Masham's Repose* (London, Cape, 1947), Harmondsworth, Penguin, 1972.

White, T. H., *The Sword in the Stone,* 2nd edition, London, Collins, 1957 (considerably revised from the first edition, London, Collins, 1938).

White, T.H., *The Once and Future King* (London, Collins, 1958), London, Collins, 1962. (This contains, as its first part, a further revision of *The Sword in the Stone*.)

Secondary Sources

Alexander, Lloyd, 'The Flat-Heeled Muse', in *Children and Literature,* ed. Virginia Haviland, pp. 241–5.

Aquinas, St Thomas, *Summa Theologiae,* gen. eds Thomas Gilby and P. K. Meagher, 60 vols, London, Blackfriars, with Eyre & Spottiswoode, 1964–76.

Barber, Dorothy L., 'The Structure of *The Lord of the Rings'*, University of Michigan PhD, 1965.

Blishen, Edward (ed.), *The Thorny Paradise,* Harmondsworth, Kestrel (Penguin), 1975.

Cameron, Eleanor, *The Green and Burning Tree: On the Writing and Enjoyment of Children's Books,* Boston, Atlantic – Little, Brown, 1969.

Coleridge, S. T., *Biographia Literaria,* ed. George Watson, London, Dent, 1965.

Coleridge, S.T., *The Complete Poetical Works of Samuel Taylor Coleridge,* ed. Ernest Hartley Coleridge, 2 vols, Oxford, Clarendon Press, 1912. Reprinted 1957.

Coleridge, S.T., *Miscellanies, Aesthetic and Literary,* ed. T. Ashe, London, Bell, 1885.

Cox, Harvey, *The Feast of Fools: A Theological Essay on Festivity and Fantasy,* Cambridge, Mass., Harvard University Press, 1969.

Crouch, Marcus, 'Chronicles of Narnia', *Junior Bookshelf,* vol. 20, no. 5, November 1956, pp. 245–53.

Crouch, Marcus, *The Nesbit Tradition: The Children's Novel 1945–1970,* London, Benn, 1972.

Dante Alighieri, *La Divina Commedia,* ed. C. H. Grandgent and C. S. Singleton, Cambridge, Mass., Harvard University Press, 1972.

Dante Alighieri, *Le Opere di Dante Alighieri,* ed. E. Moore and P. Toynbee, London, Oxford University Press, 4th edition, 1924.

de la Mare, Walter, *Animal Stories,* London, Faber, 1939.

Fisher, Margery, *Intent Upon Reading* (Leicester, Brockhampton, 1961), Leicester, Brockhampton, 1964.

Fogle, Richard H., *The Imagery of Keats and Shelley: A Comparative Study,* Chapel Hill, University of North Carolina Press, 1949.

Gale, Richard M. (ed.), *The Philosophy of Time,* London, Macmillan, 1968.

Garner, Alan, 'Coming to Terms', *Children's Literature in Education*, 2, July 1970, pp. 15–29.

Graves, Robert, *The White Goddess* (London, Faber, 1948), London, Faber, 1952.

Green, Roger Lancelyn and Hooper, W., *C. S. Lewis: A Biography,* London, Bodley Head, 1963.

Haigh, John D., 'The Fiction of C. S. Lewis', University of Leeds PhD, 1962.

Haviland, Virginia (ed.), *Children and Literature: Views and Reviews* (Chicago, Scott Foresman, 1973), London, Bodley Head, 1974.

Hedges, Ned Samuel, 'The Fable and the Fabulous: The Use of Traditional Forms in Children's Literature', University of Nebraska PhD, 1968.

Hoban, Russell, 'Thoughts on a shirtless cyclist, Robin Hood, Johann Sebastian Bach and one or two other things', *Children's Literature in Education,* 4, March 1971, pp. 5–23.

Hunter, Mollie, *Talent is not Enough,* New York, Harper & Row, 1976.

Irwin, W. R., *The Game of the Impossible: A Rhetoric of Fantasy,* Urbana, University of Illinois Press, 1976.

Isaacs, N. D., and Zimbardo, R. A. (eds), *Tolkien and the Critics: Essays on*

J. R. R. Tolkien's The Lord of the Rings, University of Notre Dame Press, 1968.

James, Henry, *The Art of the Novel* (New York, Charles Scribner, 1934), New York, Charles Scribner, 1962.

Kocher, Paul H., *Master of Middle-Earth: The Achievement of J. R. R. Tolkien* (London, Thames & Hudson, 1973), Harmondsworth, Penguin, 1974.

Lewis, C. S., 'The Dethronement of Power', *Time and Tide*, vol. XXXVI, 22 October 1955, pp. 1373–4.

Lewis, C. S., *The Discarded Image* (Cambridge University Press, 1964) Cambridge University Press, 1967.

Lewis, C. S., *An Experiment in Criticism*, Cambridge University Press, 1961.

Lewis, C. S., 'The Gods Return to Earth', *Time and Tide*, vol. XXXV, 14 August 1954, p. 1083.

Lewis, C. S., 'It All Began with a Picture', in *Of Other Worlds*, p. 42.

Lewis, C. S., 'Kipling's World', in *They Asked for a Paper*, pp. 72–92.

Lewis, C. S., *Of Other Worlds: Essays and Stories*, ed. W. Hooper, London, Bles, 1966.

Lewis, C. S., 'On Stories', in *Of Other Worlds*, pp. 3–21.

Lewis, C. S., 'On Three Ways of Writing for Children', in *Of Other Worlds*, pp. 22–34.

Lewis, C. S., *A Preface to Paradise Lost*, London, Oxford University Press, 1942.

Lewis, C. S., 'Sometimes Fairy Stories May Say Best What's to Be Said', in *Of Other Worlds*, pp. 35–8.

Lewis, C. S., *Surprised by Joy*, London, Bles, 1955.

Lewis, C. S., *They Asked for a Paper*, London, Bles, 1962.

Lockley, R. M., *The Private Life of the Rabbit* (London, André Deutsch, 1964), London, Corgi, 1976.

Manlove, C. N., *Modern Fantasy: Five Studies*, Cambridge University Press, 1975.

'The Myth Makers', *Times Literary Supplement*, 1 July 1955, Children's Book Supplement, pp. i–ii.

Parker, Douglass, 'Hwaet We Holbytla', *Hudson Review*, vol. 9 (1956–7), pp. 598–609.

Plimmer, Charlotte, and Plimmer, Denis, 'The Man Who Understands Hobbits', *Daily Telegraph Magazine* (no. 181), 22 March 1968, pp. 31–2, 35.

Raban, Jonathan, *The Technique of Modern Fiction*, University of Notre Dame Press, 1969.

Ratchford, F. E., *The Brontës' Web of Childhood* (New York, Columbia University Press, 1941), New York, Russell & Russell, 1964.

Rees, Alwyn, and Rees, Brinley, *Celtic Heritage: Ancient Tradition in Ireland and Wales* (London, Thames & Hudson, 1961), London, Thames & Hudson, 1973.

Ryan, J. S., *Tolkien: Cult or Culture?*, Armidale, N.S.W., University of New England, 1969.

Sayers, Dorothy L., 'Chronicles of Narnia', *Spectator*, 22 July 1955, p. 123.

Shelley, P. B., *A Defence of Poetry*, in *The Complete Works of Percy Bysshe Shelley*, ed. Roger Ingpen and Walter E. Peck, 10 vols (vol. VII, pp. 109–40), London, Benn, 1965.

Shippey, T. A., 'The Magic Art and the Evolution of Words: Ursula Le Guin's Earthsea Trilogy', *Mosaic*, X/2, Winter 1977, pp. 147–63.

Swinfen, Ann, 'The Sub-creative Art', University of Dundee PhD, 1979. (This contains a considerably more comprehensive bibliography than the present work.)

Thompson, Stith, *Motif-Index of Folk Literature: A Classification of Narrative Elements in Folktales, Ballads, Myths, Fables, Mediaeval Romances, Exempla, Fabliaux, Jest Books and Local Legends*, 6 vols, revised and enlarged edition, Bloomington, Indiana University Press, 1975.

Tillyard, E. M. W., *The Elizabethan World Picture* (London, Chatto & Windus, 1943), Harmondsworth, Penguin, 1974.

Tinkler, John, 'Old English in Rohan', in *Tolkien and the Critics*, ed. N. D. Isaacs and R. A. Zimbardo, pp. 164–9.

Tolkien, J. R. R., 'Beowulf: The Monsters and the Critics', *Proceedings of the British Academy*, vol. XXII (1936), pp. 246–95.

Tolkien, J. R. R., *Tree and Leaf*, London, Allen & Unwin, 1964.

Townsend, J. R., *Written for Children* (London, Garnet Miller, 1965), revised edition, Harmondsworth, Kestrel (Penguin), 1974.

William-Ellis, Amabel, 'Traditional Tales', *Spectator*, 8 July 1955, pp. 51–2.

Wilson, Edmund, 'Oo, Those Awful Orcs', *Nation*, 182: 15, 14 April 1956.

Wind, Edgar, *Pagan Mysteries in the Renaissance*, London, Faber, 1958.

Index

249